W9-BTJ-381

68.25526 (1/2/69)

This volume is the eleventh of a number in which are being published the results of research carried on by the faculty and research scholars working at Yale University in the field of Foreign Area Studies. In 1953 there was published THE MULTI-STATE SYSTEM OF ANCIENT CHINA by Richard L. Walker and in 1954 there were published THE RUSSIAN HEXAMETER by Richard T. Burgi and CHINA'S MARCH TOWARD THE TROPICS by Herold J. Wiens, followed in 1960 by the INDEX TO CH'ING TAI CH'OU PAN I WU SHIH MO, edited by David Nelson Rowe, in 1961 by BRITAIN'S IMPERIAL ROLE IN THE RED SEA AREA 1800-1878 by Thomas E. Marston, and WHAT CHINA POLICY? by Vladimir Petrov, and in 1964 by UNITED STATES FOREIGN POLICY TOWARDS SOUTH AFRICA 1948-1963 by Leon M. S. Slawecki, in 1965 by TAIWAN IN CHINA'S FOREIGN RELATIONS, 1836-1874 by Sophia Su-fei Yen, and INDEX TO SU-LIEN YIN-MOU WEN-CHENG, edited by David Nelson Rowe and Sophia Su-fei Yen, and in 1968 by THE OPENING OF KOREA: A STUDY OF CHINESE DIPLOMACY, 1876-1885 by Fredrick Foo Chien. Subsequent volumes will include studies in the various disciplines, both Humanities and Social Sciences, in respect to East Asia, Southeast Asia and the Soviet Union. The undersigned are acting as general editors for the purpose of securing and approving the best possible results of research in these fields at Yale. In the various disciplines or areas to which the special skills of this committee do not directly apply, it is planned to secure supplementary advice from both inside and outside the University.

David Nelson Rowe
Chairman, Editorial Committee
Professor of Political Science

William S. Cornyn
Professor of Slavic and
Burmese Languages

THE FILIPINO REACTION
TO AMERICAN RULE
1901-1913

By

Bonifacio S. Salamanca

The Shoe String Press

1968

WINGATE COLLEGE LIBRARY
WINGATE, N. C.

Copyright © 1968, The Shoe String Press, Inc.

Library of Congress Catalog Card Number: 68-25526
Printed in the United States of America

TABLE OF CONTENTS

41299

LIST OF TABLES

THE FILIPINO REACTION TO AMERICAN RULE

INTRODUCTION

Before the past century came to an end, the American people made a historic departure from their tradition and values and, as a consequence of the Spanish-American War, acquired the Philippines from Spain. How and why the fateful decision to annex the Philippines was finally made by President William McKinley has been treated in an impressive body of historical and biographical literature with such convincing thoroughness that it would be needless to dwell on it anew in this work.[1] Suffice it to state that out of a combination of economic, political, and strategic motives and the impact of the belief in "Manifest Destiny," Secretary of State John Hay informed the American Peace Commissioners in Paris on October 28, 1898, that Spain should relinquish the Philippines and cede them to the United States.[2] This decision was incorporated in the Treaty of Paris, signed on December 10, 1898, and ratified by the United States Senate on February 6, 1899.[3]

Thus was inaugurated almost half-a-century of American rule in the Philippines, of direct and intensive Filipino-American contact and relations, with profound consequences on Philippine history and civilization. After three centuries of exposure to Western civilization of the Hispanic type, the Filipinos would henceforth be exposed to another mainstream of Western civilization, the Anglo-American variant.

This work is a preliminary inquiry into the impact of American civilization on Philippine institutions. It is viewed from the standpoint of the Filipino reception of, or reaction to, American policies and institutions during the period 1901-1913. The period 1901-1913 aptly deserves to be called the Taft Era or the Taft Regime. From 1900 to 1901, William Howard Taft was president of the Taft, or Second, Philippine Commission; he was Civil Governor from 1901 to 1903; Secretary of War, exercising general supervision over the Philippines, from 1904 to 1908; and finally President of the United States, sharing with the Congress of the United States ultimate responsibility for

the adoption of policy, and carrying sole responsibility for
the implementation of that policy, from 1909 to 1913.
The terminal date of this study is not without significance in itself. The temper, if not the official policy, of
the United States government toward the Philippines under-
went an important change after the Taft Era. Considering
the importance of attitudes and policy in shaping the Filipino
response during the Taft Era, the Filipino reaction subsequent to 1913 must have been different, and indeed it was.

It is now generally accepted that American colonial
policy differed greatly from that of the older colonial powers. It had to be, partly because of the spirit of American
institutions themselves, and partly because Philippine
society on the eve of the American impact was different
from the societies upon which the older colonial powers had
imposed their rule. There already existed an articulate
political and economic elite in the Philippines, behind whom
stood the other ninety percent of the people in opposing,
first, the continuation of Spanish rule and, second, the
imposition of yet another colonial rule, that of the United
States. Recognizing this, the United States decided to
govern the Philippines through the elite. The latter, in
turn, determined what substantive policies should be adopted
by the United States and which institutions should be accepted
in full, rejected in part, or rejected in full. The Filipino
reaction to American rule, therefore, was essentially the
response of the Filipino elite or upper class. Our greater
focus on the response of this class has also been dictated by
the dearth of reliable historical data on the attitudes or response of the lower classes to all phases of American policy
and institutions. Needless to say, where available, I have
not hesitated to present such data in their proper perspective.

Unlike Spanish rule, American rule was more effective
and widespread throughout the Philippines. The mountain
peoples and the Muslim Filipinos were reached by American authority. However, because they were not active determinants of the overall American policy and, again, because
of the absence of source materials, I have almost completely
excluded the non-Christian Filipinos from this study, except
in the case of the Muslims under the subject of religion.

In discussing the reaction of the Filipino elite, greater emphasis has been placed on the response to the political aspects of American rule. The formulators of American policy seem to have considered political growth as the standard of accomplishment; and the Filipinos themselves were more preoccupied with politics, especially with the issue of independence.

As a minute contribution to a historiographical study of the Philippines in the twentieth century, this work derives its importance not so much from its pioneering nature as from the writer's attempt to review the first era of American rule from the standpoint of the Filipino response[4] and from the perspective of fifty years. It derives an added importance from the utilization of later monographic studies and especially of manuscript materials which were not available to earlier students of American rule in the Philippines. Most of these scholars relied on published documents, periodical sources, and their own personal, but at times, biased, knowledge of men and events.[5]

It is hoped that this study will lead more enterprising and capable students to make further inquiries into the entire Philippine experience under American rule.

THE PHILIPPINES ON THE EVE
OF THE AMERICAN OCCUPATION

Introduction

Basic to a clearer understanding of the Filipino reaction to American rule is a knowledge of Philippino society on the eve of the American occupation. The internal structure of that society — its institutions and even its aspirations — helped to shape the range and condition the nature of Filipino responses to the introduction of American institutions and ideas into the Philippines.

At first glance, undertaking a description of Philippine society at the end of the nineteenth century seems an easy task. After all, Spain had been in continuous occupation of the Philippines since 1565, and the Filipinos had been Hispanized according to the degree of their exposure to Spanish institutions.[1] Therefore it should be fairly easy to obtain insights into Philippine life by simply discussing the legacy of Spanish rule. Unfortunately for the student however, just before Spain relinquished the Philippines to the United States, the Philippine Revolution broke out, resulting in changes in Philippine society. As we now know, the Philippine Revolution was not merely a movement to overthrow Spanish rule, but was also a social movement aimed at transforming Philippine society.[2] In other words, the Philippine Revolution was an instrument of institutional change. Consequently, to be accurate, a description of Philippine society on the eve of the American impact must include the heritage of the revolution, either as social changes or aspirations, although the revolution was but a brief period in the life of the Filipino people.

Social and Political Institutions under Spain

At the time of the Spanish conquest in the sixteenth century, the Filipinos had but one distinctive form of political organization. This was the barangay, a kinship unit, varying in size from 30 to 100 families, and governed

by a hereditary datu.[3] The Spaniards did not destroy the
barangay, but instead made it the basis of village government. The datu was retained as the cabeza de barangay
(village headman) and served as the intermediary between
the Spanish political and religious authorities and his people.
With slight modifications, therefore, the pro-Spanish Filipino political system survived the impact of Spanish rule.

Spanish administrative innovations included the formation of towns, and establishment of provincial and central
governments. [4] At the apex of the administrative hierarchy
was the all-powerful Governor-General and, below him, a
number of lesser officials of the central government.

A number of barangays constituted a town (pueblo).
This meant a regrouping of the population into larger units
than heretofore. The town government was, in appearance
at least, in the hands of Filipinos. The gobernadorcillo
(petty governor) was a Filipino, chosen by an electoral
board drawn from the principalia, or body of prominent
residents of the town. These were the active and former
cabezas de barangay and previous officeholders. Filipino
participation in the government stopped at the municipal or
town level, and it was even severely curtailed, as we shall
presently indicate, by the active role of the Spanish parish
priest in municipal affairs.

A group of towns formed a province, which was under
a civil governor who earlier carried the title of alcalde-
mayor. [5] Appointed by the Governor-General of the Philippines, the provincial executive was but an agent of the
central government. It is perhaps important to point out
that one basic weakness of local and provincial governments under Spain was the absence of local autonomy.

Throughout the period of Spanish rule, a lawmaking
body in the Philippines was conspicuous by its absence.
The formulation of laws for the country was the prerogative of the Spanish Government and their applicability to
the Philippines was determined by the Governor-General.

Although pre-Spanish customary law and procedure
were not totally swept aside, Spanish legal procedures and
substantive law were inevitably introduced. A judicial
machinery was also established. Toward the end of the
Spanish regime, it consisted of the following: a territorial

supreme court in Manila, two superior courts in Cebu and
Vigan, courts of first instance in each province (including
Manila), and justices of the peace courts in each municipality. In addition, there were ecclesiastical, military,
naval, and commercial courts. [6]

Under Spanish rule, Church and State were united,
with the State providing financial and other forms of support to the Catholic Church. The Governor-General, as
Vice-Royal Patron, meddled in Church affairs while the
Church bureaucracy performed political functions at all
levels of the civil administration. In fact, the ecclesiastical bureaucrats have been regarded as the "real vital
organs of the Philippine governmental system" under
Spain. [7]

The political system introduced by the Spaniards was
perhaps appropriate and even desirable for the first century of Spanish rule in the Philippines, but in its continuance
ance, it became oppressive and repressive. It is no wonder
that in the latter part of the nineteenth century, a concen-
trated effort was waged by the Filipino upper class to
reform the regime, and when this campaign failed, a
revolution took place to oust the Spaniards.

One of the most important social institutions during
the Spanish regime was the Roman Catholic Church. In
addition to its interlocking relationships with the State,
another of the Church's outstanding features was the role
played by the regular clergy — particularly the Dominicans,
Augustinians, Franciscans, Recollects, and Jesuits — in
political organization and activities. According to Majul,

> The friars represented and exercised the pre-
> rogatives of the Church in Philippine society.
> They were the agents through which the Church
> dominated the schools, higher education, and
> sometimes, even the political affairs of the
> country. [8]

Circumstances of history accounted for the special
position of the friars, or members of the regular clergy,
in Philippine life. For one, well into the nineteenth century, there were not enough secular or diocesan priests

to replace the regulars who had been administering the
parishes since the beginning of Spanish rule under a special
dispensation from the Pope.[9] There was no choice but to
keep the friars as parish priests, even though this practice
was contrary to sound administration and the decrees of
the Council of Trent in the sixteenth century.[10] Furthermore, the friars were usually the only Spaniards to be
found in the distant towns and, as such, the only visible
evidence of Spanish authority. Given the union of Church
and State at that time, this placed them in the natural position to be political instruments of control.

It was the intention of the Spanish monarchs, as Royal
Patrons, to replace the friars with secular priests as soon
as possible, and various attempts were made to do so before the nineteenth century. But at the time when the
Spanish government and the Church were earnest in pursuing "secularization,"[11] there were not enough qualified
Spanish or Filipino seculars who could replace the friars.
This fact and the reluctance of the friars to give up their
parishes prevented early efforts to secularize the parishes
from being successful. When, in the latter part of the nineteenth century, there was already a well-developed Filipino
secular clergy, the Spanish government and the Church had
already abandoned the policy of secularization; in fact, a
countersecularization policy, or despoliation, was applied.[12]
This backward step was probably instigated by the friars,
although it may have been partly due to the fact that in the
nineteenth century, the Spanish government came to rely
increasingly on the Church organization, or the friars, to
govern the Filipinos as its own civil bureaucracy grew
more inefficient and corrupt.

The Filipino clergy naturally harbored deep resentment against both the Spanish government and the Church
for their failure to enforce the secularization of the parishes,
given the availability of native priests. After all, the principle that seculars should administer the parishes had been
laid down by the Council of Trent.

The friars were also an economic force, owning huge
tracts of the richest agricultural lands in the country.[13]
At the time of the Revolution in 1896, the Dominicans,
Augustinians, and Recollects owned the following:[14]

Province of	Acres
Cavite	121,747
Laguna	62,172
Manila	50,145
Bulacan	39,441
Morong (now Riza)	4,940
Bataan	1,000
Cagayan	49,400
Cebu, island of	16,413
Mindoro, island of	58,455
Isabela	56,433
TOTAL . .	460,146

In the first five provinces listed above, the friars owned more than one-half of the total agricultural land, although not all was cultivated land. Hence, it is not surprising that these provinces were the cradle of the revolution against Spain as well as the scene of serious agrarian troubles before the revolution.[15]

The friars were also prominent in the educational field. Their parochial schools were the forerunners of the public primary school system under Spain. They also established secondary institutes, colleges and the University of Santo Tomas. They determined the content of the curriculum and later supervised the public primary schools, as will be seen below.

In 1863, the Spanish government finally decided to systematize primary instruction in the Philippines. A royal decree issued that year — which was fairly, if not thoroughly, executed[16] — provided for at least two public primary schools in each town,[17] one for boys and another for girls. The influence of the Church in the formulation of the educational decree is very much evident from the following portion of the decree which stated that the government was establishing the primary schools for the main purpose of

disseminating as far as possible, the instruction in the Holy Catholic Faith, in the mother

tongue, 18 and in the elementary branches of
knowledge... [and] considering that the basis
of all education is the solid diffusion of our
holy religion... it establishes a normal school
in charge of the Fathers of the Society of
Jesus.... The immediate supervision of said
schools is entrusted to the parish priests who
are given sufficient powers to make it efficient
and the instruction of Catholic doctrine and
morals is placed under the exclusive direction
of the prelates. 19

This discussion on the friars shows clearly that they
constituted a privileged group in Philippine society. As
such, they were expected to resist any movement to alter
the status quo which might result in a diminution of their
social, economic, and political power. With so much power in their hands, they were bound to commit abuses both
against the Church and the government and, more injuri-
ously, against the Filipinos. It is no wonder, therefore,
that the friars should be looked upon with unmitigated con-
tempt by the "Propagandists" or reformists — notably Dr.
Jose Rizal, our national hero, and Marcelo H. del Pilar
and Graciano Lopez-Jaena20 — and by the revolutionists,
who went to the extent of treating the friars as prisoners
of war and killing forty-three of them. 21

Social stratification. Pre-Spanish Philippine society
was structured into a small upper and governing class of
nobles, a larger class of freemen, and a still larger "ser-
vile, dependent class whom the Spaniards misleadingly
called slaves. "22 In common with some other societies of
pre-European Asia, the class structure was based on landownership and birth, although in the Philippines the social
strata were not as rigid as the castes of India.

Three centuries of Spanish rule naturally modified,
but did not totally alter, the basis of the social system. To
the traditional bases of class structure were now added
occupation and education. In the colonial Philippine society,
racial origins were a determining factor in locating one's
social position.

If one excludes the Chinese, who really formed a

special group, Philippine society during the Spanish regime
actually consisted of two different societies: the Filipino
and the Spanish. In the Spanish society were the Peninsu-
lares or European-born Spaniards, the Insulares or Philip-
pine-born Spaniards, and the Spanish mestizos (born to
Spanish-Filipino parents), [23] as well as high government
officials, Church prelates, and officers of the military
establishment. Rich merchants and plantation managers
formed a small middle class, and lower-ranking government officials, clerics, and non-commissioned officers of
the army, most of whom were probably not well educated,
constituted the lower class among the Spaniards. But
regardless of their place of birth and social origin, occupation and education, the Spaniards and Spanish mestizos
belonged to the upper stratum of Philippine society as a
whole. They were, after all, the colonial masters and
enjoyed vast economic and political power.

The Filipino society had its own aristocracy, made up
of the caciques and the more opulent and highly educated
ilustrados. The term cacique was applied to a local chief
in Haiti at the time the Spaniards arrived there, and they
also used the term to denote the datus of the various barangays in the Philippines. [24] The caciques were the tax-
gatherers, administrators of justice in their localities,
and the intermediaries between their people and the Spanish
authorities. They were the principalia or prominent residents at the local level, [25] and during the Spanish regime,
were in a position to increase their wealth. This has been
pointed out very clearly by Professor Pelzer:

> By recognizing them, the Spaniards helped
> the caciques to preserve their power over the
> people and gave them the opportunity of getting
> more and more land into their hands, of making
> more and more people financially dependent
> upon them (inasmuch as they were the tax-
> collectors), and of reducing freeholders to
> the status of tenants. Thus many of the lead-
> ing families of pre-Spanish days kept their
> favorable social and economic position, and
> often strengthened it by intermarriage with the
> Spaniards. [26]

In Spanish times, the term ilustrados applied to the
highly educated and professional Filipinos, although technically speaking anyone who had an education, high or low,
was an ilustrado. 27 In a way the ilustrados formed a distinct class: since education was the distinguishing mark,
this class cut across economic lines. We may, however,
consider the ilustrados as belonging to the Filipino upper
class, since most of them must have come from well-to-
do families to be able to afford a university education in
Manila, and, in some cases, even in Europe. Many, if
not all, of the ilustrados were probably mestizos. 28

The ilustrados were excluded from membership in
the upper class of Philippine society in spite of their education and, in some cases, wealth; they were not accorded
the same political and ecclesiastical privileges as the
Spaniards. They were, however, given some for of social
recognition denied the uneducated caciques. And in the
smaller Filipino society, they definitely shared with the
caciques privileges of membership in the upper class.

A middle class as understood in European society was
probably non-existent in the Filipino society. At any rate,
even for Philippine society as a whole, the middle class
was woefully limited. The great majority of the Filipinos,
then as now, were peasants. Some of them were free-
holders, but the bulk of the peasantry probably consisted
of part- or full-time tenants as well as agricultural
hands. 29

Taxation and tariff relations with Spain. Before discussing the changes brought about by the Philippine Revolution in the society whose features we have sketched in
the preceding pages, it may be pertinent to discuss the
taxation system and the tariff relations between Spain and
the Philippines on the eve of the revolution.

There were four main types of internal taxes: (1) the
cedulas personales, or capitation tax, (2) documentary
stamp taxes, (3) the urbana tax, or tax on rentals of urban
property, and (4) the industria tax, consisting of commercial, corporation, occupation, professional, and income
taxes. 30 As can readily be seen, there was no real estate
or land tax as such. 31

The cedulas personales ranged from ₱37. 50 down to

WINGATE COLLEGE LIBRARY
WINGATE, N. C.

₱0.50.[32] depending upon the amount of industria and urbana taxes one paid. Exempted from the cedulas personales
were priests and nuns, privates of the Spanish armed forces
and of the civil guard, paupers and individuals serving jail
terms, and the following clase privilegiada: town chiefs
and their wives as well as cabezas de barangay, their wives,
and first-born sons. Such exemption was "in recognition of
their services in the administration and collection of the
tax."[33] Thus, those who were in a better position to pay
the tax were the ones exempted.

Another unfair feature of the system of taxation may be
seen in the case of the industria tax. Commercial establishments in the same line of business paid the same amount of
tax, regardless of the volume of sales or net profits. Furthermore, some of the richer people probably escapted payment of taxes, or at least secured a substantial reduction of
them, through collusion with tax officials. Worse, only a
small percentage of the taxes and other revenues[34] was
spent on public welfare projects, as may be seen from the
fact that of the total expenditures, in 1880-1881 and 1885-
1886 less than 3 percent was allotted to such projects; in
1894-1895, it was less than 5 percent.[35]

Philippine-Spanish trade relations were based on a
system of tariff preferences. Spanish products were admitted into the Philippines duty-free if imported in Spanish
bottoms; a slight duty was levied if they were brought in
foreign vessels. Foreign merchandise imported in Spanish
vessels also paid lower duties than if brought in non-
Spanish ships. Correspondingly, Philippine products exported to Spain were admitted duty-free.[36]

The Heritage of The Revolution

Background: The Propaganda Movement.[37] The colonial society of Spanish times was rigidly stratified, mainly
on the basis of racial origins. The Spaniards monopolized
the political and ecclesiastical power over a country in
which they were a very tiny minority. The ilustrados were
not accorded a share in political power, a fact which deeply
frustrated the more radical ones among them because they
could claim equal, if not better, professional and educational

backgrounds than most of the Spanish officeholders. Having
assimilated some notions of European liberalism of the
eighteenth century variety from foreigners and some Spanish liberals who came to the Philippines during the liberal
regime of Governor Carlos Maria de la Torre (1869-1871),
the ilustrados naturally desired a more broadly based
regime.

The ilustrados' clamor for greater political power also
had another mainspring: their desire to be in an advanta-
geous position to preserve their economic and social position in Philippine society, which was undergoing important
changes in the nineteenth century. Professor Majul puts it
as follows:

> With the possible changes in the economic
> structure of the country, due to commerical
> penetration from abroad and agricultural im-
> provements within, they [i. e., the ilustrados]
> desired a definite and secure place in order
> that their interests would be better protected.
> It was to secure this place that political re-
> forms were deemed essential. 38

It was not to be expected that the defenders of the
status quo would meekly give in to the desires of the
ilustrados. Power is seldom shared and hardly ever relinquished voluntarily. On the contrary, the champions of
the old order, notably the friars, branded the ilustrados
as opportunists who were merely interested in personal
aggrandizement. In refutation of this claim, the ilustrados
asserted that they were speaking for the entire Filipino
people. To justify this assertion, and to win the support of
the other Filipinos for their cause, the ilustrados were
obliged to demand more than simply political power for
themselves. Their expanded set of demands eventually
came to include the extension of a more liberal regime
and governmental institutions, a more efficient, honest
administration, more and better schools, and "the speedy
replacement of the friars by Filipino priests. "39 The
latter demand was no doubt included in an attempt to capi-
talize on the resentment of the Filipino secular clergy over

the failure of the government and Church to secularize the parishes.

The ilustrados worked hard to make the masses understand their ideas and program, thereby establishing an ideological bond between the Filipino upper class and the lower classes. 40 Thus, the Propaganda Movement, as the reform movement is more popularly known in the country's history, assumed two forms: a campaign for reforms, waged mostly in the mother country, and the awakening of the masses. The propagandists or ilustrados proposed to accomplish their program within the framework of the Spanish regime, not outside it.

The Philippine Revolution. 41 Unfortunately for the propagandists, the Spanish government remained impervious to their demands, and the Propaganda Movement ended in dismal failure, unable to achieve any of its desired reforms. Nevertheless, out of this failure emerged the Katipunan, a secret society which proposed to attain the objectives of the ilustrados or propagandists through a revolution, and the separation of the Philippines from Spain.

The violent upsetting of the status quo was not welcomed, however, by the ilustrados, who were adverse to bloodshed. Furthermore, as Professor Majul claims, there was a "basic conflict involving economic interests and the claims of. . . [some] ilustrados that they should inherit the prerogatives of the past colonial masters. "42 Consequently, the ilustrados, with very rare exceptions, refused to joing the Katipunan or even to give it financial support. Some ilustrados, like Apolinario Mabini and Antonio Luna — who were to play leading roles during the later phase of the revolution — went to the extent of denouncing the Katipunan. 43 The Katipunan therefore remained a plebeian organization and the Revolution of 1896 was truly a "revolt of the masses. "

The Philippine Revolution passed through two phases. The first phase started in August, 1896, and was terminated in December, 1897, by the Pact of Biyak-na-Bato, which proved to be merely a truce. 44 The second phase started in the early months of 1898 and ended as an armed resistance against the imposition of American sovereignty over the Philippines. The second phase of the revolution concerns us more, for it was during this period that the Filipinos took concrete steps to change the undesirable features of the old regime and succeeded in realizing some of their aspirations.

The most important change, as far as the Filipinos were concerned, was the liberation of the Philippines from Spain and the establishment of a Filipino government culminating in the Philippine Republic of 1899, which is more popularly referred to in historical literature as the Malolos Republic. [45] Under the Malolos Republic, the major institutional change in the government was the creation of a Congress of legislature. The political divisions of the old regime were retained.

The institutional arrangements at all levels of the government assured the ilustrados and the caciques a controlling position in the revolutionary government. [46] This calls for some explanation, since they had refused to join the first phase of the revolution. Quite apart from the natural revulsion against bloodshed, the Filipino upper class had kept aloof from the Katipunan and the Revolution of 1896 because they still hoped that Spain would grant some of their demands and therefore maintain their predominant position in the Filipino society. They also doubted, and perhaps so did some of the Katipunan leaders themselves, whether the Filipinos — lacking arms — could really defeat the Spaniards. This actually turned out to be the case. A revolution that had no prospect of success had no attraction for the upper class, who stood to lose everything they owned, perhaps their very lives, if a vengeful Spanish government found out that they had supported the revolution.[47]

It was different in the case of the second phase, which had all the makings of a successful revolution. Spain had been humbled by the United States, whose naval forces stood ready to cut off any Spanish re-enforcements from abroad. The Filipinos were also much better equipped this time. They had more arms, thanks to Admiral George Dewey, who had turned over to General Aguinaldo captured guns from the Cavite arsenal. Ironically, tne Spaniards themselves were also responsible for providing more weapons. In December, 1897, they had paid ₱400,000

to General Aguinaldo, who used the money to procure arms.[48]
Adding to the certainty of the revolution's success were
earlier American professions of friendship and unofficial or
unauthorized avowals of disinterest in the Philippines.[49]
Thus, when General Aguinaldo issued the call for unity among
the Filipinos on July 15, 1898,[50] in the hope of attracting
more ilustrado talent into the revolutionary government,
the latter immediately grabbed the opportunity to show their
patriotism or to protect their own interests.

But let us return to the arrangements which gave the
upper class a most decisive role in the revolutionary government. In the municipalities, only those residents "distinguished for high character, social position and honorable
conduct" were entitled to vote for town officials.[51] This
provision of the electoral law alone was sufficient to dis-
qualify most of potential electors and confined the choice
of officials to a very limited circle.[52] Since the town
chiefs elected the provinical officials, provincial governments were likewise under the control of the provincial
gentry. At the central or national level, the Filipino upper
class was equally well-entrenched. Among its ranks were
members of the cabinet, army officers, and congressmen.
It was probably as members of the Congress that the upper
class as a body came very close to being the dominant
group in the revolutionary government. This was so because the governmental system that was later adopted was
of the cabinet rather than the presidential type, with the
legislature dominating the other two branches of the government. Since the members of the Congress from each
province were chosen — in places where it was possible to
hold elections — by the town chiefs, it was only logical for
the upper class to dominate the Congress.[53] From that
vantage point they were able to make their influence prevail over the President and the judiciary. The system was,
after all, designed to work that way. The "author" of the
Malolos Constitution had this explanation, long familiar to
students of Philippine political history, to offer for the
arrangement adopted at Malolos:

> Being fully convinced, . . . that in case of ob-
> taining our independence, we were for a long

time to have a really oligarchic republic in
which the military element, which was ignorant
in almost its entirety, would predominate, I
preferred to see that oligarchy neutralized by
the oligarchy of intelligence, seeing that the
Congress would be composed of the most intelligent elements of the nation. This is the principal reason why I vested Congress with such
ample powers, not only within the legislative
sphere, but also in its control of the executive
and the judicial branches. In one word, where
oligarchies were concerned, I preferred the
oligarchy of the intelligence to an ignorant
oligarchy.54

The above shows, first of all, that at Malolos class
consciousness was rather pronounced. It also indicates a
significant division within the upper class. Although some
army officers were doubtless ilustrados and intelligent
caciques, like General Luna, General Manuel Tinio, and
Aguinaldo himself, it was believed by the ilustrados that
most of the army officers were ignorant, or liable to be
controlled by the ignorant rank and file of the military establishment. Moreover, the latter were also "have nots,"
economically speaking. The prospect of a government
dominated by an ignorant and impecunious military element,
confiscating the properties of the substantial ilustrados,
must have been dreadful. To stop legally any confiscatory
move, the ilustrados designed a parliamentary form of
government in which they would be the dominant group.
This abundantly illustrates that on the eve of the American
Occupation, there was already an articulate and cohesive
group of conservative-nationalists who knew what they
wanted and who were experts in the techniques of safe-
guarding their vested interests.
    One of the changes brought about by the revolution was
the removal of the friars from their position of power. The
revolutionary government treated the friars within its territory as prisoners of war,55 an unorthodox measure which
was defended on the grounds that the friars had actually
been the cause of the revolution, that they had aided

Spanish soldiers, and that their convents had been trans-
formed into strongholds and pockets of resistance against
the forces of the revolutionary government.[56] It was also
defended on the ground that if released, the friars might
start a "counter-revolution."[57] The real reasons, however, may have been the desire of the revolutionary government to keep the Filipino priests on its side and to take
over the friar lands.

It was not enough that the revolutionary government,
by the forcible removal of the friars, had enabled the
Filipino clergy to take over the parishes and thereby
realize their dream of secularization. The revolutionary
government also encouraged and assisted in the establishment of the National Church, which was envisioned as an
entirely Filipinized chapter of the Roman Catholic Church,
from accolyte to archbishop.[58]

The idea of a National Church was conceived by Mabini
as early as October, 1898. Political considerations were
apparently uppermost in his mind when he proposed to
Father Gregorio Aglipay y Labayan that he organize the
Filipino priests into a National Church.[59] Mabini probably
wanted to be sure that even as the revolutionary government proceeded to confiscate the friar lands and to propose the separation of Church and State and the equality of
religious worship, the Filipino clergy would still support
the revolutionary movement just as strongly as if it had
not undertaken any of these measures. He must have
assumed that the Filipino priests expected to succeed to
the former religious perquisites of the friars as well as
to their properties, and that if they did not, they might remain loyal to the Archbishop of Manila, who was not only
a Spaniard but also a friar! That would not only be anoma-
lous but might even prove disastrous to the unity of the
Filipino people, since the Filipino priests were also influential in their respective parishes. On the other hand,
Mabini argued that if the Filipino clergy did not unite and
negotiate an agreement with the Pope that only Filipino
priests and bishops were to be appointed to the Church in
the Philippines, the religious gains of the revolution might
be forfeited after the conclusion of peace; the Pope would
still have the unencumbered power to appoint non-Filipinos,

perhaps even Spaniards, as bishops and priests of the Catholic Church in the Philippines. The revolutionary government promised to assist the Filipino clergy in securing a concordat with the Vatican which would preclude that possibility.60 In other words, Mabini proposed to place the power and prestige of the State behind the efforts of the Filipino clergy to keep the positions in the Church exclusively to themselves.

On October 23, 1899, twenty-seven Filipino priests, led by Father Aglipay, assembled at Paniqui, Tarlac, and adopted the constitution of the National Church. The Paniqui Assembly formally decided to send a delegation to the Holy See to secure papal recognition of the National Church, canonical validation of the actions of the Paniqui Assembly and of the clergy — especially of Father Aglipay before the Assembly — and the concordat as proposed by Mabini. As expected, Father Aglipay was chosen provisional head of the National Church.

Although no open break with the Roman Catholic Church was decided upon at Paniqui, the tendencies of the National Church were definitely schismatic, for it represented a declaration of independence by a portion of the Filipino clergy from their diocesan superiors in the Philippines. The National Church was, in fact, the direct precursor of the Philippine Independent Church.61

The revolutionary government confiscated the friar lands and an article added to the Malolos Constitution officially declared these as having "been restored to the Filipino government."62 They were not distributed among their tenants, but instead were used as sources of government revenue. Toward this end a law was passed in February, 1899, which provided for the administration of the friar lands "by men of means" to be designated by the Secretary of the Treasury, with preference to be given to "local chiefs," "who will furnish such security, in cash or in bond, as the secretary of the treasury may deem necessary."63 The administrators of the friar lands were paid for their services according to a schedule fixed by law. Here again was one arrangement which redounded to the benefit of the gentry. But it must have been quite a disappointment to the masses who "joined Aguinaldo in the

hope of acquiring possession of a piece of land" from
among the properties of the religious orders.64

One other important legacy of the revolution remains
to be noted: the steps taken in the field of education. At
the primary level, the revolutionary government continued
more or less the same system of education in effect before
the revolution.65 Now, however, the role of the Spanish
friar was gone. The creation of the Literary University of
the Philippines by a decree of October 19, 1898, was the
most important single educational innovation instituted by
the revolutionary government. This was the first time that
a secular, state-supported institution of higher learning
was established in the Philippines. During the university's
short life, it was able to hold its graduation exercises in
Tarlac on September 29, 1899, when degrees in medicine
and law were awarded.66

Filipino Aspirations

The Filipino response to American rule was determined not only by the objective conditions of Philippine
society at the time of American annexation, but also by the
aspirations of the Filipinos. It is therefore necessary to
point out what these aspirations were, especially since the
Filipinos were striving hard to realize them when the
United States decided to acquire the Philippines from Spain.

These goals of the Filipinos were expressed in their
writings, their constitutional programs, and their testimonies as recorded by their American interlocutors.
Professor Majul's statement that these "originated from
the social class in the Philippines historically known as
the ilustrados"67 is perfectly understandable. Only the
ilustrados, by virtue of their education, were in a position
to reflect on the social and political issues of the day and
to challenge the Spanish authorities with ringing demands
for reforms.68

On the whole, Filipino aspirations were concerned
primarily with individual freedoms, the relation of individuals in society to their political institutions, the proper
functions of government, the limits of governmental
authority in a free society. One looks in vain for com-

parable expressions of Filipino economic aspirations because the ilustrados were already economically well off.
What they wanted most was a share in political power.

The emphasis on political rights may also be explained
by the orientation of the ilustrados toward European liberal
philosophy. By European philosophy is here meant the
philosophy of the Enlightenment, which laid greater stress
on political equality than on economic equality. This in
turn may be explained by the fact that the political philoso-
phers of the Enlightenment were generally from the middle
class and so, given their already favored economic position,
were obsessed with wresting political power from the aristocracy. The latter, in spite of their diminishing wealth
and usually inferior educational and professional backgrounds, had continued to monopolize the "corridors of
power" simply because they were born to the governing
class (which then included the clergy).

While many of the Filipino aspirations were mere
abstractions, others had roots in the political and social
realities of the day. Thus, the desire for greater local
autonomy had its roots in the extreme centralism of Spanish rule, that for separation of Church and State stemmed
from clerical control of essential areas of governmental
activity, and so on. Finally, the demand for independence
developed with the realization that the bulk of Filipino
aspirations were unattainable within the framework of
Spanish sovereignty.

The writings of the ilustrados — notably Rizal, del
Pilar, Lopez-Jaena, 69 and Mariano Ponce 70 — and even
those of the Katipunan leaders, such as Andres Bonifacio
and Emilio Jacinto, 71 all contained sections on the necessity of recongizing individual rights and of conferring upon
the individual the privilege of participating in decision-
making. The numerous constitutional plans of the Filipinos
all contained a Bill of Rights. 72 Considered as the goals
of the revolution, those enumerated rights were a warning
that the Filipinos would not tolerate a return to the des-
potism and absolutism of Spanish rule.

The Filipino's ideal of the relationship that should
exist between units of the government was expressed in the
following provision of the Malolos Constitution:

> The administration of the private interests of
> the towns, provinces, and the state, correspond
> respectively to the municipal (populares) assem-
> blies, the provinical assemblies and the admini-
> stration in power according to the laws, and
> upon the basis of the most ample decentralization
> and administrative autonomy.[73]

Local and provincial autonomy was qualified, however, by
another provision of the Malolos Constitution which would
allow

> The intervention of the government, and in a
> proper case by the Assembly in order to pre-
> vent the provincial and municipal corporations
> from exceeding their powers, to the prejudice
> of general and individual interests.[74]

The desire of a sizable portion of the Filipinos, particularly the ilustrados, to do away with the union of Church
and State and to enjoy the freedom to profess forms of
religious worship other than Roman Catholicism was embodied in the brief Article 5 of the Malolos Constitution,
which reads as follows:

> The state recognizes the freedom and equality
> of all religious worships, as well as the separa-
> tion of the church and the state.

To be sure, this was not the original proposal contained in
the Calderon draft of the Malolos Constitution, and it was
adopted only after a second balloting by a majority of one
vote.[75] Probably because of this, and the desire of the
revolutionary leaders not to alienate the support of the
Filipino clergy, a temporary provision of the Malolos
Constitution was adopted suspending the execution of
Article 5. The same article also stated that in the meantime, the municipalities or places which might need "the
spiritual services of any Filipino priest, shall provide for
his necessary support. "[76]

Finally, there was the Filipino aspiration to remain

independent of alien rule upon the termination of the Spanish-
American War. In fact, as far as the Filipinos were concerned, the reality of independence existed during the last
six months of 1898 and early months of 1899. The desire
for independence was not widespread during the early phase
of the revolution, but during its second phase, it became
practically universal.77 As an American students of early
Philippine history puts it:

> We should be far from the truth if we should
> say that this Tagalog rebellion [i. e. , Philip-
> pine Revolution], and the demonstrations of
> sympathy with it in other provinces, brought
> the Filipino people together in a unanimous
> sentiment for independence. That it did greatly
> stimulate this feeling is certain. He would be
> a bold man who would now assert that <u>indepen-
> dence</u> was not the common aspiration, when
> outside pressure suddenly pricked the bubble
> of Spanish sovereignty in 1898 and released
> the people for the free expression of their
> sentiments.78

As we shall see in the rest of this thesis, Filipino
aspirations for independence, and indeed all other Filipino
aspirations, had a decisive influence upon the policy of the
United States as well as on the nature of Filipino-American
relations during the Taft Era.

THE BIRTH OF AMERICAN
POLICY TOWARD THE PHILIPPINES

The outbreak of the Filipino-American War on February 4, 1899, was the immediate Filipino response to the American decision to acquire the Philippines. It was the response of a people who, desiring recognition as a nation, were made all the more brutal by feeling that the United States had betrayed an earlier trust. Filipino-American relations did not begin with outright violence; the hostilities of 1899-1902 were preceded by an Indian summer, as it turned out to be, of friendly relations between General Aguinaldo and certain high American consular, naval, and military officials. While the de facto collaboration had simply been the result of a common short-run interest — the defeat of the Spanish forces — the Filipinos were wittingly or unwittingly made to believe that the United States would recognize their independence upon the conclusion of peace.

The direct aftermath of the Filipino-American War was smoldering Filipino distrust of Americans, a situation which could erupt into open violence at any time. It became the objective of American policy to prevent such an eruption.

The result was the formulation of a policy calculated to reconcile the Filipinos to American rule as quickly as possible and to win back their confidence without promising them independence. This could be accomplished only by meeting some of their demands. From the outset, therefore, Filipino aspirations became important determinants of American policy.

Early Attempts to Reconcile the Filipinos

The American decision to acquire the Philippines, highlighting the failure of Filipino diplomacy to influence the outcome of the Paris peace negotiations,[1] completely shattered the Filipinos' faith and confidence in the intentions of the United States to bring back General Aguinaldo from exile in 1898. 2 It was the last of a series of actions which made the Filipinos suspect that the United States did not intend to recognize Philippine independence at the end of the war. Among these actions had been Dewey's failure to attend, or send a representative to, the proclamation of Philippine independence at Kawit, Cavite, on June 12, 1898,3 and the refusal of the American military commanders to address General Aguinaldo as President of the Revolutionary Government.4 But most important of all, the Filipinos had been prevented from participating in the "battle" of Manila on August 13, 1898. Since the Filipinos had considered the capture of Manila as the major battle in their way for independence, they were extremely bitter at this cavalier treatment by their American allies.5 In fact, Filipino-American hostilities on August 13 were avoided "only with great difficulty. "6

The actions of the American forces subsequent to August 13 did nothing to restore Filipino confidence. Elwell Otis, Wesley Merritt's successor as American Military Commander, was overbearing in his relations with Aguinaldo, adding insult to injury.7 Disgusted, the latter moved the seat of his government from Cavite to Malolos, where the historic Malolos Congress soon took place.

This, in brief, was the situation when the Treaty of Paris was signed in December, 1898, President McKinley must have been fully aware of the Filipino attitude, for even as he took steps to establish more firmly the military regime, whose replacement with a civilian authority was the first concrete step taken to reconcile the Filipinos, he emphasized:

> The earnest and paramount aim of the military administration [should be] to win the confidence, respect, and affection of the inhabitants of the Philippines by assuring them in every possible way that full measure of individual rights and liberties which is the heritage of free peoples, and by proving to them that the mission of the United States is one of benevolent assimilation, substituting the mild sway of justice for arbitrary rule. 8

President McKinley repeated the above purposes of the military administration in identical messages to Otis and Dewey on January 8, 1899, 9 doubtless with the aim of inducing the Filipinos to accept American rule without a fight.   It was also for this purpose that he appointed and sent the First Philippine Commission to the Philippines. The desire to conciliate the Filipinos is plain from President McKinley's instructions to the Schurman Commission, as the First Philippine Commission is commonly known. For instance, President McKinley instructed the Commission to determine what improvements in the condition of the Filipinos and in the public order might be adopted. The Commission was also to make recommendations for the "perfection of present administration. " Finally, President McKinley urged the members of the Commission to emphasize always in their dealings with the Filipinos "the just and beneficent intentions of the Government of the United States. "10

But the Filipinos cared neither for "benevolent assimilation" nor to hear more about the "beneficent intentions of the American government. What they wanted was to be left alone to consolidate the gains of the revolution, or, if the United States really wanted to do something for them, a declaration that it would protect an independent Philippines from aggressors.11

As fighting went on, the United States now came out with more than proclamations of intentions. On May 12, 1899, it offered the so-called Hay Plan, with a Philippine government to

> consist of a Governor-General appointed by
> the President; cabinet appointed by the Governor-
> General; a general advisory council elected by
> the people, the qualifications of electors to be
> carefully considered and determined; and the
> governor-general to have absolute veto. Judi-
> ciary strong and independent; principal judges
> to be chosen from natives or Americans, or
> both, having regard to fitness. 12

Secretary Hay added that President McKinley wanted an

early cessation of hostilities, and that the Filipinos would be given "the largest measure of local self-government consistent with peace and order."13 The Schurman Commission had recommended the offer of this more or less autonomous form of government after ascertaining the views of the conservative Filipinos in Manila and also after conferences with a commission from the Malolos Republic.14 The latter, however, eventually rejected the Hay Plan as falling far short of the expectations or aspirations of the Filipinos.15

With the rejection of the Hay Plan, America's early efforts at conciliating the Filipinos collapsed. The Schurman Commission therefore returned to the United States without accomplishing its objectives of facilitating the "most humane, pacific, and effective extension of [American] authority throughout these islands...."16 Meanwhile, President McKinley declared that "the settlement of the Philippine problem would be accomplished by force of arms, and not be efforts of conciliation."17

The Steps at Reconciliation

The replacement of the military regime. Despite the superior military forces which had demolished organized Filipino resistance in November, 1899, there remained considerable opposition to American sovereignty. Guerrilla warfare, in many cases more exasperating to the American soldier, was widespread. It was at this juncture that the Americans renewed their efforts to conciliate the Filipinos who remained hostile to American rule. Two steps were crucial: the replacement of the military regime and the formulation of a more concrete Philippine policy. We shall discuss these two changes in order.

The Schurman Commission recommended that the Military Government should be replaced by one staffed by civilians. Part of their argument for proposing the change was that military rule was incompatible with the Filipino's desire for local home rule, "for it is an axiom with all Filipinos...that there is no genuine freedom where the military power is not subordinated to the civil."18 The Commission put it more cogently:

It is also believed that the general substitution
throughout the archipelago of civil for military
government (though, of course, with the retention of a strong military arm) would do more
than any other single occurrence to reconcile
the Filipinos to American sovereignty, which
would then stand revealed, not merely as
irresistible power, but as an instrument for
the preservation and development of the rights
and liberties of the Filipinos and the promotion
of their happiness and prosperity.19

It is not without significance that the Second, or Taft,
Philippine Commission, which followed very shortly upon
the return of the Schurman Commission, was specifically
instructed to establish civil municipal and provincial governments, and to perform the legislative and some minor
executive functions of the Military Governor effective
September 1, 1900. 20
Taft had barely touched Philippine soil for the first
time when, sizing up the situation, he came to the conclusion that although necessary, the "Army... is not an agent
to encourage the establishment of a well-ordered civil
government, and the Filipinos are anxious to be rid of
policing by shoulder straps...."21 In Taft's view, the
great majority of the Filipinos were not opposed to the
United States at all; their hostility was simply directed
against the Military Regime. He therefore concluded that
the Filipinos would "welcome the civil authorities."22
Taft's colleagues shared his views, adding in their
first report to the Secretary of War that until the establishment of a civil government, it would be impossible for the
Filipinos "to realize the full measure of the difference between a government under American sovereignty and one
under that of Spain."23 This was a hint that just as the
Filipinos had eventually reached the point of staging a
national revolution against Spain, so would the vast majority of them continue to challenge openly the imposition of
American authority if the Military Regime were not replaced by a civilian one. It never occurred to any of the
American commissioners that the Filipinos might dislike

even civil government under American rule, and that it mattered not whether their ruler was styled dictator or president, and a general at that, provided he was a Filipino. They were in the Philippines to establish a satisfactory working arrangement between Americans and Filipinos within the framework of American sovereignty, and not to find out whether the Filipinos wanted American rule or not.

With President McKinley's re-election in 1900 assuring the continuation of American rule in the Philippines for at least the next four years, 24 Taft renewed his plea for a change in the character of the Philippine government. If he could have his way, such a change should take place before McKinley's second term. 25 Once a civil government was established, the Filipinos would, in his view, abandon their support of and sympathy for the insurrection 26 and welcome American rule. Such was Taft's faith in the wisdom of instituting civil government at once that he thought any extension of the tenure of the military regime "would be a fatal mistake. " 27

To counteract the claims of the military that the Filipinos had no real desire either for peace or to cooperate with the American Government, and hence military rule should continue for another decade, Taft penned the following letter to Root:

> The truth is, Mr. Secretary, that the situation here has never been properly represented to the public. The disposition of the Army is to distrust any evidence of popular feeling in favor of the American Government [and it]... has discounted tremendously all evidences of a willingness of the people to come to peace and to American sovereignty. 28

When Taft wrote the above lines, he had just returned from the Commission's first journey to organize provinces in Central Luzon in accordance with the provisions of the Commission-enacted provincial act. He could therefore claim some familiarity with conditions outside the city of Manila. It might be pointed out here that everywhere it went, the Commission was reportedly very warmly received by the people. 29

The necessity for a revised policy was buttressed by citing concrete evidence that the Filipino attitudes toward the United States had changed from total revulsion to enthusiastic acceptance. Taft attributed the change to the Commission's arrival and assumption of legislative powers hitherto wielded by the Military Governor, coupled, perhaps, with the Filipinos' recognition that a sustained struggle against the United States was hopeless. Writing to Root, Taft said that the Commission's system of adopting measures only after public hearings, unlike the arbitrary method the Military Regime used to make its decisions, had furnished "a substantial evidence of the civilian methods which would become all-controlling if peace were brought about. " Taft also asserted without hesitation that the formation of the pro-American Partido Federal[30] would not have occurred

> but for the presence of the Commission, or
> the hope which their presence and their legis-
> lative functions have given to the people of
> the beneficial changes which would follow the
> reduction of the military power to an auxiliary
> force in the government.[31]

"I know, " he concluded, "that this is the opinion of the entire Directory of the Federal Party. " To Theodore Roosevelt, soon to succeed McKinley as President of the United States, Taft wrote of the "most gratifying" temper of the Filipinos, "specially toward the Commission and those who are engaged in establishing civil [i.e., provincial and municipal] governments. "[32]

The man President McKinley entrusted with the refinement — if not also the formulation and implementation — of the Philippine policy of the United States was Elihu Root, the able Secretary of War.[33] Root was at the receiving end of communications emanating from both the Commanding General of the American Forces in the Philippines, who was also the Military Governor, and Taft, the President of the Philippine Commission. While the former strongly favored a continuation of military government, Taft, as we have seen, worked earnestly to have that regime

supplanted by civilian rule as soon as possible.34 Root may
have been partial to Taft, a fellow lawyer, when he chose
to oppose General Arthur MacArthur.35 But there was more
than partiality toward a fellow lawyer involved.

Root himself believed that the results of efficient,
honest, and just government — such as adequate revenues
to ensure the performance of the civil functions of government, good schools, good means of transport, etc. — were
the main instruments for convincing the Filipino people that
the United States was sincere in its "profession of interest
in their welfare." In Root's opinion, these could be
achieved only with accelerated commercial and industrial
activity, for which there must be "mining laws, homestead
and land laws, general transportation laws, and banking
and currency laws." "Such laws," Root emphasized,
"the military government can not supply;" only a civil
government could because it could project its authority
into the future. Root continued:

> The great agency to bring industrial activity
> and awakened enterprise and prosperity and
> contentment to the country of the Philippines
> must be, not a military government, but the
> same kind of individual enterprise which has
> built up our own country.36

President McKinley endorsed Root's recommendations
to Congress in late January, 1901. Congress responded by
passing the "Spooner Amendment" to the Army Appropriation Bill in March, 1901, enabling the President to proceed
with the establishment of civil government.37 On June 21,
1901, Root issued the order relieving the Military Governor of his civil executive authority over the pacified provinces and transferring such authority to the President of
the Philippine Commission, who now also carried the title
of Civil Governor, effective July 4, 1901.38 In another
year's time, Congress passed the Philippine Organic Act,
of which more will be said presently. Implementing its
provisions, Root issued another order on July 4, 1902,
placing the entire Philippines, save the Moro provinces in
Mindanao and Sulu and Southern Palawan, under the civil

government.[39] It was believed then that this step, which
was indeed quite significant, had been warranted by peaceful conditions made possible by the twin forces of military
power and the gradual bestowal of civil government upon
the Filipinos.[40]

Supporters of civil government were apparently justified in their motive — that the end of military rule and the
consequent implementation of civil government would reconcile the Filipinos. A significant change in Filipino
attitudes, especially the elite's, toward Americans may
at least be inferred from the following observations of an
American missionary in the western part of the Visayas:

> Our work has been hindered among the upper
> classes by a bitter feeling toward the Ameri-
> cans, which includes us missionaries. So long
> as the military authorities are so active, these
> classes are careful to conceal this feeling from
> us....
> ....
> On the whole I notice a great change in the
> feeling of the upper classes toward America
> from what we met when I came here thirteen
> months ago. Whether it is the rise of the civil
> Government under Governor Taft, or the influ-
> ence of the civilians, or merely the soothing of
> time that has effected the change, I am not
> certain. Certain it is that the change within a
> year is very marked in this part of the
> Visayas.... [41]

Understandably, the provincial governors appointed by the
Taft Commission in 1901 were more effusive in their asser-
tions on the change in Filipino sentiments as a result of
terminating the military regime and establishing civilian
government.[42]

Policy to reconcile the Filipinos. The replacement of
the military administration was undertaken in an effort to
reconcile the Filipinos to American sovereignty as rapidly
as possible. An inquiry into the philosophy and content of
the Philippine policy of the United States during the Taft

Era suggests that to a great extent the United States was also motivated by the desire to win the friendship of the Filipinos.

The constitutional basis of the Philippine policy of the United States during the Taft Era (1901-1913) was laid down in the Philippine Organic Act of July 1, 1902, otherwise known as the Philippine Bill.[43] This law was in great measure an elaboration of the Letter of Instructions of 1900 to the Taft Commission as well as a ratification of what the Taft Commission had accomplished in the Philippines under these Instructions. The law's important contribution to Philippine policy was the provision for an elective Philippine Assembly. As we shall later see, however, this was mainly due to Taft's efforts. For all practical purposes, therefore, the Philippine policy of the United States during the Taft Era was laid down in 1900, with some refinements in 1902.[44] Our main concern is with the background of that policy.

It is important to point out at the outset that American policy was formulated at the time when the Filipinos were still engaged in guerrilla warfare against American soldiers. A Philippine policy that would prolong such resistance, active or passive, was obviously out of the question. A policy had to be formulated that could help end the hostilities and establish an atmosphere of confidence. In other words, the policy to be enunciated and applied should enable the United States to govern the Philippines without so much reliance upon the military.

The nature of that policy was suggested vaguely by the Schurman Commission which President McKinley had sent to the Philippines in 1899:

> The United States can succeed in governing
> the Philippines only by understanding the
> character and circumstances of the people
> and realizing sympathetically their aspirations
> and ideals.[45]

Specifically, the Schurman Commission said, the government to be devised for the Philippines should, "to the utmost extent possible,... satisfy the views and aspirations

of the educated Filipinos. "[46] Happily for the United States,
the Commission pointed out:

> The more one studies the recent history of
> the Philippines and the more one studies by
> conversation and intercourse with the Filipinos
> to understand and appreciate their political
> aims and ideals, the more profound becomes
> one's conviction that what the people want above
> every other thing, is a guarantee of those funda-
> mental human rights which Americans hold to
> be natural and inalienable birthright of the in-
> dividual but which under Spanish domination in
> the Philippines were shamefully invaded and
> ruthlessly trampled upon. Every scheme of
> government devised by the Filipinos is in its
> primary intent, a means to secure that end.[47]

The Schurman Commission placed at the disposal of
President McKinley and Secretary of War Elihu Root data
on the Philippines which until then had not been available
in comprehensive form, as well as suggestions for future
action.[48] A serious handicap to objective policy-making
had thus been partly overcome. And although some of the
Schurman Commission's recommendations were not immediately considered for adoption, such as the one on the
central government,[49] it was not long after the submission
of its Report that a fairly specific colonial policy assumed
shape in the form of President McKinley's Letter of Instructions to the Taft Commission.

The Letter of Instructions to the Taft Commission has
long been hailed as a landmark in the history of tropical
colonization and as "a model of constructive statesman-
ship."[50] Root's biographer did not hesitate to pontificate
that the Instructions constitute the "most important single
document in American colonial history."[51] In Philippine
political history, it is of cardinal significance.[52]

A state paper so epochal in significance as the Letter
of Instructions deserves a little background history, even
if it means digressing somewhat from the main theme of
this chapter. Fortunately, unlike the Monroe Doctrine,

no debate as to its authorship has to tax the historian's
efforts.

Root and Taft were primarily responsible for drawing
up the Instructions, although there were contributions from
others. This is perhaps better seen by quoting Taft's letter
to LeRoy when Taft was still Secretary of War:

> The real history of the instructions... by Presi-
> dent McKinley, is this:
> By direction of the President, the Commission
> met in Washington and held a number of sessions
> and there discussed at great length the powers,
> functions and duties which the President should
> confer on us if we went to the Islands. Mr.
> Worcester, who had had the experience of
> membership in a previous commission, made
> us realize very clearly that unless we had more
> power than the previous commission, our visit
> would be without profit to the country or the
> administration. Accordingly we held a number
> of meetings with the Secretary of War, in which
> many suggestions were made to him and dis-
> cussed with him. The chief suggestion I remember
> now making was that we should have control of
> the purse strings in civil matters. This you will
> remember was embodied in the instructions.[53]
> Of course many other matters were touched upon.
> The Secretary made memoranda of those things
> which he deemed important, and drafted the
> instructions and sent them to me after the Com-
> mission had adjourned to meet in San Francisco.
> I was able to read them before I left Washington,
> and expressed to both the President and Secre-
> tary my high estimate of their weight and value.
> They were drawn by the Secretary, and I do not
> think Mr. McKinley made more than one or two
> verbal changes. The formulation of them, and
> substantially all their contents, are to be
> credited to Mr. Root.[54]

It is unnecessary to add to this account.

Quite apart from the promise to grant fundamental
freedoms to the Filipinos — something which earlier pronouncements of policy had only stated implicitly — the
Letter of Instructions sought to impress upon the Filipinos
that they would be given the widest possible opportunity to
manage their own government, commensurate with their
growing capabilities, within the framework of American
rule. As I have pointed out earlier, the Letter of Instructions paved the way for civilian government by removing
legislative power as a prerogative of the Military Governor
and lodging it in the Philippine Commission, that is, the
Taft Commission. The Instructions also conferred upon
the Commission executive functions pertaining to appointments. 55

The underlying principles which were to guide the
Commission in the performance of their mandate are contained in the following portion of their Instructions:

> In all the forms of government and administra-
> tive provisions which they are authorized to
> prescribe, the Commission should bear in mind
> that the government which they are establishing
> is designed not for our satisfaction, or for the
> expression of our theoretical views, but for the
> happiness, peace, and prosperity of the people
> of the Philippine Islands, and the measures
> adopted should be made to conform to their
> customs, their habits, and even their prejudices,
> to the fullest extent consistent with the accom-
> plishment of the indispensable requisites of just
> and effective government. 56

The influence of the Schurman Commission is unmistakable
at this point.

In many instances during its lifetime, especially during
the period 1901-1913, the Commission was both praised and
criticized by Filipinos and Americans, as well as by foreigners, for either zealously adhering to or arbitrarily
departing from the Instructions. Nevertheless, one can
still safely claim that the desire to conciliate the Filipinos
was an over-riding — although unwritten — goal of the

Instructions. Certainly, the spirit of the Instructions
negates President McKinley's "no-quarter" speech before
the veterans of the Philippine-American war in August,
1899. 57

The contention that conciliation was the guiding spirit
behind the Philippine policy of the United States may be
further substantiated by focussing our attention on two
specific features of that policy. We recall that the Hay
Plan had embodied a "general advisory council elected by
the people" as a feature of the Philippine government until
Congress should decide otherwise. 58 Included in the Schurman Commission's final recommendations was a provision
for Congress to establish a legislative body for the Philippines consisting of an elected lower chamber and an upper
chamber, one half of whose membership was to be elected,
the other half appointed. 59 The Schurman Commission
hastened to add that the Filipinos, i.e., the elite, had asked
for such a legislature. 60

In addition to asking that Congress declare United
States policy with respect to the Philippines, the Taft Commission also strongly urged that this policy incorporate a
provision for the establishment of a popular assembly.
They even recommended that such an assembly start sharing lawmaking functions and powers with the Philippine
Commission beginning January, 1904. 61 The Taft Commission sought to strengthen their recommendation with the
following observation:

> What the Filipino people desire is a definite
> knowledge of the intention of Congress with
> respect to this country, and the passage of a
> law such as the one here indicated would place
> before them within a definite period the oppor-
> tunity for that which they wish — a popular
> assembly. With definite knowledge of the time
> of its creation, they will be satisfied during the
> two years of the interval in which the government
> ... may be rounded out and completed. 62

Taft was more explicit in his covering letter, transmitting a copy of the Commission's recommendations to

Senator Henry Cabot Lodge, Chairman of the Senate Committee on the Philippines. Evidently unsure of Lodge's
position on the assembly, Taft marshalled cogent reasons:

> I feel sure that this promise of a popular assembly
> in two years will greatly facilitate the pacification
> of the Islands, and... will go a long way toward
> satisfying even the most intransigent with our
> rule.[63]

Taft repeated the above when he appeared before Lodge
Lodge's committee in February, 1902. He also said at
that time that if the Filipino people were given a forum
where they could give official expression to their views,
share in the making of laws directly affecting their lives,
and thereby have "a part in the government," they "will
have confidence that our statement to them, that we desire
to educate them in self-government and give them a measure of self-government,.. is true. "[64]
The Philippine Bill with the provision for the Philippine Assembly was passed by the House of Representatives
amidst excited partisan debates, but in the Senate the provision for the Assembly was dropped, at least momentarily.
The American Senators, it appears, did not think the time
had come for the Filipinos to be given such an important
share in their government. If they were waiting for "per-
suaders" to change their votes, these were not slow in
coming forward. From the Philippines, where he was
Acting Civil Governor, Luke E. Wright wrote to the War
Department that such partisan debates over the Philippine
Bill were agitating the Filipinos. While he thought that the
Filipinos had become more or less convinced that the
United States was not going to relinquish the Philippines to
them, Wright nevertheless emphasized the desirability of
Congress' adopting an "authoritative declaration... of a
permanent policy and the establishment of a territorial
government as recommended by the Commission" (i.e.,
with an elective Philippine Assembly) as these "would have
more real effect in the way of pacification than anything
else that could be done. "[65]
On his part, Taft wrote Lodge another strong letter in

support of the provision of the bill establishing the popular
assembly: Taft contended that, in many respects, he regarded this section as "the most important feature of the
bill" because of the training it would afford the Filipinos
and also for its political effect in convincing them that the
United States meant to prepare the way for a truly popular
government. He sought to persuade Lodge who actually
was against the Assembly provision that[66]

> The [Filipinos] count on this: the Federal Party,
> which is the strongest aid we have in the Islands,
> is committed to it, and the Commission has rec-
> ommended it. If Congress shall withhold the
> provision now, I very much fear discouragement
> on the part of our friends in the Islands. . . . I am
> very sure that the granting of such a Popular
> Assembly will have a good effect. . . in the Philip-
> pine Islands. It will be an expression of confi-
> dence in the people. . . , and it will do so much
> to help along our labors that a denial of it will
> greatly discourage me in going back.[67]

The Philippine Bill eventually passed the Senate, but
it contained the stipulation that the Assembly could be
organized — not in 1904 as the Commission had recommended — but only two years following the publication of
a census, and then only if peace had reigned throughout
the Philippines during those two years. As it turned out,
the census was not published until 1905,[68] and the Assembly project did not materialize until 1907.[69] Nevertheless,
the fact that a popular assembly had been provided for in
Congress' first real attempt to formulate Philippine policy
was a victory for the Administration and especially Taft,
who had personally labored for the Assembly in the honest
belief that the dangers would be far outweighed by the political and psychological effects of its creation upon the
Filipinos.[70]

Before discussing the Filipino reaction to the passage
of the Philippine Bill, it is pertinent to add at this point
that in recommending the establishment of the Philippine
Assembly, the Taft Commission also asked that Congress

provide for the joint election by the Assembly and the Commission of "two delegates to represent the interests of
these islands and the Filipino people before Congress and
the Executive at Washington. " The Commission said that
"this is something which the Filipino people have very
much at heart;"[71] and Taft also informed Senator Lodge
that this measure, as well as the establishment of the
Philippine Assembly, would help end the opposition of even
the more irreconcilable Filipinos to American rule.[72]
Probably the Filipinos did not want a repetition of their
experience under Spanish rule, when their real interests
were never represented before the Spanish Cortes, or, for
that matter, before any other branch of the Spanish Government.[73]

Congress responded to the Commission's recommendation by providing in Section 8 of the Philippine Bill for "two
Resident Commissioners to the United States, who shall be
entitled to an official recognition as such by all departments" of the American Government.[74]

The Resident Commissioners sat in the House of Representatives of the American Congress, and although they
did not enjoy voting privileges, they could speak on matters
that directly affected the interests of the Filipino people.
They were in constant touch with the Bureau of Insular
Affairs, which prepared the Administration's bills on the
Philippines for enactment by Congress, and which kept a
close check of their affairs and activities while in the
United States. Furthermore, they also made good use of
their presence in the mother country to explain the "Filipino cause" to the American public through personal
speeches, newspaper interviews, and the publication of
books and magazines. This was particularly true in the
case of Resident Commissioner Quezon.[75]

The presence of two Filipino Resident Commissioners
in the United States made American colonial policy rather
unique. To my knowledge, no other dependent peoples had
ever enjoyed such a privilege vis-à-vis the mother country,
although the institution was nothing new to the United States:
the territories organized under the Northwest Ordinance of
1787 each had one non-voting delegate in the American Congress. However, such territories were not regarded as

colonies but were marked for eventual admission, and were in fact later admitted, into the Union.76 For the Philippine colony, the establishment of the offices of Resident Commissioners was a happy blending of American practice and Filipino aspirations.

It is now clear that at least the political features of the Philippine policy of the United States were strongly influenced by Filipino desires. The Filipino reaction to the Philippine Bill is, in this context, quite easy to understand. The Philippine Commission wrote of it as follows:

> The Filipino people of the better class have received the passage of the Philippine act with great satisfaction. The provision for the legislative assembly has attracted much attention, and its passage has been interpreted as an earnest of the desire of the United States Government to test the growing capacity of the people and of the sincerity of its promises to extend to them self-government as rapidly as they shall show themselves fit for it.77

That the "better class" Filipinos should welcome a popular assembly is perfectly understandable. They had had it at Malolos, or at least provided for it in the Malolos Constitution. And although they entertained no illusions as to the powers of the Assembly in a colonial environment, they realized it was at least better than no popular assembly at all. There was no doubt that in the majority of cases, men from the "better" class would be chosen by a highly restricted electorate to serve in the Assembly. Therefore, even if they could not hope to dominate the government through the Assembly,78 the upper class would still gain social recognition through membership in it. Furthermore, the Filipino elite probably recognized that the Assembly could be utilized as a forum for demanding a broader interpretation of the Organic Act, or even a revision of American policy through another organic act that would provide for complete autonomy, if not independence. In fact, this was what happened.

Were the hopes and expectations of the architects of

American policy as embodied in the Philippine Bill vindicated? Or, to put it another way, did that policy, soon to acquire fame as the "Philippines for the Filipinos" or the "policy of attraction," help generate Filipino enthusiasm for American rule amidst the fresh memories of war?

The following observations of General James F. Smith, made on the eve of the inauguration of the Philippine Assembly in 1907, may perhaps supply part of the answer. General Smith had been in the Philippines since 1898, except for a few months' vacation in the United States;[79] his observations therefore had the benefit of a little perspective.

General Smith was extremely generous in his estimate of the impact of the "policy of attraction" upon Filipino attitudes. This may be attributed to the fact that he was Governor-General at the time. Moreover, he was writing to Taft, then Secretary of War and one of two individuals most directly responsible for the framing of American policy. Nevertheless, after making allowance for pardonable optimism not unusual among officials interested in the success of a given enterprise — although Smith confessed that he had doubted the expediency of civil government when it was established[80] and "thought that the concession of a popular assembly was a bit premature — we may consider that Smith's views are fairly accurate.

After correctly stating that the "policy which made the Philippine Assembly a possibility was a novel one in the world's history," Smith went on to say:

> The policy, new as it was, "did things;"...
> and notwithstanding the prophesies to the contrary it charmed the rifle out of the hands of the insurgent and made the one time rebel chief the pacific president of a municipality or the staid governor of a province. It brought peace to the islands, constituted out of those lately in arms against the sovereign power a constabulary force for the maintenance of public order and made feasible the establishment of civil government while every barrio and municipality was still smoking hot with insurrection and rebellion. In a word the policy of attraction, the policy of

giving to the Filipino people as large a measure
of local self-government as they might be capable
of exercising and enjoying proved successful and
accomplished all and more than was expected
of it.[81]

A less direct and more restrained answer to our questions may also be obtained from the following words of one
of the leaders of the Partido Federal in 1904:

> [American sovereignty] has been accepted in the
> belief that it would give the Filipinos a chance
> to pursue their own development, to acquire ex-
> perience for themselves, and to face the responsi-
> bilities that history rightfully places upon those
> peoples who hold their destinies in their own
> hands.[82]

The grant of political concessions as a means of ending
Filipino opposition and reconciling the Filipinos to American
rule was accompanied by the far-reaching decision to secure the withdrawal of the friars from the Philippines and
to purchase their estates.   This policy amounted to a recognition of the most important grievance of the Filipinos
against Spain and an implementation, though less drastic,
of the program of the Malolos Government.[83]
At the risk of over-simplification, it may be asserted
that America's friar policy, and for that matter its entire
religious policy, was at least as decisive as the political
concessions in tempering Filipino reaction to American
annexation and in reconciling the Filipinos to American
sovereignty.   This was so because Filipino aspirations in
this area were met almost completely.   The twin features
of the friar policy promised a definitive solution to the
vexatious friar question; and the application of the principle of separation of Church and State, the adoption of the
Faribault Plan in the schools,[84] and the policy of religious
toleration foreshadowed the end of the centuries-old
imporium of the Roman Catholic Church over Philippine
life, a goal which the Filipinos had long wished to accomplish by themselves.

While the United States was unwilling to recognize
Philippine independence in any form, since it was considered incompatible with America's political and economic
interests at the beginning of the twentieth century, the
religious aspirations of the Filipinos were viewed in a
different light. Here was an opportunity to make a really
substantial effort toward pacifying the recalcitrant Filipinos without sacrificing American interests. The purchase
of the friar lands would preclude the possibility of serious
agrarian unrest in the friar estates, especially since the
friars would probably insist on collecting unpaid rentals
since 1896 if allowed to repossess their properties. Furthermore, such a policy would be pleasing to the Filipino
propertied class, who might want to purchase some of the
friar lands. The removal of the friars would enable the
Filipino priests to realize their aspirations without having
to form a schismatic Church, and they would therefore be
grateful to the United States. Adherence to the principle
of the separation of Church and State would satisfy the
Filipino political elite, especially at the local level, since
they could then succeed to the political preferments and
perquisites of the friars. Finally, the recognition of the
freedom of religion and the provision for optional religious
instruction in the public schools would gratify those who
disliked Catholicism on purely doctrinal grounds as well as
those advocating freedom of conscience.

The friar policy concerns us most at this point, since
Filipino attitudes on this issue were more vocal and articulate. It led to a novel American mission to the Vatican,
headed by no less than Taft himself, to secure the Holy
Father's assistance in the sale of the friar lands and in the
withdrawal of the friars from the Philippines. If Roosevelt,
Root, and Taft believed that this unprecedented mission
would in one stroke settle the friar question, they were
mistaken and extremely naïve about the policy of the
Church.[85] But they were convinced that the settlement of
the friar question along the lines they had outlined would
effectively reduce the opposition of the Filipinos and help
to reconcile them to American sovereignty.

It its early stages America's friar policy, perhaps
unconsciously, was favorable to the Church and the friars.

This is shown by General Otis' efforts to secure the release of the friars emprisoned by the revolutionary government, [86] and by the Treaty of Paris, which recognized the properties and rights of the Church and the friars in the Philippines.[87]

The Schurman Commission made a very superficial study of the friar question.[88] This did not prevent it from urging that early consideration be given to the purchase of the friar lands by the government and from stating that it might be advisable for the Catholic Church to withdraw the friars.[89] "Considering the strong feeling of the natives concerning the lands held by the friars," the Commission said, "this policy would have good results."[90] The Commission further stated that Article VIII of the peace treaty did not constitute a barrier to the purchase of the friar lands.[91]

Root instructed the Taft Commission to undertake a thorough and careful investigation of the "titles to the large tracts of land held or claimed by individuals or by religious orders."[92] He did not recommend outright that the Commission purchase the estates, although he probably had such a step in mind. This may be inferred from the portion of his famous instructions enjoining the Taft Commission to "seek by wise and peaceable measures a just settlement of the controversies and redress wrongs which have caused strife and bloodshed in the past," and from his reminder that "our Government...prohibits the taking of private property without due process of law." Root could not have known of any strife except on the friar haciendas. A "just settlement" would seem to be for the tenants of these haciendas to own the parcels which they had been cultivating. And if these could not be acquired à la Malolos, they could at least be bought.

Unlike the Schurman Commission, the Taft Commission heard testimony for and against the friars, including testimony from the friars themselves. Taft personally conducted the hearings,[93] the transcripts of which constitute the most complete presentation of the friar question at the time of the American annexation.[94]

In summarizing the evidence before it, the Commission reported to the Secretary of War:

All the evidence derived from every source but
the friars themselves shows clearly that the
feeling of hatred for the friars is well-nigh
universal and permeates all classes. [95]

Taft added that what the report disclosed was "mild compared to what might have been said. "[96]

The Taft Commission concluded that the revolution
against Spain had started as an anti-friar movement,
though the Commission was careful to point out that the
people were not anti-Catholic Church and that they would
willingly accept American priests.[97] Since to the Filipino
"the government. . . under Spain was a government of the
friars, " it was but natural that the anti-friar movement
was also a political movement.[98] Therefore, to help in
pacifying the Philippines, the Commission recommended
that the Americans should not only avoid doing anything
that might be construed as favoring the friars in any way,
such as even giving them the ordinary police protection
extended to all individuals, but also recommended that the
government ask the Roman Catholic Church to recall the
friars from the Philippines. The Commission was sure
that the friars could return to their parishes only at the
point of the bayonets of the American Army. In the
Commission's view, this would bring the wrath of the
entire Filipino people upon the Americans, including those
Filipinos "who are in sympathy with the American
cause. "[99]

As regards the properties of the friars, the Commission made the following recommendation:

It would avoid some very troublesome agrarian
disturbances between the friars and their quon-
dam tenants if the insular government could buy
these large haciendas of the friars and sell them
out in small holdings to the present tenants. . . .[100]

The Taft Commission repeated its views on the purchase of the friar estates in its report to the Secretary of
War for 1901, [101] but remained silent on the subject of
removing the friars. Nevertheless its president, William

H. Taft, writing at about the same time in one of his numerous personal and confidential letters to Root, said:

> If we, the Americans, could rid the Islands of
> the friars the gratitude of the people for our
> action would be so deep that the slightest fear
> of further insurrection would be entirely
> removed.[102]

Meanwhile, the Vatican, through its Apostolic Delegate, Archbishop Placido L. Chapelle, formerly of the
New Orleans diocese, had been keeping a close watch over
the affairs of the Church in the Philippines.[103] Unfortunately, Archbishop Chapelle disagreed strongly with the
Taft Commission on the real feelings of the Filipinos
tward the friars and hence opposed the policy recommended
by the Commission.[104] In April, 1901, he left for Rome,
never to return. The Vatican, sensing greater trouble if
the friar question remained unsettled, indicated to the
United States Government, through Archbishop Ireland in
May, 1901, that it would be happy to hear from its authorized representative the proposals of the United States. The
Holy See was perhaps hinting at a mission, since it had no
formal diplomatic relations with the United States.[105]
Ireland, who was the American prelate of his day
closest to the Republican Administration, lost no time in
contacting Root and Taft. He did not know Taft personally,
but they both had a common friend in Mrs. Bellamy
Storer.[106] He also got in touch with Roosevelt, who had
become President upon McKinley's assassination in September, 1901. On November 7, 1901, James Cardinal
Gibbons, Archbishop of Baltimore, also entered the picture when he discussed the friar question with Roosevelt
on his courtesy call at the White House. The sum of
seven million dollars was even mentioned as a probable
purchase price for the friar lands.[107] A month later,
Ireland and Roosevelt had lunch together. Later in the
day, the latter asked Root the following:

> Have you though over the matter of sending some
> envoy — by preference a Catholic, to find out at

Rome what the Holy See, as a corporation, is
willing to do with the Philippine property?[108]

The mission to the Vatican was taking form. It became
final after a White House meeting on February 18, 1902,
between Roosevelt, Root, Taft,[109] and Ireland.[110]

The mission was to consist of Taft, Bishop Thomas
O'Gorman of Sioux Falls — who, fortunately for students,
has left a memorandum of the negotiations at Rome[111] —
General James F. Smith,[112] and Major John Biddle Porter,
as Secretary.[113] Although the proposed mission was not
announced as a diplomatic mission, since there were no
diplomatic relations between the United States and the
Vatican, the Vatican probably considered it as one anyway.
As Roosevelt put it:

It is simply that the Governor of the Philippines
will stop at Rome on his way to the Philippines
in order to go straight to the headquarters of the
business corporation with which he has got to
deal in acquiring that business corporation's
property.[114]

The Taft Mission, which arrived at Naples on May 29,
1902,[115] had as its objectives the consummation at Rome
of the sale of the friar lands and the immediate recall of
the friars from the Philippines.[116] The mission failed to
accomplish either of its goals. The Vatican was willing
to consider the sale of the friar lands, but insisted that the
transaction take place in Manila. For this purpose, it
promised to appoint a new Apostolic or Papal Delegate;
hard bargaining lay ahead. As regards the withdrawal of
the friars, the Vatican emphatically rejected the American
proposal. Taft sailed from Naples for the Philippines on
July 22, 1902, but not before informing Root that "the
answer of the Vatican was a great disappointment and
surprise to me."[117]

Nevertheless, the Taft Mission was not without
immediate results. It was a convincing proof to the Filipino elite that the United States meant to consider some
of their legitimate demands in governing the Philippines.

The first task of the American regime was precisely to convince the Filipinos that their aspirations would be realized within the framework of American sovereignty. The intrinsic value of America's friar policy, therefore, was not lessened by the failure of the Taft Mission. Furthermore, as we shall later see, the mission's objectives, to a great extent, were eventually realized.118

THE FILIPINOS
AND AMERICAN POLITICAL INSTITUTIONS

A well known American historian has written that American civilization made its greatest impact upon Philippine institutions from 1901 to 1913.[1] It would have been surprising had this not been the case.

First of all, as I have pointed out very briefly in Chapter II, the Propaganda Movement and the Philippine Revolution had already started to change some features of Philippine life before the advent of American rule. Philippine society on the eve of the American Occupation was, therefore, a society in ferment and relatively susceptible to institutional changes.

Secondly, exhausted as a result of the revolution against Spain and the even more costly war against the United States, the Filipinos were hardly in a position to reject forcefully the American program for the political, social, and economic reconstruction of their country, which involved discarding some of their institutions and ideas and introducing some American ones in their place. Fortunately, some of the latter coincided with the expectations of the more sophisticated and leading Filipinos.

Third, the period 1901-1913 was the period during which the United States exercised the strongest control over policy, administration, and public instruction in the Philippines.

Fourth, American administrators during this early period of American rule, as well as American teachers and leading private groups and individuals, such as churches and missionaries, were imbued with an "Americanizing" mission[2] that was certainly less conspicuous among the personnel of the succeeding administration of Francis Burton Harrison (1913-1921). [3]

Finally, this "Americanizing" mission was buttressed by a policy which did not consider the possibility of Philippine independence until the Filipinos had gone through a long period of apprenticeship in the methods of operating a democratic and efficient government. [4] It was assumed

that in the course of the period of tutelage — one generation or probably longer[5] — as the Filipinos learned more
about American institutions, they would be less eager for
independence.[6] In other words, Filipino-American affinity
— in this case based on some similarities in the institutions of the two peoples — was envisioned as the coupling
pin of the future order of Philippine-American relations.
It was assumed, furthermore, that Philippine-American
affinity would be all the more desirable because of mutual
economic benefits which would ensue from such a relationship.[7]

But however sincere and earnest the Americans of the
Taft Regime may have been in their attempts to introduce
American institutions and ideas, in the final analysis, the
realities of Philippine life determined the limits, speed,
and outcome of the confrontation between American civilization and Philippine institutions. This cardinal fact and
the other considerations mentioned above should be con-
stantly borne in mind as we proceed to analyze the Filipino
response to American rule.

American policy emphasized more than anything the
political development of the Philippines.[8] This was due to
several reasons. In the first place, the political development of the Philippines toward self-government was the
most important aspiration of the Filipinos, particularly the
elite, whose cooperation was essential to the success of
the American regime. We have seen in the preceding chapter how the United States eagerly sought to convince the
Filipino elite that many of their demands would be realized
under American rule.

Another reason was that it would have been highly in-
consistent with the American political tradition had the
United States not announced that the paramount aim of her
policy was to prepare the Filipinos for self-government.
At the outset it was even doubted whether, under its constitution, the United States could actually hold other nations
as colonies.[9]

It must also be pointed out that the American annexation of the Philippines did not have the endorsement of the
entire American people. Americans could afford to dis-
agree because colonies did not constitute a real national

interest, unlike the case of the European colonial powers.
There were also those who strongly disapproved of the excesses of pacification measures. In order to disarm the
critics of his policy, as well as to ensure continued Republican control of the government, President McKinley had to
enunciate a policy with the political tutelage of the Filipinos
as its focal point. Such a policy was formulated and
announced shortly before the presidential elections of
November, 1900. 10

Also to be taken into account was the conviction, that
had evolved from America's own experience, that the
solution of national problems was to be found in the democratic process. Since, from the beginning, the Americans
had considered that the Filipinos lacked the necessary experience to participate in their own government, the aim
of American policy had to be their political education.

As outlined in the Letter of Instructions of April 7,
1900, the political development of the Philippines was to
be undertaken along democratic lines, with as much Filipino participation in the government as possible, and
within the framework of administrative decentralization.
A system for determining the "merit and fitness" of
aspirants for civil positions was to be established. There
was to be minimum interference with the body of Philippine
civil law, but changes were to be made in the criminal laws
and the laws of procedure to facilitate trials and to make
those trials more impartial. The ends of government were
to be the happiness of the Filipinos and the guarantee of
their enjoyment of their basic human rights.

This political program clashed head-on with the
existing conditions in Philippine society, discussed briefly
in Chapter II, which could not be easily changed. The
result was accommodation and compromise on all aspects
of the American political program.

Shortly after the Taft Commission arrived in the Philippines, it held extensive hearings in Manila "as to the form
of government best adapted to these islands and satisfactory
to the people."11 Many of the witnesses appearing before
the Commission were members of the Filipino elite, who
demanded recognition of their political and social aspirations, such as local self-government and a large voice in

the central, or insular, government. The Commission, however, realized that the elite, for all their professed democratic ideals, had not really had experience under a democratic regime. The Commission also found what it called dense ignorance and credulity of the masses, who comprised 90 per cent of the population, and submissiveness to the Filipino upper class.12 From the Commission's standpoint, therefore, the main problem was how to strike a balance between the elite's demand for self-government and social realities.

The dilemma was resolved by the adoption of a very conservative guide which the Commission was to follow in establishing a civil government. In its own words:

> The theory upon which the Commission is proceeding is that the only possible method of instructing the Filipino people in methods of free institutions and self-government is to make a government partly of Americans and partly of Filipinos, giving the Americans the ultimate control for some time to come.13

Thus, while the municipal governments were completely in the hands of the Filipinos, they were subjected to the "scrutiny and criticism of a provincial government in which the controlling element [was] American. . . ."14 The effect of this dual arrangement was to lessen the autonomy that municipal governments were supposed to enjoy under the Letter of Instructions. In fact, the history of municipal governments under American rule was one of progressive diminution of local autonomy.15 In this respect, wrote Hayden, "the process of local government in the Philippines differs most strikingly from that in America. "16

The popular election of municipal officials was explicitly provided for in the Letter of Instructions and was faithfully carried out by the Taft Commission. In doing this, however, the right to vote was given only to males who were at least 23 years old, had held municipal offices before August 13, 1898, were literate in either English or Spanish, and who either owned real property valued at

least at two hundred and fifty dollars or paid an annual tax
of fifteen dollars.[17] "In fixing these qualifications, " the
Commission reported, "we followed the recommendations
of the Filipinos whom we consulted, except that there were
many of them who advocated a higher qualification. "[18]

The same conservative philosophy was applied to the
provincial governments, at times even to a higher degree.
Yet, municipal officials were all Filipinos and chosen by
popular vote, however small that might be. In the provincial board, until 1906, only the governor was a Filipino,
and until that year he was chosen by the vice-presidents
and councilors of the towns comprising the province. Thereafter, the governor, together with the Filipino "third member" who replaced the supervisor on the board, was elected
in the same manner as municipal officials.[19] The appoin-
tive treasurer and supervisor, the two other members of
the board before 1906, were usually Americans. Until 1907,
all treasurers were Americans; in 1913, as the following
table indicates, they still outnumbered their Filipino colleagues 18 to 13.

TABLE 1

TREASURERS IN REGULAR PROVINCES,
1907-1913[a]

Year	Filipino	American
1907	1	30
1908	5	26
1909	7	26
1910	10	21
1911	11	20
1912	11	20
1913	13	18

[a]Figures obtained from Philippine Commis-
sion Reports (1907-1913).
Treasurers in the special provinces, including
Moro Province, were all Americans.

What is important to point out at this stage was the
limited role played by Filipinos in the provincial govern-

ment and the lack of provincial autonomy. Although the position was prestigious, the provincial governor actually exercised very limited powers. The fact that his salary was less than that of the treasurer testified to the few responsibilities and powers of the office. The treasurer controlled the funds, provincial as well as municipal, while the supervisor handled contracts, internal improvements, and provincial property. "In this way," Taft explained, "we expect to keep those functions in the hands of Americans, which if exercised by the natives, would be a source of a great deal of abuse."[20] At times the provincial governor was also placed in the embarrassing situation of being under the control of the Senior Inspector of the Philippine Constabulary, who was for a long time an American.[21]

The provincial treasurer and supervisor were appointed by the central authorities and, in that respect, were officials of the national, or insular, government. The independence of the provincial governments from the central government was further weakened by the supervision and control exercised over it by the Executive Bureau, under the office of the Governor-General and headed by an American.[22]

As a result, while the central government's institutionalized supervision over provincial and municipal governments insured that as much as possible these units of government performed their duties the way Americans wanted, it also meant a significant departure from the Letter of Instructions.

Three other important observations on the system of local governments during the Taft Era may be made:

First, the political subdivisions, or administrative units, that had existed under Spanish rule were retained. In this respect, the Americans introduced nothing new.

Second, the Americans failed to remedy a fundamental weakness of local governments in the Philippines that was a carryover from Spanish times. Because the municipal and provincial governments, for the most part, were mere extensions or instrumentalities of the central government, they failed to generate local initiative in the management of local affairs. During the second phase of the Revolution,

the Filipinos had prescribed a scaffolding to solve the
problem, but the war with the United States prevented
them from carrying it out.

Third, the Filipino elite became the immediate beneficiaries of the system of local governments; the high qualifications for the exercise of suffrage confined meaningful
participation in the electoral process to the leading residents of the towns, or the caciques. As LeRoy puts it:

> The traditional caciques of the people were
> definitely recognized as the governing class,
> a recognition of existing fact which, under one
> form or another, would have to be made.[23]

The base of political participation was of course now
considerably broader than during the Spanish and revolutionary periods.

It is against this latter observation that we must look
for an explanation of the following report made by the
Commission describing Filipino reaction to the municipal
and provincial codes:

> On the whole it may safely be said that the peo-
> ple have received the municipal code in a most
> friendly spirit, have taken a commendable inter-
> est in its provisions, and in the majority of
> cases have attempted in good faith to carry
> them out.[24]

The Filipinos appeared to have also responded warmly to
the provincial code, as may be gathered from Taft's testimony before the Senate Committee of the Philippines in
1902:

> Filipinos flocked to us with expressions of
> gratification that we had thought it wise to pro-
> vide in the provincial code for an election of a
> governor, something that had not been known
> in Spanish time, and something that introduced
> into the provincial government a strong [sic]
> Filipino element. [25]

A group which benefits from a given system will hardly ask for a change in that system, or even criticize its operations too strongly for fear that any reforms will undermine advantages currently being enjoyed. This might help to explain the rather generally glowing reports of the work of municipal and provincial governments by Filipino provincial governors, although reports of American provincial executives26 and other sources of information tended to impart a different picture.27 Thus, the following report of the American governor of Samar in 1908:

> Every town has a certain number of people whose sole occupation is governing....
> . . . .
> In some municipalities many councilmen are completely ignorant of their duties and responsibilities.... There are towns which for this reason regulate their municipal ordinances in an illegal manner, committing oppression upon the inhabitants in such a way that many can do nothing with their own personal interests without previous permission from the president, councilman, or lieutenant of the barrio.28

The governor of Mindaro, also an American, reported in the same year with some bitterness: ''How is any government going to protect a man against himself...? The powers given the municipal councils are not bettering his condition.''29

On the other hand, we have the following excerpts from reports of Filipino provincial governors. Here is what the governor of Cagayan reported in 1907:

> I have noted with great satisfaction that all branches of the government of this province are making progress, not only so far as their administration is concerned, but also as to their interior organization and to the prompt dispatch of their business, thanks to the initiative and activity of the officers in charge of its several branches. 30

During the same year, the governor of Bulacan reported:

> It is my great pleasure to record in this report
> the prodigious progress of the municipal officials
> in the administration of public affairs, all of
> whom have worked in conformity with the duties
> which the law imposes on them....31

And still in the same year, the governor of Bataan wrote
that "with few exceptions all the municipal officers are
working for the good of their respective municipalities,
and good understanding prevails between them and the
people."32

While it is entirely possible that differences in political development between the provinces may have been a
basis for the differences in the reports, it is rather remarkable that Filipino provincial chiefs in general should
find not much, if anything, to criticize in the performance
of municipal governments. Perhaps this was so because
municipal officials, like provincial officials, belonged to
the upper class, and so any criticism of one group by the
other would only serve to put the class as a whole in a bad
light. As leaders of the Filipinos, the upper class knew
that the Filipino capacity for self-government was on trial
and was being carefully watched by the Americans. Any
adverse report on the operations of municipal and provincial governments emanating from the Filipino leaders
themselves would only be taken as a confession that they
were really unprepared for self-government and would
therefore strengthen American resistance to the Filipino
clamor for more powers of government, especially at the
national level.

While it may be true that from the American point of
view local and provincial governments of the Taft Era were
far from satisfactory,33 one should not ask too much from
the Filipinos of that period. They were still living in a
social milieu that was partly native and partly Castilian,
with ideas and practices that had been inherited practically
intact from the days of Philip II. Neither practice nor
instruction could have possibly altered this society to any
extent within a mere decade. On the contrary, the great

wonder was that municipal and provincial governments in
the hands of Filipinos worked at all without attendant con-
vulsions in society.

The conservative temper of the Philippine Commission
was more clearly demonstrated by the unusually limited
Filipino share in lawmaking and administration during most
of the Taft Era. The appointments of T. H. Fardo de
Tavera, Benito Legarda, and Jose de Luzuriaga to the
Commission took place only after the major legislation
for the political reconstruction of the Philippines had been
completed by the original five American members of the
Taft Commission.[34] In addition, the records show that the
appointments were made in an attempt to disarm possible
Filipino criticism of the Commission as a small body of
Americans governing seven million Filipinos and to prove
that the United States meant to "consult Filipino sentiment"
in governing the Philippines.[35]

The latter aspect of American policy may have helped
to reduce the colonial nature of lawmaking, but in some
respects Tavera, Legarda and Luzuriaga were in the Commission merely as "consultants." The American members
of the Commission simply outvoted, hence disregarded, the
Filipino commissioners when the latter would not listen to
arguments in support of proposed measures. This was particularly true during the administration of Governor Wright
and later of Ide,[36] and well illustrated in the enactment of
the Internal Revenue Law in 1904 and in the suspension of
the land tax in 1906.[37] With the establishment of the Philippine Assembly in 1907, however, the almost exclusive power of lawmaking exercised with patent arbitrariness by
Americans was greatly reduced.

The Philippine Assembly was perhaps the most important single political novelty introduced by the United States
in the Philippines. It was the matrix from which real
Philippine autonomy evolved and served as the school for
national leaders, such as Sergio Osmena and Quezon. Because its members came from various parts of the Philippines, the Assembly was also a vital link of social communications among the Filipino people. In the halls of the
Manila ayuntamiento, where the Assembly's sessions were
held, the members of the Filipino elite met face to face,

probably for the first time, to deliberate freely on matters affecting the Philippines. As such, the Assembly was a useful instrument of political socialization and, therefore, of nation-building in the Philippines.[38]

These considerations warrant an extended treament of the Assembly, whose historical background we have discussed in the preceding chapter. Its projected creation was the most important provision of the Philippine Bill of 1902, and was a major concession to the aspirations of the Filipino elite for self-government. Since the Assembly was to exercise coequal legislative powers with the Philippine Commission, except over the special provinces,[39] it represented a radical departure from prevailing colonial practice in the opening decades of the twentieth century. Taft considered its establishment of such extraordinary importance that he made another trip to the Philippines as President Roosevelt's Secretary of War to preside over the inaugural ceremonies, on October 16, 1907.

The eighty popularly elected members of the Assembly were apportioned among the thirty-four regularly organized provinces in 1907 on the basis of population, but each province was entitled to at least one assemblyman (diputado), regardless of the size of its population. Manila was regarded as a province for purposes of representation in the Assembly.[40] Under the Philippine Bill, members of the Assembly held office for two years. The term of office was extended to four years by a law passed by the United States Congress on February 15, 1911.[41] The Assembly held annual sessions, beginning on the first Monday of February,[42] which lasted for ninety days, excluding Sundays and holidays. It could also be called into special and even extraordinary special sessions by the Governor-General.[43] The Assembly conducted its proceedings in Spanish and its journal was therefore kept in that language.[44]

As in the case of other American institutions introduced in the Philippines, the nature of the Philippine Assembly during the Taft Regime was determined by several factors. Because there were no established antecedents other than the short-lived Malolos Congress and its successor, the Legislative Assembly of the Malolos Republic, it was comparatively easy for the members of the Assembly to

adopt the organization and procedure of the House of Representatives of the American Congress; in appearance the
Philippine Assembly was more an adaptation of the House
of Representatives than of the Spanish Cortes, whose rules
of procedure had been adopted by the Malolos Congress.[45]
Reasons of strategy also probably motivated the proponents
of the American system. The Filipino leaders were deeply
aware that their attempts to organize the Assembly were
being carefully watched by the Americans. They felt that
it would be easier for the latter to judge their performance,
and their growing capacity for democratic self-government,
if they adopted procedures familiar to Americans. As the
Secretary of the First Philippine Assembly put it, "should
success crown our efforts, it would be hard for them to
evade recognition of the successful trial."[46] The leaders
of the Assembly, most of whom were members of the
Nacionalista Party[47] which advocated "immediate" independence, probably also thought that their cause would be
greatly helped if their Assembly appeared to work like the
American House of Representatives.

It was, of course, inevitable that the Philippine Assembly
in operation should differ from its American model. Its
colonial status, the experience, background, and tempera-
ment of its leaders and members, the American policy of
conciliating the leadership of the Filipinos, the nature of
social relations in Philippine society, and the character of
Philippine society in general — all these helped to endow the
Philippine Assembly with characteristics peculiar to itself
and to influence its actual behavior.[48]

Thus, the demonstrated voting appeal of a platform
of independence — especially "immediate" independence
— inevitably resulted in the assemblymen frequently
employing the·Assembly as a forum for the expression
of their official views on that issue. Although there is
reason to believe that at least a few prominent leaders
of the Nacionalista majority were not really for "immediate" independence,[49] a considerable number of the
Assembly's sessions were unavoidably spent on speeches
or resolutions endorsing "immediate" independence.
This has led Hayden to observe that to a great extent
the Assembly evolved "as an instrument for the

attainment of indepence rather than as a normal lawmaking body. "50

In addition, during the Assembly's first six years the
American-controlled Philippine Commission insisted on
determining the final shape of legislation, and, claims
Hayden, members of the Assembly developed "a feeling of
irresponsibility for the actual process of legislation. "51
They were quite willing to let the Executive branch, in
consultation with the Speaker of the Assembly, formulate
the major bills. This situation, coupled with the Speaker's
recognition as the second most important official of the government — next only to the Governor-General52 — Speaker
Osmena's personality, and Filipino traditional deference to
institutionalized leadership, led the office of the Speaker to
evolve, in some respects, as a "legislative cacique. "This
development was augmented by the administration's adherence, particularly under Governors-General Smith and
Forbes, to the policy of conciliating as much as possible
the Filipino leaders, which meant at this particular time
the Nacionalistas, especially Speaker Osmena.53 Such a
policy was of course imperative if the administration
wanted to get the cooperation of the Assembly. As Commissioner Elliott puts it:

> During the later years of the Forbes adminis-
> tration legislation became largely a matter of
> private arrangement between the governor-general
> and the speaker. The governor-general was, of
> course, anxious to secure the passage of neces-
> sary laws. Mr. Osmena,... was greatly inter-
> ested in his party and his own position and in
> legislation which would bring nearer the day of
> independence.... The Filipinos regarded him as
> the real head of the government. The situation
> was very difficult and probably the governor-
> general can not properly be criticized for showing
> excessive deference to the speaker and his party.
> It was necessary in order to secure legislation
> which was required to carry out the policy of the
> administration. 54

Here probably lies one of the keys to the Filipino's successful experiment in lawmaking even during the formative years of the Assembly. The Filipinos were after all not left to their own devices when it came to the formulation of major legislation, for they were under the tutelage of the Philippine Commission. On the other hand, they were not completely subservient to the Philippine Commission or the Governor-General, since the Speaker of the Assembly, whom they regarded as their leader and spokesman, saw to it through "private arrangements" with the latter that their prerogatives as lawmakers were given formal recognition. If this was hardly democratic from the American standpoint, it was nevertheless what the circumstances allowed.

We now move to a consideration of the Assembly's position in regard to the society as a whole. It is to be assumed that only those who belonged to the upper class, who had ample educational background or previous experience, could hope to be elected to the Assembly. The skills necessary for membership in that body could not have been provided by the lower classes. In this respect, at least, the Philippine Assembly may be considered as an oligarchic body representing the dominant and leading families in the Philippines. They were outwardly distinguishable from each other only, as we shall later see, by their respective stands on the issue of Philippine independence, that is, whether they were for "immediate" or "ultimate" independence. And although the members of the Assembly were popularly elected, the qualifications for voting, which were similar to those for municipal electors, restricted the suffrage to a minute percentage of the total adult population. This may be better appreciated by taking a careful look at the table on page 66.

The Philippine Assembly, whose members were elected by only three per cent of the population, could hardly be considered truly representative in the strict sense of the word. However, the small body of electors made for stability and order because it confined the area of competition to the leading and conservative families in the provinces who recognized, so to speak, the same rules of the

TABLE 2

NUMBER OF REGISTERED AND ACTUAL VOTERS ELECTIONS OF 1907, 1909, 1912[a]

Election Year	No. of Registered Voters	Per cent of Population	No. Actually Voting	Per cent of Registered Voters	Per cent of Population
1907	104,966[b]	1.15	98,251	94.00	1.41
	172,624[c]	2.59	161,697	94.21	2.42
1909	208,845[d]	3.03	192,975	92.40	2.81
1912	248,154[d]	3.50	235,792	96.00	3.30

a   Figures obtained from Reports of the Philippine Commission: 1907, Pt. 1, pp. 169-70, 203; 1908, Pt. 1, p. 87; 1910, pp. 45-46; 1912, pp. 46-48; and 1913, p. 7.

b   For special elections to the First Philippine Assembly, July 30, 1907; does not include results from three towns.

c   For first popular provincial elections, November 5, 1907.

d   For combined Assembly, provincial, and municipal elections.

game. This was so despite the fact that elections in the Philippines were accompanied by great agitation. The organization of the Philippine Assembly gave an impetus to the development of the party system in the Philippines, although it was not the reason for the rise of political parties.[55] Again, like many other Philippine social and political institutions, American policies greatly influenced the characteristics of the party system during the Taft Regime.

The conservative American policy with respect to suffrage meant that those entitled to participate in the electoral process belonged to the same social class, with practically the same interests. The political parties, be they Federal or Nacionalista, were inevitably elite parties. Since they represented or appealed to the same social class, ideologically speaking, they were identical.

The colonial setting in which the party system operated, coupled with the equivocal Roosevelt-Taft policy toward Philippine independence,[56] provided the only meaningful dividing line between the major parties, at least during the first half of the Taft Regime. Thus, officially, the Partido Federal originally advocated statehood within the United States and later "ultimate independence. The Partido Nacionalista, on the other hand, officially endorsed "immediate" independence from the very beginning. While such party labels as "ultimate" and "immediate" independence outwardly connoted great differences, in reality they meant the same thing. Nevertheless, it was claimed that they were fundamentally different, as may be seen in Legarda's letter to Taft a few months before the elections for the First Philippine Assembly:

> The political campaign now going on is very interesting, because really the division between the Progresista (old Federal) and Inmediatista (old Nacionalista) parties consists in that the first is favorable to Americans, and the second is opposed to them. The real division consists in this, because the final object of both is the same, the first deeming preparation for independence necessary, while the second says that they

are at present prepared for it. . . . But it is really
curious to note that besides these great differences
there is a very remarkable one, and that is all
persons of good moral character and responsibility
have gone to the Progresistas, while the worst
elements of society have gone to the others.[57]

Legarda was wrong, for his own party (Progresista)
included men whose attitudes toward independence were as
radical as those of some Nacionalistas, while some Nacionalistas were even more conservative than some of the
Progresistas. And certainly, not even Legarda himself
would admit that Osmena, Quezon, Rafael Palma and other
prominent Nacionalistas were persons of questionable moral
character, irresponsible, or members of "the worst elements of society."[58] In fact, as we shall point out later,
in 1910 the Progresistas almost went to the extent of
coming out openly for "immediate" independence because
of the slogan's proven ability to bring in votes. In contrast,
the Nacionalistas, or at least their party stalwarts —
Quezon and Osmena — were not really for "immediate"
independence. Under these circumstances, party membership became largely a question of likes and dislikes, of
where one's compadres were, or how one's personal
interests could best be served, regardless of party labels.
Philippine political parties during the Taft Era, therefore,
may be considered more as coalitions of the principal
families in the provinces and towns than as political parties
in the strict sense.[59] Quite naturally, elections were decided on the basis of "personal" or "family" issues,
rather than on the basis of "party" issues or social programs. Needless to say, since the political parties did not
differ in ideology, switching from one party to the other
seemed only too natural, and presented no embarrassment
do either the defector or the recipient party.[60]
But let us return to the Philippine Commission's efforts to reconstruct the Philippine government and the
application of its conservative theory.
The Americans were willing, for political reasons and
because they had no choice — given the lack of American
personnel — to have the municipal governments completely

in the hands of Filipinos. Eventually, the Filipinos were to be given the majority on the provincial boards. Also for its political effect, they granted the Filipinos ample participation in lawmaking, first by the appointment of Filipinos to the Philippine Commission beginning in 1901 and, more significantly, by the establishment of the popularly-elected Philippine Assembly in 1907. Finally, as we shall discuss presently, the Americans agreed to accord the Filipinos a far more substantial share in the judicial branch of the government, including the prestigious position of Chief Justice of the Supreme Court. Again, such a concession was partly, if not primarily, dictated by political considerations.

When it came to Filipino participation in the inner councils or top levels of the insular administration, however, the Americans were comparatively conservative — perhaps too conservative. Only one Filipino was appointed secretary of an executive department during the entire Taft Era. This took place in 1908, seven years after the appointment of the first Filipinos to the Philippine Commission and almost a year following the inauguration of the Philippine Assembly.[61] American reluctance to appoint Filipinos to high administrative posts is also attested to by the fact that, as of 1913, Filipinos were directors of only four out of some thirty government bureaus, and these bureaus were administratively and politically the least important: Weather, Archives, Patents, and Copyrights.[62]

The predominance of Americans in the top administrative posts helped instil standards of bureaucratic behavior that combined the best features of the civil service systems in the United States with the ideals of the men who were chiefly responsible for introducing the civil service system into the Philippines.[63] The validity of this view is not greatly diminished by the fact that Filipinos had started to outnumber Americans in the regular and permanent civil service from 1904 onward,[64] for the Civil Service Bureau and departmental chiefs exercised rigid and effective supervision over the performance of Filipino officers. It must also be pointed out that the civil service was insulated from partisan politics throughout the Taft Era and was therefore spared the pernicious effects of the "spoils system."[65]

The beginnings of an efficient civil service system were thus laid down during the Taft Regime. Since, under Spanish rule, public office had been considered a private perquisite, the new Philippine civil service system with its emphasis on efficiency and honesty, with appointments and promotions based exclusively on merit, must have been a novelty in its own right. That it was able to shield itself during the Taft Era from the pressures of the Filipinos' previous experience with bureaucracy was undoubtedly due in large measure to the predominance of idealistic Americans at the higher levels of the insular government.

But Filipino cooperation, as in other phases of the American program, was also indispensable to the success of the civil service program of the Taft Era. This may have been the result, claims Hayden, of efforts by the highest officials to teach government employees and the people in general the need for an honest and efficient civil service.[66] Perhaps the upper class were persuaded to accept the original American program, in spite of its theoretically egalitarian feature, by means of concessions in the form of political offices and unclassified appointments.[67]

The Americans retained the basic institutions of the Spanish judicial system in the Philippines: justices of the peace courts, courts of first instance, and the Supreme Court. They introduced a new type of court, the Court of Land Registration.[68] Only slight changes in the body of Philippine substantive law, which was based on the civil law, were effected;[69] from the beginning there was never any thought of introducing the common law into the Philippines.[70] It was felt, however, that the Criminal Code and the Code of Criminal Procedure needed to be revised drastically because they were oppressive and cumbersome, outmoded and unjust. Taft also doubted the integrity of the great majority of the Filipino lawyers, many of whom had been appointed to the bench during the Military Regime.[71] Taft therefore proposed to create an "American judiciary here." If that could not be done, he told his friend Judge Howard Hollister of Cincinnati:

I should feel like giving up the task of securing

any progress among these people. It is the
basis of all civil right and liberty, and no Filipino judiciary could have any adequate conception
of what practical civil liberty is.72

The execution of these two programs met with firm
opposition from the Filipino lawyers, organized into a bar
association (Colegio de Abogados) and led by Felipe
Calderon, the author of the Malolos Constitution. They
strongly objected to the Wright draft of the Criminal Code,
which was based largely on American law,73 "on the ground
that it changes the theory of the law which has been long in
operation in the Islands."74 A committee was therefore
appointed to prepare another draft. According to the
Secretary of Finance and Justice in 1904:

> The code, as drafted by the committee, retains
> as much of the Spanish code as was deemed
> feasible,... [and] with some modifications that
> have already been found to be necessary will
> doubtless be enacted at an early date.75

Before leaving the subject of the law, it might be well
to point out that one of the greatest concessions to reality
was the adoption of Spanish as the official language of the
courts. This was undertaken despite the insistence of
American lawyers that English should be the official language since, after all, English was the language of the
public schools and of the insular administration.76 But
Taft, already faced with mounting opposition to his program of an "American judiciary here" (more about this
presently) and the probable alienation of the loyal support
of the influential Filipino lawyers "which they had largely
given to the American Government,"77 elected to compromise. Thus, it was provided in Section 12 of the new
Code of Cibil Procedure that until January 1, 1906,
Spanish should be the official language; after that date it
should be replaced by English.78 For this act of the
Commission, Taft wrote, "we were at once praised to the
skies" by the Filipino abogados.79

Taft encountered serious obstacles to his plans for an

"American judiciary" in the Philippines. There was the
problem, first, of recruiting enough American lawyers who
could speak Spanish for the various judicial posts in the
islands; second, there was the need, for political reasons,
of appointing or reappointing a few Filipinos to responsible
positions in the judiciary; and third, there was the apparent
injustice of imposing alien judges unfamiliar with the customs and institutions of the Filipinos.[80]

The result was an accommodation that made the judicial branch of the government relatively the most Filipinized
of all branches.[81] With very rare exceptions, Filipinos
were appointed to the peace courts in the municipalities.
However, the jurisdiction of these courts was extremely
limited.[82] Also, the justices were appointed for very short
terms, at least at the beginning, and they could be removed
by the Governor-General.[83]

In the higher courts, Americans were in the majority,
but the number of Filipino judges was significant. By 1912,
the Filipinos had an equal share of the key judgeships of
First Instance; they had an equal share in the Court of Land
Registration from its inception in 1903.

The Supreme Court of the Philippines during the Military Regime was composed of six Filipinos (including the
Chief Justice) and three Americans.[84] The Philippine Commission reorganized the Court, reducing its membership to
seven and appointing four Americans and three Filipinos
(including the Chief Justice) to compose it.[85] To our knowledge, the Filipinos did not resent the change, drastic though
it was. Perhaps this was because they regarded the Supreme
Court as the least powerful organ of the government at that
time, since it lacked powers of judicial review; what the
Filipinos wanted most was to control the political organs
which were the mainsprings of power and the lower courts,
which were closer to the daily lives of the people.

Before attempting to assess the influence of American
ideas and practices on the Philippine judicial system, it is
well to point out that concern for individual rights was a
keystone of America's Philippine policy. That is why the
United States conferred upon the Filipinos, through the
Letter of Instructions and the Philippine Bill, all the rights
guaranteed to Americans by their own constitution, except

TABLE 3

NUMBER OF JUDGES OF FIRST INSTANCE AND OF LAND REGISTRATION, 1902-1913[a]

	Judges of First Instance		Judges of Land Registration[b]	
Year	American	Filipino	American	Filipino
1902	10	6	---	---
1903	15	6	1	1
1904	15	5	1	1
1905	15	8	1	1
1906[c]	--	--	1	1
1907	13	10	1	1
1908	13	10	1	1
1909	14	9	1	2
1910	12	10	3	3
1911	12	11	3	3
1912	12	12	3	2
1913	12	12	3	4

a Forbes, op. cit., I, 311, n. 2.
b The Court of Land Registration was abolished in 1914, and its functions were transferred to the Courts of First Instance. Ibid., I, 322.
c Number of judges of First Instance for 1906 not available.

the right to bear arms and the right to trial by jury. Concern for peace and order, and perhaps the possibility of another insurrection, prompted denial of the right to bear arms. As regards trial by jury, even leading Filipinos, like Chief Justice Cayetano Arellano, did not think that it would be feasible to introduce the system into the Philippines.[86] This led Finley Peter Dunne, one of the foremost journalists and wits of the era, to comment through Mr. Dooley, who is here supposedly quoting Governor Taft, as follows:

I have not considhered it advisable to inthrajooce anny fads like thrile be jury iv ye'er peers into

me administhration. Plain sthraight-forward
dealin's is me motto. A Filipino at his best
has on'y larned half th' jooty iv mankind. He
can be thried but he can't thry his fellow man.
It takes him too long. "[87]

According to Forbes, "the spirit infuzed by the American administration in the whole judicial system was little
short of marvellous. "[88] A later study, however, would
seem to indicate that Forbes' observation applied only to
the higher courts.[89] This, in itself, is an indication of the
ease with which the few Filipino jurists who served in the
Courts of First Instance and on the Supreme Court during
the Taft Regime readily acquired American judicial ideas
and practices. It also shows that Taft's earlier apprehensions about the rectitude of Filipino lawyers once on the
bench were unsubstantiated.

When we turn our attention to the justices of the peace,
we get an entirely different picture. Hayden's description
of them is very apropos:

> In too many municipalities they were the tools
> of the local cacique who used their courts to
> oppress the poor, collect usurious debts, pun-
> ish enemies, reward friends, win elections,
> and in general control the community.[90]

It would have been surprising if this had not happened,
given the structure of local society and its established
practices, some of which had been implicitly accepted by
the system of local governments. To prevent the caciques
from utilizing the institutions of local justice the way they
did would have required changing the conditions of society
and educating the people rapidly and well. But as Taft
observed as early as 1903,

> Our great difficulty is in reaching the people
> and in having it understood what we are doing.
> We advertise our laws in a number of papers,
> have an official gazette published in English and
> in Spanish and circulated about the islands, and

we assist as far as we can the publication of
friendly newspapers in Tagalo[g]; but the people
are so densely ignorant that it is very difficult
to get into their heads just what it is we are
doing, and are so bound with their former bonds
of a kind of quasi slavery called caciquism to
the educated and wealthy men in their immediate neighborhood that our great problem is to
teach the people what their rights are.91

Taft noted practically the same conditions of "dense
ignorance" — at least 80 per cent of the population, he
said — and of caciquism in 1908. 92 He also made the
following observation at that time:

The efforts of the American Government to
teach the ignorant their civil rights and to up-
lift them to self-governing capacity finds only
a languid sympathy from many of the "ilustrados."93

Without the masses' awareness of their rights, the
machinery of local justice was naturally controlled by the
upper class, cacique or ilustrado. Inevitably, therefore,
the judicial system which more than any other aspect of
the American political program was intended to benefit all
Filipinos, became, like other political institutions of the
Taft Era, an instrument for strengthening the position of
the Filipino upper class. In fairness to the upper class,
however, it ought to be stated that it was as much the
social conditions and circumstances of the time as their
own machinations which made this development possible.
A great amount of social learning, as well as unlearning,
on the part of the Filipinos as a whole would have been to
prevent the Filipino elite from being the sole beneficiaries
of the judicial system introduced by the Americans during
the Taft Era.

THE FILIPINOS AND AMERICAN
EDUCATIONAL POLICIES AND INSTITUTIONS

The United States considered public education second in importance only to the political development of the Filipinos; as a matter of fact, it was regarded as the handmaiden of political progress. Given the importance attached to education, it was natural for the United States to introduce far-reaching innovations in Philippine education. Such changes will be the subject of this chapter. As in the case of political adjustments, they will be viewed within the context of the Filipino reception of, or response to, specific educational policies and institutions.

The Letter of Instructions enjoined the Taft Commission to promote, extend, and improve the educational work initiated by the Military Regime, and to give first priority to "the extension of a system of primary education which shall be free to all," such education "to fit the people for the duties of citizenship and for the ordinary avocations of a civilized community."[1]

The Commission enthusiastically carried out this mandate, within the limitations imposed by its financial resources.[2] It established public primary schools in almost every Philippine barrio, intermediate schools in the principal barrios (poblaciones) of municipalities, and at least one secondary school in each province. In addition, a Normal School, an Arts and Trade School, a Nautical School, and a Nursing School were established in Manila, an Agricultural Institute in the island of Negros and, finally, the University of the Philippines in Manila[3] — all in the span of less than a decade. The Commission brought over from the United States hundreds of American teachers, collectively called the Thomasites because most of them crossed the Pacific on board the transport Thomas.[4] It revised the curricula of the public schools and gradually induced the private schools to harmonize their curricula with that of the public schools so as to bring the Filipinos into contact with the mainstream of modern life. Finally, the Philippine Commission sent about 300 of the brightest high school graduates to the United States for higher and professional education at government expense — hence, they were called "pensionados." These fortunate young men and women later served, some with unusual distinction, in the government and taught at the state supported colleges and professional schools and at the University of the Philippines.

The educational structure was of course not a novelty to the Filipinos. As we have seen in Chapter II, all the types of educational institutions introduced by the Americans had existed in the Philippines in one form or another before the American Occupation. In practically all other respects, however, the American educational program represented a decided and fundamental break with tradition. Its values were secular, not religious. Correspondingly, the methods, content, and supervision, if not the entire personnel, of the educational establishment had to be changed to attain the secular objectives of education. The impressiveness of the changes, as well as their striking contrast with the previous educational experience of the Filipino people, may be more readily grasped when it is recalled that education under Spain had been the almost exclusive concern of the Roman Catholic Church, except financially, and had consequently emphasized "the glory of God."[5]

In formulating its educational policy, the United States could not simply ignore the Roman Catholic tradition of the Spanish public school system in the Philippines. Nor could it disregard the fact that, nominally at least, the vast majority of the Filipinos were Roman Catholics who, presumably, would want religious instruction for their children. Although such instruction could well be obtained through the parochial schools, these were not readily available except in the rich parishes.[6] Since 1863, there had been no urgent need for them because religious instruction was offered in the state schools, which the American government had now taken over. What the Catholics wanted was for the state to subsidize religious instruction in the public schools.

On the other hand, there was the injunction laid down in the Letter of Instructions that "no form of religion and no minister of religion shall be forced upon any community," and that, furthermore, ''the separation between state and church shall be real, entire and absolute. '' In addition, many articulate Filipinos were hoping for the separation of state and church, expressed in the Malolos Constitution, and for secular education.[7] These sentiments, too, the United States had to take into consideration.

The above factors resulted in the adoption of the so-called Faribault Plan[8] under Section 16 of the educational act, which reads in part:

> No teacher or other person shall teach or criticise the doctrines of any church, religious sect or denomination, or shall attempt to influence the pupils for or against any church or religious sect in any public school established under this act. If any teacher shall intentionally violate this section, he or she shall, after due hearing, be dismissed from public service.

> Provided, however, that it shall be lawful for the priest or minister of any church established in the pueblo where a public school is situated,... to teach religion for one-half an hour three times a week in the school buildings to those public-school pupils whose parents or guardians desire it and express their desire therefore in writing filed with the principal teacher of the school,
> ...[9]

The reception of the Faribault Plan. It is impossible to state categorically what the Filipino reception to the Faribault Plan was. That it remained on the statute books throughout the Taft Era would seem to indicate that, in Elliott's words, ''there was general acquiescence in the new order of things. ''[10] I came across only one report of a school superintendent who emphatically recommended, at the request of parents, that native teachers be allowed to give religious instruction in the school.[11] The Catholic Church and doubtless many devout Filipino Catholics, however, were against it, although they did not say so openly. This is borne out by the criticisms of various aspects of

the American educational program made by the American
prelates, who most likely voiced the sentiments of the
majority of Filipino Catholics. Thus, Archbishop of
Manila Jeremiah Harty wrote:

> The unfriendly disposition of the [school] offi-
> cials, some of them ex-preachers and mission-
> aries, has given me annoyance beyond language.
> The unspeakable Barrows has published a his-
> tory which is an offense to every decent Catholic.
> I wish to see the passing of Barrows and the
> personnel whom he stands for.[12]

Bishop Frederick Z. Rooker of Jaro (Iloilo) was no less
critical. He wrote to President Roosevelt that the personnel of the public schools, from classroom teacher to the
Director of Education, were, "with the exception of an
insignificant number, hostile to the Catholic Religion...."
He further claimed that the Filipino teachers, most of
whom were appointed by municipal boards, were "professed
haters of the Catholic Church." Describing one of his trips
through Occidental Negros, which was a part of his extensive diocese, Bishop Rooker continued:

> Complaints were made to me in nearly every
> town that the native teachers were exercising a
> perverting influence religiously and parents
> came to me with tears rolling down their faces,
> begging that I try to do something to have
> Catholic teachers placed in the schools so that
> the faith might not be taken from their little
> ones.[13]

In the view of the American prelates, the government
was pursuing an entirely wrong policy and was not even
correcting fast enough what they thought were its faults in
application. Finally, in 1908, Bishop Thomas A.
Hendrick of Cebu flatly told Major Frank McIntyre, then
Assistant to the Chief of the Bureau of Insular Affairs:

> My objection to the school system there is

broader than the appointment of Catholics or
protestants as teachers, you understand? It is
on the general principle that there is no religious
education given in the schools, and I think the
people must deteriorate without religious
education.[14]

It would have been surprising, indeed, had the Catholic hierarchy and staunch Filipino Catholics meekly
accepted the secularization of the public schools as represented by the Faribault Plan. For three centuries,
religious instruction had been part of the curricula of the
schools; and lay teachers had been obliged to teach religion
to the children because the priests had other duties,
wordly and otherwise, to attend to. The change to an
entirely new system seemed to be not only robbing the
people of their taxes,[15] but also a disguised attempt to
convert their children to Protestantism or Aglipayanism.[16]
However, the Catholic hierarchy did not publicly advocate
scuttling the Faribault Plan. As perhaps befits the guardian
of the souls of more than three-fourths of the Filipinos, they
merely demanded a more benevolent attitude on the part of
the government.[17]
  Why the Catholic Church did not ask for an outright
rejection of the Faribault Plan may be explained by a number of reasons. Elliott thinks that it was because the
"Vatican put in charge American trained bishops who were
familiar with the American school system."[18] The evidence we have just presented does not sustain this view,
however. The American prelates may indeed have been
familiar with the American school system, but they did not
like it applied to the Philippines; tolerant at home, they
became almost zealots and bigots abroad. If they did not
openly ask for an abandonment of the Faribault Plan, perhaps it was because the plan was the "brainchild" of Archbishop Ireland, the Catholic prelate of his day closest to the
Republican administration in the United States and to whom
the latter turned for assistance in resolving far larger
religious issues between the United States and the Catholic
Church in the Philippines — such as the friar question[19]
and property claims arising out of the Aglipayan Schism.[20]

It would have been highly embarrassing to Archbishop
Ireland and probably to the Holy See, also, which had
implicitly though belatedly approved the Faribault Plan in
1892,[21] if the American bishops in the Philippines had
demanded the abandonment of the plan and insisted on
direct Church influence in the public schools in the
islands.

There was another, and perhaps more cogent, reason
why the Catholic Church reconciled itself to the Faribault
Plan: the realization that it could not count upon the support
of the leading Filipinos, many of whom had served in the
Malolos Government and directed it toward secularism, and
whose opinions were sought on almost all aspects of American policy. These leading Filipinos, under the banner of
the Partido Federal, strongly endorsed the Faribault
Plan,[22] and endorsement reflected in Barrows' report on
the Filipino reception to the American educational program
in 1903:

> Thoroughly American as our school system is,
> it represents the ideas which theoretically com-
> mand the desires of the Filipino. His request
> was for free, secular schools, open to all inhabi-
> tants and teaching the English tongue and the
> elementary branches of modern knowledge.[23]

Looking more closely at the reception given to the
public schools in general, we get the following impression
from the official reports of school officials: the residents
of Manila were excelled by the residents of the provincial
towns,[24] and the latter by the residents of the barrios,[25]
in their enthusiasm for the American public school system;
and "as a rule the poorer and more ignorant people were
first attracted permanently to the public schools...."[26]

It would be a gross mistake, however, to assume that
the enthusiasm shown by the Filipinos least exposed to
Spanish civilization was due to the secular features of the
public schools. It is probably closer to the truth to say
that such a favorable reception was due to the establishment, at last, of free public schools in their midst, something which only the poblaciones and large barrios had

enjoyed in Spanish times, i. e. , since 1863. This may also
explain why the less favored members of society were
happier than the richer ones with the introduction of the
American public school system. For example, the lack
of enthusiasm among the residents of Manila was explained
by the Assistant to the General Superintendent of Education
in the following manner:

> Here the old regime had a firm footing, and pri-
> vate and church schools have been for years in
> successful operation with large enrollment.
> The people have been slow to accept the radical
> innovations of the American educational system.[27]

Curricular adaptations. Dr. Barrows boasted in 1903
that the American educational system was "the most
typically American institution which our government has
established" in the Philippines.[28] However, the particular
needs of the Filipino people made it necessary to change
the curriculum so that gradually the substance of Philippine education differed considerably from its American
counterpart. Describing the differences between the two
curriculums, Dr. Barrows wrote:

> Larger place is given to science work than is
> usual in the public schools of America. Training
> in the English language and literature supplies in
> the Philippine system the place of classical
> studies of American school programmes. Time
> is thereby gained for that training in exact
> methods and concrete subject-matter for which
> there is peculiar need.[29]

Adaptability, in fact, was a chief feature — and virtue —
of the Philippine educational system under American rule.
Reception of the English language. The first Philippine school under American rule opened on Corregidor
Island, off Manila Harbor, in May, 1898, followed by the
reopening of city schools when Manila "capitulated" to
the Americans in August, 1898. Within about a year, the
Military Regime had in operation a school system con-

sisting of over thirty schools with a total enrollment of
about 5,000 children. Catholic Chaplain William D.
McKinnon of the First California Volunteers was made
superintendent of schools.30 He reinstated the former
teachers and hired American soldiers to fill the gaps.
The curriculum established under Spanish rule was retained with some changes, such as the elimination of
religion and the introduction of courses in English.31
Since the textbooks were in Spanish and the former
teachers probably did not speak or write English, Spanish
had to be the medium of instruction.32

The Taft Commission had specific instructions to
employ the vernacular in the primary schools. It also had
instructions to establish "a common medium of communication" among the Filipinos, who spoke different languages.
"It is obviously desirable," Root advised the Commission,
"that this medium should be the English language."

Taft and his colleagues went beyond their instructions,
for they also made English the medium of instruction in all
the public schools.33 This decision was inevitable. First
of all, the governmental system demanded that English be
the language of administration because most of the higher
officials were Americans who, at the outset, probably
knew very little Spanish, let alone any Philippine language.
Second, to implement the government's amitious educational program, a corps of American teachers had to be
employed. They, too, in all likelihood, had a very limited
command of Spanish and no knowledge whatever of any
Philippine language. Also, the cost of translating textbooks and other reading materials would have added tremendously to the financial problems of the Department of
Public Instruction.34 Third, many Filipinos whose opinions
were asked on the matter evidently preferred English as the
medium of school instruction. The Taft Commission reported to the Secretary of War that "English is desired by
the natives, and undoubtedly it should be the language
basis of public-school work,..."35 Another reason may
very well have been the desire of Americans to impose
their own language since, after all, they were the rules
and not the ruled, coupled with a reluctance to study the
languages of the Filipinos. As Finley Peter Dunne's

"Mr. Dooley" pointed out in January, 1899: "We will
erect schoolhouses,...an' we'll larn ye our language,
because 'tis sisier to larn ye ours thin to larn oursilves
ye'ers,... "36

The Filipino reception of the English language varied.
On the one hand there was popular enthusiasm, prompted
in part by curiosity, in part by pragmatic considerations
(since English was the predominant language of the government), and, perhaps, in part by psychological reasons,
drawn from the fact that Filipinos had been denied instruction in the language of their overlords until 1863 — three
centuries after the establishment of Spanish rule in the
Philippines.37 As Dr. Frei has suggested:

> It may well be said that the Filipinos had not
> only no antipathy toward the language of the con-
> querors, but to a large extent they were eager
> to learn it.... English...was looked upon by
> the Filipinos in the same way as they looked
> upon Spanish before. It was the "Open Sesame"
> for cultural, economic, and political advance-
> ment and achievement. 38

Against this background we should read the reports
and letters of government officials, which tend to exag-
gerate the eagerness of the Filipinos to learn the English
language. For example, the Secretary of Public Instruction boasted in 1902, a year after the introduction of
English as the language of the public schools, that "note-
worthy results" had been achieved.39 Four years later,
Forbes, then Secretary of Commerce and Police, asserted
that the Filipinos "are perfectly crazy to learn the English
language. " "In my travels about the provinces, " he added,
"I find more English spoken a good deal than Spanish. "40
By 1910, government sources were claiming that more
Filipinos "speak and write the English language than speak
and write any other language or dialect. "41

In contrast to these typical reports by individuals who
had every reason to justify government policy and present
its accomplishments in a good light, the following evidence
tends to impart quite a different impression of the Filipino

reception to the English language: (1) the reports, among
others, of two special investigators on Philippine conditions; (2) the attempt of the Filipino leaders in the Assembly in 1908 to provide for the use of the vernacular in the
primary grades; (3) the successful resistance to the imposition of English as the language of the courts and, of
course, the exclusive use of Spanish by the Assembly; and
(4) the early, if moribund, efforts to promote the scientific
study of Philippine languages with a view to developing a
common vernacular. We shall discuss each of these
briefly, except the last, which is not really as germane to
this inquiry as the others. Besides, the subject has been
adequately treated elsewhere.[42]

The reports by Henry Parker Willis and Henry Jones
Ford, both prominent members of the academic world of
their day,[43] are perhaps the most generally critical studies
by Americans of early American rule in the Philippines.[44]
Given their distinguished backgrounds, one would expect the
expositions of these two political economists to be models
of impartiality and factual precision. But the very purpose
of their investigations and the persons for whom they were
undertaken, the types of data available to them and the
amount of time they actually had to obtain and evaluate this
data, lead one to suspect their impartiality and accuracy.

Professor Willis went to the Philippines in 1904 and
spent several months in the islands at the request of
Morefield Storey of the Anti-Imperialist League, which
was opposed to the American occupation of the Philippines.
He sent Mr. Storey periodic reports which were widely
publicized, doubtless with a view to discrediting the Re-
publicans in the 1904 presidential election.[45] These
reports and Willis' subsequent refinements were eventually
published in a handy volume in 1905.[46]

Professor Ford spent exactly sixty-six days in the
Philippines (March 14 to May 19) in 1913, as President
Wilson's special investigator. Like Willis, he traveled
extensively throughout the Philippines. In addition, Ford
had access to the confidential files of at least the Philippine Constabulary (which, unfortunately, had no bearing on
the language problem!), something which Willis did not
have. Shortly upon his return to the United States,

Ford submitted two reports, neither of which has been
published.[47]

We can assume that Willis and Ford, particularly
Willis, did not embark upon their Philippine assignments
with open minds. Still, one must not belabor this or other
obvious shortcomings of their reports. They were not
sympathetic to the Taft Era, to be sure; but neither were
they apologists. My own personal view, however, is that
they were overly critical on the language question, and
tended to interpret lapses in speech and comprehension on
the part of the Filipinos whom they met as proof of an
unfavorable Filipino attitude toward the English language

We are now ready to present Willis' and Ford's
observations. Here is what Willis wrote:

> The fact is that the enthusiasm of the natives
> in learning English is largely a myth. While
> it is undoubtedly true that more progress is being
> made by the natives than in any other branch of
> study, it is also true that this progress is largely
> attributable to the general desire to pass civil
> service examinations or to be able better to trade
> with American visitors. . . . Far from its being
> the fact that an understanding of English is per-
> colating through all classes of the community,
> and is being sought for by people of all grades,
> the truth is that an adequate knowledge of English
> is possessed by very few even of the educated
> classes in the Philippines, while the proportion
> of the population which comprehends as much as
> a few simple words is extremely small. . . . the
> desire to learn English, save for the motive al-
> ready suggested, is non-existent or limited to
> a very small class.[48]

Willis was correct concerning the practical considerations
which underlay the favorable acceptance of the English
language by Filipinos, but, as I have just pointed out,
they were not the only motivations.[49]

In the section of his report dealing with education,
Ford made the following remarks on the Filipinos and the
English language:

There is,... another aspect of the case that should
be considered.... Although on the basis of school
statistics the statement is made that more Filipinos now speak English than any other language,
no one would think so on the testimony of one's
own ears. Everywhere Spanish is the speech of
business and social intercourse. To receive
prompt attention, Spanish is always more useful
than English and outside of Manila, is almost
indispensable.... Taking together municipal and
provincial offices as they happened to come in
the course of my travels, Spanish seems to me to
be indubitably the prevailing language. Outside
of the schools, it was the exception to hear English.[50]

Ford's observation would seem to imply that English had
not made much headway, even in the government, during
the entire Taft Era. But if civil service examinations are
any indication, Professor Ford would seem to be in error:
In 1906, for the first time, the number of Filipinos
examined in English outnumbered those who were examined
in Spanish; more English language examinees passed the
examinations two years later.[51] If Professor Ford encountered more Spanish-speaking municipal and provincial
officials, it was probably because they had obtained their
formal education during the Spanish regime; since they
were then too old to learn English or knew only a smatter-
ing of it, they probably could have engaged Ford in con-
versation only through an interpreter.[52]

On February 27, 1908, the Philippine Assembly passed
Bill No. 148, which provided that instruction in the public
primary, or elementary, schools should be given in the
language or dialect of that province or region.[53] The
Philippine Commission unanimously rejected the bill on
the general theory that it proposed a drastic alteration of
the whole scheme of public instruction in the Philippines,
and that it would create unnecessary confusion, waste, and
inefficiency, with consequent detrimental effects upon the
educational growth of school children. The real reason,
however, was that the proposed amendment to the educational act (Act No. 74 of the Philippine Commission)

would have hampered the rapid spread of the English
language.[54]

The Commission's action was undoubtedly resented
by the Assembly: Ford noted it as late as 1913.[55] Ford
also claimed that Speaker Osmena had told him that upon
the attainment of Philippine independence, "instruction in
the vernacular would be introduced in the elementary
schools, but instruction in the use of English would certainly be continued."[56] Ford further said that Speaker
Osmena "was emphatic on this matter of English, remark-
ing that that was settled, that there was no difference of
opinion among them on that point."[57] In short, while the
Filipino leaders wanted English to be the common language,
they did not want it at the price of excluding the native
languages from the primary schools.[58]

If the Americans could insist upon English in the public schools and in the executive branch of the government,
they were powerless in the case of the judiciary and of the
Assembly during the Taft Era. Here Spanish was the official language and, in the case of the Assembly, the
exclusive language.

As I have pointed out earlier, Spanish was scheduled
to be replaced by English as the official language of the
courts after January, 1906.[59] Filipino opposition, however, resulted in several two-year postponements of the
substitution. Finally, in 1911, the Philippine Assembly
passed a bill seeking to postpone to January 1, 1917, the
use of English as the language of the courts.[60] This was
too much for the then Acting Governor-General, who was
also Secretary of Public Instruction and an ardent advocate
of the use of English as the official language in all the
branches of the Philippine government. Largely because
of his own efforts, therefore, the Philippine Commission
did not act on the Assembly's measure, and so English
became the official language of the courts by default. The
Nacionalista paper, El Ideal, probably voiced the general
consensus among influential Filipinos when it declared:

> The Philippine Commission, that is, the American
> government, in failing to pass the bill of the popu-
> lar House [Assembly] postponing the time for

the imposition of the use of the English language
in the courts of justice, has committed a tremendous political and administrative error which
seriously wounds the liberal prestige of this regime and infuses doubt and suspicion in the people
regarding the intentions of this administration.61

Vigorous Filipino opposition finally resulted in a compromise in the form of Act No. 2239, which stipulated that
"while English was to remain the primary official language
of the courts Spanish should... be also an official language
until January 1, 1920."62

Spanish was also the language of the Philippine Assembly, an understandable state of affairs since the generation
or generations to which the members of the Assembly
belonged had been educated in Spanish. This also explains
why almost all Filipino-owned newspapers of the Taft Era
were in Spanish.63 We must also assume that those who
had facility with the Spanish language nurtured a deep pride
in having acquired it. It is therefore clear that in the case
of the courts and of the Assembly, the linguistic imperialism of American rule was moderated by the heritage of the
Spanish regime in the Philippines. Nevertheless, the
linguistic character of American rule, however gradual,
was assured. The educational system was the instrument
toward this end, and the American regime provided the
incentives for the acquisition and mastery of the English
language.

The Filipinos and the American teachers. A discussion
of the Filipino reaction to the American educational program
must include a brief mention of the attitude toward the
American teachers by the people in general and the Filipino
teachers in particular. A typical attitude of the people is
expressed in the following words by one of the Thomasites
himself, Mr. William R. Hamme:

As far as I have observed the attitude toward
the American teachers was excellent. Every
place we went we were treated with high regard.
We were given preference at banquets, fiestas
and dances. The graciousness of the Filipino

people was par excellence. Many times we
were embarrassed at the attention paid us.[64]

Like the rest of their countrymen, the Filipino teachers
welcomed the American teachers warmly. On this point it
might be worth quoting from the report of the school superintendent of Batangas which, next to Samar province, suffered most from the hardships of pacification:[65]

> The native teachers have almost invariably
> been exceedingly friendly with the American
> teachers. The one or two only exceptions are
> to be laid at the door of the American teacher.
> The native teachers have cheerfully accepted the
> American teachers as their instructors, and
> they are coming more and more to realize the
> value of English to them in their positions.
> Their conviction that their promotion depends
> upon their steady progress has made them very
> eager. They are more influential in the com-
> munity than formerly.[66]

This reception was in sharp contrast to the Filipino lawyer's
lawyer's reception of the American judges at the beginning
of the Taft Era. The reason, of course, lies in the fact
that the Filipino teacher's position was never seriously
threatened by the arrival of the American teacher, who
soon helped organize vacation normal institutes to improve
the training of native teachers.[67] The latter feature of the
educational program probably made the Filipino maestro
feel that he was important, and consequently he became a
loyal supporter of the public school system and a close
friend of the American teacher and school administrator.[68]
This did not, however, prevent him from demanding a
salary equal to that of the American teacher.

Higher education. The training of public school
teachers was only part of the program to enable Filipinos
to acquire higher education and professional courses in
English. More far-reaching were (1) the pensionado program, or the sending of government scholars to study in the
United States and (2) the creation of the University of the Philippines.

The pensionado program started in 1903.[69] In November of that year, about 100 of the most promising young Filipinos arrived in California, accompanied by the first superintendent of Filipino students in the United States.[70] Four or five senoritas and a few more senoritos were added in the following year to bring the complement closer to the authorized number of 125 pensionados.[71] The program was still going on when the Taft Era came to an end, but on a much smaller scale.[72] Two hundred and nine Filipinos and Filipinas had obtained degrees or advanced training in the United States by 1912, with a total government expenditure of 479,940 dollars.[73]

A proper assessment of the role of the pensionados as agents of social change during the American regime as a whole has yet to be undertaken. In later years, many of them became top administrators, successful professionals, and scholars.[74] Their total exposure to American life for an average of over four years, and the fact that all the first pensionados attended non-Catholic institutions and state colleges and universities, must be taken into proper account in any evaluation of their overall impact on Philippine life.[75] Although they were a novelty during the period under review, the recency of the program of government scholarships makes it difficult to pinpoint the tangible effect of the pensionados upon Philippine society of the Taft Era.

One thing, however, is certain. The pensionado program helped enhance the position of the leading members of Philippine society. Although we do not know the exact backgrounds of all the pensionados, it is not hard to establish the fact that, with very few exceptions, they belonged to the leading families of each province and of Manila. For one thing, all the pensionados had to be high school graduates, and so they must doubtless have been almost exclusively scions of rich families. As late as 1923, the majority of high school students continued to be drawn from such families.[76] For another, social status was one of the factors considered in the selection of scholars. This is abundantly clear from Taft's telegram to the provincial governors concerning the selection of the first pensionados:

After conference with the Division Superintendent

of Schools select for appointment as Students
in the United States at the expense of the government... Filipino Students of the public schools,
between sixteen and twenty-one years of age.
Each candidate is subject to examination in
Manila.... Each student must be of unquestionable
moral and physical qualifications, weight being
given to social status.[77]

Needless to say, the pensionado program was welcomed
by the people at large, but it is probable that the Filipino
upper class welcomed it more.[78] It is not without significance that Tavera, a plutocrat, was the "author" of Act
No. 854, which authorized the pensionado program.[79]

The University of the Philippines was the "capstone"
of the public educational system under the United States.[80]
Like the lower public schools, it represented a departure
from established practice. The Spanish government had
not maintained a public, secular university, and so at the
time of American annexation, higher learning was in the
hands of the religious corporations.[81]

The establishment of the university in 1908, a logical
development of the non-sectarian public school system, was
warmly received, especially by the upper class. This
enthusiasm is demonstrated by the "very active and earnest
interest" of the Filipino members of the Philippine Legislature, who belonged to the upper class, "in the establisment
and operation" of the various units of the university.[83]

The reasons for this reaction are not hard to find. Most
of the public high school graduates came from the upper
class.[84] If these graduates could not be assured of an
opportunity to pursue advanced and professional instruction
in English, upper class support of the public school system,
mild as it was, might be entirely lost. These families
would then send their children to the sectarian high schools
in preparation for collegiate studies under the supervision
of the friars. That would be tantamount to a perpetuation
of the old system of higher education, especially since the
government had no control over the curricula of the private
schools; it could suggest revisions but it could not enforce
compliance. Moreover, many members of the upper class

who eagerly wanted professional training so as to be in a position to justify their demands for a more rapid Filipinization of the higher governmental offices, preferred state-supported advanced secular education, as evidenced by the creation of the Literary University under the auspices of the revolutionary government.[85] Finally, they preferred such advanced education to be in English, since English was the language of the government and was expected to be the language of the courts.[86]

The American authorities, on the other hand, did not want the public educational program weakened by the continuing predominance of the sectarian preparatory colleges and the University of Santo Tomas, where Spanish continued to be the medium of instruction. The need for a secular university was also made imperative by the financial impossibility of maintaining the pensionado program at the authorized levels indefinitely, let alone expanding it to provide training for more young Filipinos. The urgency of training more Filipinos, in turn, was dictated by Filipino demands for a greater share in the administration, particularly at the higher levels. The Americans could not completely ignore such demands because the avowed goal of their policy since the Taft Administration had been ''the Philippines for the Filipinos.''[87] There was therefore a convergence of American and Filipino interests behing the creation of the university — one of the most effective instruments of institutional change and the most outstanding landmark of secular education.

Despite the fact that the University of the Philippines was patterned after the various state colleges and universities in the United States, some features of higher educational institutions with which the Filipinos were familiar also influenced the early life of the university. For instance, until 1919, its organization was patterned after the European model, which the Spanish friars had adopted for their own educational institutions. The College of Liberal Arts conferred bachelor's degrees after two years of college work, instead of four. Thereafter, the students entered any of the professional schools of the university.[88] Once again, the heritage of the Spanish regime determined the early forms of the American educational program in the Philippines.

Education as an instrument of social change. The Americans considered caciquism under the American flag unthinkable. But however much they may have wanted to abolish it, they possessed neither the spirit nor the know-how to do it effectively, since agrarian reform had never been one of their socio-economic problems at home. Furthermore, a dynamic program looking toward the abolition of caciquism would have been resisted by the Filipino upper class, many of whom were caciques, and upon whose cooperation and support depended the success of the United States in the Philippines.

Inevitably, the Americans turned toward the public schools as a means to abolish caciquism. "There is no real difference between the educated and ignorant Filipinos that can not be overcome by education of one generation," Taft informed President Roosevelt in 1908.[89] Even the acquisition of English was regarded as an important factor of change. As the first Secretary of Public Instruction put is: "The knowledge of English which the public schools offer to the youth... will contribute materially to the emancipation of the dependent classes...."[90] How, the Secretary did not precisely indicate, except that to him, if the lower classes did not know English, the caciques would exploit them more.[91]

Forbes, the Governor-General of the Taft Era who was the strongest advocate of material development, considered the emancipation of the common tao (peasant or laborer) as "the crux of the efforts of the Americans in the Philippines." In his opinion, this goal could be achieved only through a guarantee of the tao's right to enjoy the fruit of his labors and through education. From education, Forbes asserted, the tao would "know his rights and obtain them," and so emancipate himself from the caciques![92]

Quite apart from assuming that the caciques were bad and, consequently, the other ninety percent of the Filipinos wanted to cast them off as incongruous relics of a past ear, American policy also exhibited a marked naiveté about the roots of caciquism and a tendency to attribute great catalytic powers to their institutions. Caciquism was as much the result of the ignorance of the common tao as of his economic dependence upon the cacique. And while the

Americans established a public school system which was far more extensive and more egalitarian than that of the past, they did not appreciably alter the economic status quo, which lay at the foundation of caciquism.[93] The result was that although public schooling of four years' duration at the most may have made the tao less ignorant than before, his economic dependence upon the cacique was sufficient to present his limited schooling from making any appreciable improvement in his status vis-à-vis the latter.

RELIGIOUS DEVELOPMENTS DURING THE TAFT ERA

From the beginning of American rule in the Philippines, it was officially announced that a cardinal principle of policy would be, consonant with a fundamental rule of American life, to keep the separation between Church and State "real, entire, and absolute."[1] As a corollary, there was also going to be absolute religious freedom. American imperialism, therefore, was not conceived as a state-supported missionary enterprise to spread any particular faith, in contrast to the colonial rule which it had just replaced in the Philippines.

Strictly speaking, therefore, a study of the Filipino response to American rule from the religious standpoint lies outside the immediate scope of this study because there was no religious policy, or policies, per se, to which the Filipinos had to respond. The great dicta of the separation between Church and State and of the equality of religious worship were as much expressions of political ideals as of religious convictions.

Ironically, however, conditions in the Philippines at the time of annexation forced the United States to adopt what amounted to a religious policy. Thus, because of Filipino antipathy toward the friars, the Schurman and Taft Commissions were compelled to recommend their expulsion from the Philippines.[2] Such a recommendation was complicated by friar ownership of vast haciendas, some of them the richest agricultural lands in the country. Indeed, the friar question led to an unprecedented American mission to the Vatican in 1902.[3]

Furthermore, although the centuries-old edifice of State-Church unity seemed to have crumbled beyond repair under the impact of the secular tendencies of the Philippine Revolution, the Filipinos not only did not have the time to appreciate fully what separation of Church and State actually meant in practice, but were still Catholics, except for the Muslims and pagans, at the time of the American occupation. The application of any policy embodying the principle of the separation between Church and State and of religious freedom, therefore, was bound to assume the aspect of a religious policy. It inevitably resulted in far-reaching religious developments, which again ironically entangled the United States in religious questions.

American policy led directly to the introduction of Protestantism and contributed indirectly to the early success of the Aglipayan Movement. The presence of Protestants and Aglipayans, in turn, complicated the controversy over the educational policy of the United States.4 Further still, the rise of Aglipayanism compelled the United States to step right into the middle of controversies involving ownership of religious property as Aglipayan schismatics seized or claimed possession of temples of worship, cemeteries, and other properties that had been possession of the Roman Catholic Church since the days of Legazpi in 1565, when the first permanent Spanish colony in the Philippines was established. Ironically, too, American policy toward the ownership of such disputed properties checked the further growth of Aglipayanism during the second half of the Taft Era; it was, in fact, one of the factors which accounted for the incipient decline of Aglipayanism thereafter.

Be that as it may, the challenge of Aglipayanism and, to a lesser extent, Protestantism catalyzed the long overdue reform movement in the Catholic Church. Such a "counter-reformation," foreshadowed by the Manila Council of 1907, helped Catholicism retain its position as the dominant religion of the Filipinos.

The religious consequences of American rule were therefore far-reaching indeed.

Iglesia Filipina Independiente (IFI)

The Iglesia Filipina Independiente (Philippine Independent Church), or Aglipayan Church (Schism or Movement), as it is commonly called, is a comparatively recent phenomenon, but its roots lie very deep in the Filipino past. It developed from the resentment of the Filipino clergy against the Spanish government and the Catholic Church for failing to carry out faithfully the secularization of the parishes, i.e., to replace the regular clergy with the secular clergy as parish priests of the Church.5 This

resentment was deeply aggravated by the unjust execution
of Fathers Jose A. Burgos, Mariano Gomez, and Jacinto
Zamora — all staunch advocates of secularization — for
alleged complicity in the Cavite Mutiny of 1872.[6]

For obvious reasons, the Filipino reformers and
revolutionists championed the cause of the Filipino clergy,
and during the second phase of the revolution, a de facto
secularization in fact took place, the revolutionary government having imprisoned all the friars within its territory.[7]
Steps were also taken to organize the Filipino clergy into a
National Church, still Catholic and loyal to the Pope, but
to be composed entirely of Filipino priests and bishops.
The National Church, however, lasted for only a couple
of months in 1899.[8] Father Aglipay, its provisional head,
soon led a group of guerrillas in the Ilocos region against
the Americans; he was not to surrender until April 30,
1901.[9]

From a simple demand for a Filipinized Catholic
Church to a complete revolt against the Catholic Church
and papal authority in 1902 is a long story that cannot be
told and accounted for in detail in this study.[10] Nevertheless, a few highlights may at least be mentioned.

First among these was the uncompromising attitude of
the first Apostolic Delegate to the Philippines, Archbishop
Placido Chapelle of New Orleans, who arrived in Manila on
January 2, 1900.[11] The Filipino clergy had hoped that this
representative of the Vatican might be more understanding,
remove the friars, and perhaps appoint some of the Filipino
priests to higher posts in the Church hierarchy.[12] They
were to be terribly disappointed, for Chapelle proceeded to
restore some of the friars to their former parishes. In
doing this, he believed that

> The opposition to the friars is an artificial propa-
> ganda fostered by the insurgents and by the Fili-
> pino priests, who are themselves leaders in the
> insurrection and are using it to obtain control
> [of] the Church in the islands.[13]

Although Chapelle left the Philippines in April, 1901,
he had stayed long enough to convince everyone that the

Vatican contemplated no reforms in the ministry of the
Church. His quarrel with the Taft Commission over the
latter's recommended friar policy for the United States[14]
also showed that he did not approve of the friars' parting
with their estates. In short, Chapelle did nothing to prevent a schism that was already developing.

On May 8, 1902, Aglipay's forty-second birthday, the
Filipino clergy in the Ilocos region met at Kullabeng, then
a barrio of Badoc, now of Pinili, Ilocos Norte.[15] The
assembly "resolved to declare their independence from
the Church of Rome and establish a Filipino Church. " In
addition, some clergymen and laymen who were present at
the meeting recommended "reforms of doctrines and religious practices. "[16] Thus, some members of the Filipino
clergy had finally decided to make a complete break with
Rome and even hinted at departure from Roman doctrine.

If the IFI was not formally launched right then, it was
because Aglipay asked for a postponement to enable him
to get in touch with other Filipino clergymen and leading
laymen.[17] Whittemore also suggests that it was because
Taft, then about to leave on his trip to the Vatican, had
asked that the Filipinos wait for the outcome of his mission
before making a final decision.[18] Probably, it was also
because Aglipay wanted to be sure that the Pope had been
given enough warning, and might still accommodate some
of the aspirations of the Filipino clergy.[19]

Whatever the real reasons for Aglipay's vacillation,
he was soon forced to make a final decision. On June 29,
1902, Aglipay's close friend and fellow Ilocano, Isabelo
de los Reyes, [20] and Pascual Poblete issued invitations to
an anti-friar rally to be held a month later.[21] Then on
July 26, "Taft cabled the [disappointing] result of his negotiations with the Pope, " which indicated that although the
Vatican had agreed to the sale of the friar haciendas, it
would not withdraw the friars. [22] Fearing violence at the
scheduled rally, the American authorities cancelled the
permit. But de los Reyes called for a meeting of his
Union Obrera Democrática on August 3, 1902, and there
formally launched the Aglipayan Schism, or the Philippine
Independent Church.[23] As expected, de los Reyes named
Aglipay as the Obispo Maximo of the new Church and

other well-known Filipino priests, like Father Jorge Barlin of Sorsogon and Father Pedro Brillantes of Ilocos Norte, as bishops. He also proposed the establishment of an executive committee of the Church, composed of prominent laymen, and headed by Taft, General Aguinaldo, and Tavera. De los Reyes, however, still left the door open to a reconciliation with the Vatican, for a portion of his "organizing" speech reads as follows:

> If the Pope acknowledges his errors and grants canonical appointment to the bishops thus designated, they will make peace with him; otherwise they will have to go without him.[24]

The schism almost collapsed just as soon as it had been launched. The Philippine Commission issued a polite but firm refusal of its president, Taft, to serve as a member of the new Church's executive committee. Others were less polite. Only General Aguinaldo indicated willingness to be of service to the IFI.[25] But the worst temporary setback came from Aglipay himself. He claimed he had nothing to do with the August meeting sponsored by de los Reyes.[26]

All eyes naturally focused upon Fr. Aglipay. His friend had evidently put him on the spot. At this juncture, the Jesuits came to his assistance by inviting him to their retreat house in Santa Ana (a district of Manila).[27] Aglipay emerged from a four or five day retreat in anger: he had been asked to sign a document stating that he permanently dissociated himself from the schismatics and another which was degrading to the Filipino clergy. In return, Aglipay was promised an archbishopric.[28]

Aglipay thus decided to accept the nomination offered to him on August 3. Meanwhile, Taft had arrived from his mission to the Vatican and confirmed the Vatican's refusal to grant the demands of the Filipino clergy. On October 26, 1902 (a Sunday), Aglipay was inaugurated as the Obispo Maximo of the IFI, and celebrated his first mass.[29] Earlier, Father Brillantes had been consecrated Bishop of Ilocos Norte.[30] The schism was now a reality.

The birth of the Iglesia Filipina Independiente was

received with great enthusiasm by a substantial number of Filipinos, although only a small portion of the Filipino clergy switched to the new Church.[31] Rivera claims that the schism, actually a revolt, "spread like wildfire" throughout the country, and that before the first year of its life was over, "the Aglipayan leaders were already claiming three million adherents,"[32] or about 44 per cent of the population of the Philippines at that time (7,000,000). Although this figure is perhaps a bit inflated, the actual number of Aglipayans before 1907 was probably not very far from 3,000,000.[33] We cannot take the figure of about 1,500,000 Aglipayans in 1918[34] as indicative of a lower number of adherents in 1903 or 1906.[35] By that time, Aglipayanism had been checked for a dozen years. In fact, Aglipayanism suffered a steep decline after 1906 when, as we shall presently see, the Supreme Court of the Philippines ruled on the disputed ownership of religious properties in favor of the Catholic Church.[36]

In attempting to account for the rapid growth of Aglipayanism, one must carefully consider the climate of nationalism under which it developed. Although the prescription "independiente" was explained to mean independence from the Vatican, it had quite an evocative meaning to the people after six years of revolution and war against Spain and the United States. It came as no surprise, therefore, when General Aguinaldo readily accepted his nomination to the executive committee of the IFI in August. He even prepared a speech for delivery at Aglipay's inauguration, in which, El Renacimiento reported,

> Aguinaldo gave his enthusiastic adhesion to the noble idea of delivering from their cruel slavery the poor Filipino priests who under the former regime, were ill treated, imprisoned, and murdered with all impunity notwithstanding their innocence.[37] He added that every Filipino ought to support Bishop Aglipay, and finished with a cheer for the Filipino Church which was heartily responded to by all present.[38]

Filipino newspapers, in general, endorsed the schism.[39]

Even La Democracia, the organ of the Federalistas, two
of whom — Tavera and Dr. Jose E. Alemany — refused
to join de los Reyes' executive committee, warmly applaud-
ed the birth of the IFI, and was even editorially more vocal
than the newspapers of the nationalists:

> The die is cast! Padre Aglipay has crossed the
> Rubican [sic] of intransigency and absolutism, . . .
> In appearance it is a matter of hierarchy. In
> reality, it is the assertion of the dignity of the
> people, the last consequence of revolution, which
> in order to be complete requires religious liberty.
> . . . We must admit that this radical solution of
> the religious crisis, coupled with the friar ques-
> tion, has stirred up the indolent multitude, which
> yesterday was a slave to the regular clergy, . . .
> The threatening schism is a fact. Is it good?
> Is it evil? As an act of valor, as a solution of
> a conflict which hitherto the Filipino clergy has
> always been the victim, our opinion is that it is
> worthy of praise.40

Leading lay adherents of the Aglipayan Church were
quick to point out Aglipay's patriotism to the people. The
Catholic Bishop of Nueva Segovia described such a scene
as follows:

> Withing the last few days the Presidente of Vigan
> and a few more Aglipayans inaugurated within the
> limits of this town a new Aglipayan Chapel. Our
> municipal band discoursed the music; ex-Gov.
> Juan Villamor of Abra made the speech. He
> hit the nail on the head when he told the assembled
> exinsurrectos that Aglipay should be followed in
> religious matters because he (Aglipay) is a
> patriot. 41

Even Taft believed that nationalism was one of the
factors contributing to the rapid growth of the Aglipayan
movement. He naturally though, however, that such a
nationalism was only religious and not directed against the

United States, a view consistent with his unyielding belief
that the Filipinos liked American rule. One might even
say that Taft was inwardly happy, for he believed that

> [Aglipayanism] has turned the thoughts of the
> people in another direction, and has largely satis-
> fied such longing as there may be for independence
> which they are able to enjoy of friar domination,
> and has led them to an attitude of complete loyalty
> to America. . . . 42

Taft's successor, Luke E. Wright, also thought that one
of the propellents of the Aglipayan Movement was nationalism, or even racism. "The strength of this movement,"
he wrote, lies in Aglipay's "appeals to the Filipino [people]
as a race to form an independent church of their own. . . ."43

To the Catholics, of course, Aglipayanism was nothing
but a political movement. "No sensible man thinks there is
a particle of religion in this new departure, " wrote the
fighting Bishop of Jaro (Iloilo), "and the very arguments
they use to induce the people to join it and become its
'priests' are arguments of a political scope and nature. "
Bishop Rooker went on to say that to join and work for the
Aglipayan Church was regarded as a "demonstration of
Filipino patriotism, " and "to fail to join it a proof of sympathy with American domination. "44

In addition to deriving strength from the nationalist
movement, Aglipayanism also gained numerous adherents
in so short a time and with so few Filipino priests because
it resembled the old Catholic Church in many ways. Its
first priests and prelates were former Catholic clergymen;
in the majority of cases the places of worship did not
change either. Perhaps more important was the fact that
a great part of the ritual and ceremony, if not the doctrine,
of the Catholic Church was retained by the Aglipayan
Church. Appeal to the emotions rather than to the mind
was a central feature of the new religion as much as it had
been of the old.45 Colorful processions and vestments and
costly celebrations of the days of saints (fiestas) were
appropriated by the new religion.46 All these resemblances
to the Catholic Church reveal the pragmatism of the early

leaders of the movement, particularly Isabelo de los
Reyes, its early theologian. For centuries the Filipinos
had been exposed to an awe-inspiring Catholicism, em-
bellished with many "unCatholic," perhaps even "un-
Christian," survivals of the pre-Spanish religion of the
Filipinos.47 To those who did not care about the theologi-
cal foundations of their religion and who did not have a
vested interest in the new religion, an entirely different
religion would probably have been less attractive. It is
very likely that the leaders of the Aglipayan Movement
were aware of this sentiment. Although known for his
impulsiveness at times, de los Reyes, who wrote the early
books of the IFI, was a keen student of social movements.

As regards clerical celibácy, which the new Church
abandoned, this was perhaps not so shocking to the Filipinos as to have made them reconsider joining the Aglipayan Church. It was common knowledge at the time that
many Spanish priests, and perhaps their Filipino coadjutors whom they despised for their "low morals," had
not been spotless paragons of priestly virtues themselves.
Besides, the Aglipayan Movement was a movement of
people, not of single individuals, into a new faith, 48 and
whatever weak points it had from the Catholic standpoint
were probably ignored by those who joined the new religion.

Aglipayanism was already well on the road to drawing
more and more adherents from Catholicism when, on November 24, 1906, the Philippine Supreme Court handed
down the precedent-setting decision on the legal ownership
of disputed religious property. It is necessary to point
out very briefly the background of this historic decision.

We recall that the Treaty of Paris had recognized the
properties and property rights of ecclesiastical bodies as
well as of individuals regardless of nationality. 49 There
was no doubt at all that the Roman Catholic Church owned
the parish churches, cemeteries, and other property
attached to the parishes which it held as of December 10,
1898. When the schism took place, however, Aglipayans
gained control over parish churches and other assets (1)
by simply taking over a vacated parish, (2) by forcible
seizure, at times abetted by municipal councils whose
members had embraced Aglipayanism, 50 and (3) when

a Catholic priest turned Aglipayan and claimed the parish for the Aglipayan Church. 51

At first Aglipay claimed ownership for his church of all religious properties on the ground that they had been built or given by their ancestors and that these should be used for the benefit of the Filipinos and not by a "foreign" church. He receded from this extreme position when he said that if a municipality or a parish had turned Aglipayan, then the church therein should also be Aglipayan property, because that had been the temple of worship for the people since time immemorial. Aglipay also argued that the State owned the churches. Therefore, the United States had become the owner of such properties when she took over the Philippines. It was the duty of the United States government, the argument continued, to turn over such properties to the Filipinos, i. e. , Aglipayans. 52

The Catholic Church dismissed such arguments as absurd and insisted upon the strict application of the Treaty of Paris. Taft, however, had no desire to antagonize Father Aglipay if he could; that would have been contrary to the policy of conciliation. Yet he knew that legally everything was in the Catholics' favor, and so he said that the courts should decide the case. He declared, however, that until a decision was reached, whoever was in peaceful possession of a church should be considered its rightful owner. 53 It must be mentioned here that Catholics also initiated counter-seizure measures, at least in the diocese of Bishop Rooker (Jaro). 54

On November 24, 1906, the Supreme Court of the Philippines handed down its famous decision in the Barlin v. Ramires case. Brushing aside the contentions of the Aglipayans, the Court held that the Roman Catholic Church was the legal owner of all the disputed churches and other parish properties. 55 A similar decision in another case was appealed to the United States Supreme Court, which upheld the decision of the Philippine Supreme Court. 56 In the words of Achutegui and Bernad, the impact of the "cold-blooded" decision 57 was "catastrophic to the Philippine Independent Church. "58 It must have been extremely humiliating to lose so many churches, conventos, and other buildings, some of them imposing structures. "The

Aglipayan church indeed survived, " continued Achutegui and Bernad, ''but it survived as a sect, ... ''[59] The great wonder, however, is that the Aglipayan Church was able to survive in any form after this crushing blow.[60]

Despite the severe setback, the rise of Aglipayanism must be recognized as one of the important religious developments of the Taft Era. Together with the coming of Protestantism, it marked the end of the monolithic religion of the Christian Filipinos. It also inspired a Catholic "counter-offensive" which we shall discuss later on.

Looking at the distribution of the Aglipayan population as of 1918 (see Tables 4 and 5 at the end of this chapter), which probably reflects the distribution, although not necessarily the number, of Aglipayans during the Taft Era, we note also another significant aspect about the rise of Aglipayanism: it was a national, and not merely an Ilocano, movement. Only Batanes, the tiny islands north of Luzon, reported no Aglipayan adherents.

As would be expected, Aglipay's home province, Ilocos Norte, became almost completely Aglipayan. If neighboring Ilocos Sur did not follow suit, it was probably because Vigan was, and still is, the captial of the Catholic diocese of Nueva Segovia. The large percentage of Aglipayans in Manila may be accounted for by the following factors: (1) Manila was the meeting ground of the radicals who launched the movement as well as the seat of de los Reyes' union which became the launching pad of the movement, and (2) Father Aglipay was inaugurated (October, 1902) and consecrated (January, 1903) Obispo Maximo in Manila.

It might also be pertinent to note that most provinces in which some of the friar lands were located also contained significant percentages of Aglipayan adherents, as can be seen from the following: Isabela, 24.3 per cent; Rizal, 23 per cent; Laguna, 22.1 per cent; Cavite, 20.7 per cent; Cagayan; 16.1 per cent; Mindoro, 15.2 per cent. The exceptions were Bataan (8.7 per cent) and Cebu (1.8 per cent). The possible explanation for Bataan is that it contained only 1,000 acres of the friar lands; in the case of Cebu, it was because it was the seat of the bishopric of Cebu.

There remains to be mentioned the social composition of the adherents of the IFI. On this point, we can only generalize; a thorough investigation of the archives or registers of the parishes of the Aglipayan Church would be necessary before any definite conclusions could be made.

On the basis of available data, however, we may safely say that the Aglipayan Movement cut across various social classes. McGavran's concept of the IFI as an example of population movements into Evangelical Christianity is therefore, correct.[61] There is also no doubt that some members of the Filipino upper class joined the IFI, or at least sympathized with it, although we do not know their precise number or proportion to the entire elite. The impression is that it was large: Briggs claims that "the leading Filipinos openly allied themselves with Aglipay."[62] Clifford's study also suggests that many IFI leaders were nationalists and politicians.[63]

Additional evidence on this point is offered by Bishops Rooker of Jaro (Iloilo) and Dougherty of Nueva Segovia. We recall that the former complained to President Roosevelt that many Filipino public school teachers, a large proportion of whom were appointed by "local political influence," were "professed haters of the Catholic Church."[64] In all likelihood, the teachers and local political leaders referred to were Aglipayans; as a matter of fact, local political leaders had a vested interest in undermining the influence of the Catholic Church. Significantly, the Aglipayan following in many parts of Bishop Rooker's diocese was relatively extensive: in Antique, 43.4 per cent; Romblon, 42.1 per cent; Occidental Negros, 33.5 per cent; Palawan, 20.5 per cent; and in Iloilo itself, 19.0 per cent. Bishop Dougherty was more explicit. He told Taft that the mayor of Vigan and ex-governor Juan Villamore of Abra,[65] and doubtless other political leaders in the north, were Aglipayans.[66] In fact, Simeon Mandac, Obispo Maximo Aglipay's secretary, was elected governor of Ilocos Norte during the Taft Regime.[67]

The Introduction of Protestantism

Students of American expansion in the Philippines are

familiar with the following story which President McKinley
reportedly told to a group of Methodist ministers who had
paid him a courtesy call at the White House:

> When next I realized that the Philippines had
> dropped into our laps I confess that I did not
> know what to do with them. I sought counsel
> from all sides... but got little help. I thought
> first we could take only Manila, then Luzon;
> then other islands, perhaps, also. I walked
> the floor of the White House night after night
> until midnight, and I am not ashamed to tell you
> gentlemen, that I went down on my knees and
> prayed Almighty God for light and guidance more
> than one night. And one night late it came to me
> this way — I don't know how it was, but it came:
> (1) That we could not give them back to Spain —
> that would be cowardly and dishonorable; (2)
> that we could not turn them over to France or
> Germany — our commercial rivals in the Orient;
> (3) that we could not leave them to themselves —
> they were unfit for self-government and would
> soon have anarchy... ; and (4) there was nothing
> left for us to do but to take them all and to edu-
> cate the Filipinos, and uplift and Christianize
> them, and by God's grace do the best we could
> for them, as our fellow men for whom Christ
> also died. And then I went to bed, and went to
> sleep, and slept soundly.... 68

In an effort to conceal the real reasons behind the acquisition of the Philippines, McKinley pretended not to know
that the Filipinos had been Christians, save for a small
minority, for three centuries. At any rate, with American
rule came Protestantism. In May, 1899, the Presbyterians
established the first permanent Protestant mission in Iloilo.
They were followed by the Methodists and Baptists in 1900,
by the United Brethren and Disciples of Christ and Episcopalians, the latter with a missionary bishop in the person
of the Reverend Charles H. Brent, 69 in 1901, by the
Congregationalists in 1902, and by the Seventh Day

Adventists in 1905 (although regular missionary work started only in 1908). [70] To avoid duplication of missionary effort and the possibility of friction among these groups, an agreement was reached on the specific provinces or cities where each should establish missions. Most, of course, had missions in Manila. [71]

Dr. Parker makes the following observation on the early growth of Protestantism in the Philippines:

> By 1904 there were [already] about fifty Protestant mission workers in a half dozen of the largest cities of the Islands. Their work had met with great success from the very beginning. With few exceptions they were given a hearty welcome by the Filipinos. Requests for the opening of new centers came in faster than they could be answered. [72]

However, if the number of Protestant converts is taken into account, it would seem that Protestantism was not as enthusiastically welcomed by the Filipinos as Parker would have us believe. There are no data or statistics readily available on the number of Protestants at the end of the Taft Era, but we have figures for the period five years later. These are shown on the tables at the end of this chapter and indicate the relative and absolute strength of Catholics, Aglipayans, and Protestants as of 1918.

According to these tables, after eighteen years of evangelical work, the Protestants had converted only 124,575 Filipinos, or 1.3 per cent of the total population. Assuming an average conversion of 7,000 a year, the Protestant population of the Philippines at the end of the Taft Era must have been no more than 90,000, or probably about 1 per cent of the total population at that time. Of this number, roughly one-third were Methodists. [73]

Such a record, though not dismal, is very unimpressive: It is even less than one-tenth of the number of Aglipayans, and we have reason to believe that the number of Aglipayans was probably larger. [74] Certainly, the poor showing of the Protestant missions strongly contradicts the statement Bishop Hendrick of Cebu made to Major

McIntyre in 1908 that "when the American Government
came into possession of the Islands, people got the idea
that they changed from a Roman Catholic to a Protestant
government. "[75]

How may the small number of Protestant adherents be
explained? Laubach mentions a number of reasons, or
probable ones: violence, including murder, and the threat
of violence against Filipino Protestant converts; ostracism
of those who chose the new faith, even by members of one's
family; obscurantism, for which Laubach blames the
Spanish friars; the overbearing attitude of "low-class"
Americans in the provinces, whose religion the Filipinos
assumed to be Protestant; and the attitude of the Filipinos
toward independence.[76]

While each of these reasons may in fact have worked
against the possibility of a more rapid rate of growth, they
were not, in my opinion, crucial. Rather, it was because
Protestantism was less attractive to the Filipinos than
Catholicism had been to their ancestors three centuries
earlier.[77] It appealed less to their emotions and feelings.
Its ritual and ceremonies were less pompous and did not
inspire awe and fear. It is not a mere coincidence that
the Methodists, with their emotion-packed revivals, accounted for over 30 per cent of all Protestant communi-
cants.[78] Protestantism also had to contend with a well-
entrenched Catholic Church. Still further, Protestantism
had to compete with an indigenous religious movement,
Aglipayanism, that derived enormous initial strength from
the nationalist movement. In this respect, the fact that
the Protestants were Americans probably placed them at
a disadvantage that was aggravated by their failure to
establish a harmonious working relationship with Aglipayanism, or to consider it as part of their own work.[79]
Finally, the exclusivism of the early Protestants probably
played a role in repelling even some of the intelligentsia.
No Filipino missionary or Protestant became a member of
the Evangelical Union for twenty years following its establishment in April, 1901.[80]

Although it posed no threat to the dominant position of
the Catholic Church, let alone its existence, the coming
of Protestantism was an important episode in Philippine

history.   Like the American administrators and teachers,
Protestant missionaries became the bearers of a more
secular outlook on life, in much the same manner as
Catholic missionaries in the sixteenth century had been
the carriers of Europe's Catholic religious outlook. And
like their Catholic counterparts of an earlier age, the
Protestant missionaries established schools and colleges,[81]
hospitals, [82] and dormitories — like the Y. M. C. A. — and
undertook other social welfare activities.[83]

The Catholic Church During the Taft Regime

The Philippine Revolution, the Aglipayan Revolt and,
to a lesser extent, the advent of Protestantism placed the
Roman Catholic Church in a very precarious situation
during the decade 1896-1906. Not only was its predominance seriously challenged, but its very existence seemed
threatened.[84] That it was able to weather the storm was
due to the energetic efforts of the Catholic hierarchy
during the Taft Regime, the Supreme Court decision of
1906 which blunted the further advance of Aglipayanism,
the presence of a hard core of unswitchables among the
Filipino Catholics, and the introduction of reforms, even
if only gradually, in the organization and discipline of the
Church.

The appointment of Chapelle as Apostolic Delegate in
1899 was a costly mistake for the Church; he only worsened
the situation by his program of friar restoration and by his
criticisms of the Taft Commission's policy toward the
friars and their estates.[85] The Vatican had finally no
choice but to recall Chapelle in April, 1901. Indications
were even given that the Vatican was willing to negotiate
with the United States government on at least the question
of the friar lands; the result was the Taft Mission in
1902.[86] The Vatican, however, hedged on the withdrawal
of the friars: they were not pieces of real estate. Their
withdrawal, in the view of the Vatican, was an internal
Church matter and not subject to negotiation with a secular
power. This attitude was officially expressed in the
apostolic constitution for the Philippines, entitled Quae
mari Sinico, [87] issued at Rome on September 17, 1902,

by Pope Leo XIII and promulgated at Manila on December
8, 1902, by the new Apostolic Delegate, Monsignor
Giovanni Baptista Guidi.[88] By that time, the Aglipayan
schism had begun to gather momentum.

Achutegui and Bernad, no critics of the Church, had
this to say of Quae mari Sinico:

> Quae mari Sinico did in fact cause disappoint-
> ment even to Catholics, and it furnished the
> schismatics a new handle with which to attack
> the Pope and the Church. Those who had ex-
> pected sweeping changes, like the removal of
> the friars from the parishes and the appointment
> of Filipino bishops, were disappointed to find
> none of these things in the apostolic constitution.
> Yet a sober examination of the document will
> reveal certain changes, which, while not imme-
> diately sweeping, were destined to be far-
> reaching. [89]

Among the latter changes were the proposed increase in
the number of bishoprics, better training for native priests
and their increasing role in Church affairs, and enforcement of ecclesiastical discipline and reforms. Last but
not least, the apostolic constitution provided for the con-
vocation of a Provincial Council as soon as possible to
discuss doctrinal and disciplinary matters.[90]

In response to the threat posed by the Aglipayan Movement, the Vatican replaced the Spanish-friar-prelates with
American bishops in 1903,[91] and appointed Father Barlin
as the first Filipino Catholic Bishop in 1905.[92] The Spanish
friars (i. e., Dominicans, Recollects, Augustinians, and
Franciscans) were also silently withdrawn from the Philippines or confined to their monasteries or to educational
work. The official figures on page 113 may give an idea of
what happened to the unwanted friars.[93]

The Provincial Council envisaged by the apostolic bull
was to have been convened in August, 1904, but Monsignor
Guidi's death in June led to its postponement until 1907. It
was finally held in Manila From December 8 to December
29 of that year. [94] The Manila Council, as the Provincial

Religious Order	Number of friars as of		
	1898	1902	1903
Dominican	233	127	83
Recollect	327	76	53
Augustinian	346	111	67
Franciscan	107	66	47
TOTAL	1,013	380	250

Council was called, was the first real gathering of its kind
in the Philippines, and it derived an added significance
from the fact that among the Church dignitaries in atten-
dance was Bishop Barlin, a Filipino. It accepted Quae
mari Sinico as the basis of the organization of the Church
in the Philippines. Its efforts, among others, led to the
creation of five new ecclesiastical jurisdictions in 1910:
the bishoprics of Calbayog, Lipa, Tuguegarao, and
Zamboanga, and the apostolic prefecture of Palawan. [95]
The Council condemned Aglipayanism in no uncertain
terms, and threatened anyone abetting "heretics" with the
anathema of excommunication. While unusually severe,
the Council declared that the Mother Church would be
willing to reopen her portals to those who had been "mis-
led" by "a certain priest not particularly illustrious for
his learning nor commendable for his way of life."[96]
    The Catholic assessment of the Manila Council is
given as follows:

> The Manila Council of 1907 marked a real turning
> point in the history of the Church in the Philippines.
> Its effects were not immediately visible. But it
> served to stiffen the backbone of the Catholic
> clergy and people and it introduced needed reforms.
> Since then, the progress of the Church in the
> Philippines has been slow indeed, but steady.[97]

Islam Under American Rule

This discussion on religious developments during the

Taft Regime may be concluded by a few remarks on the
Muslim Filipinos, or Moros, as they are more commonly
referred to in the available literature.[98]

At the time of the American occupation, the Muslim
Filipinos probably numbered 150,000.[99] They were con-
centrated in Sulu and southern and central Mindanao. Their
basic political institution was the "clan or kinship group,"
which was governed by a datu, similar to the barangays
which the Spaniards had found in the Visayas and Luzon in
the sixteenth century.[100] In addition, the Muslims had
also evolved a more elaborate political organization — the
sultanate — embracing several clans, or barangays, and
governed by a sultan or rajah, who was assisted by a number of supra-barangay officials known as panglimas. There
were several sultanates, the most well known being the
Sultanate of Sulu. Their religion was a blend of Islam and
indigenous spiritism, similar in many respects to the
syncretic Christianity among the early Filipinos. Since
the sultans, rajahs, or datus represented religious and
political authority, government among the heterogeneous
Moros resembled a theocracy.[101]

Spanish power in the Philippines was strongest in
Luzon and the Visayas along the seacoast (except on the
Pacific side) and in the lowland interior areas easily
accessible by navigable rivers and, later, by overland
transport, such as the Manila-Dagupan Railroad. In these
areas, Spain imposed a semblance of Pax Hispanica, permitting Spanish institutions to take firm root.[102] Spanish
authority was least effective and unpredictable in Mindanao
and Sulu, except along the northern coast. The Moros
successfully resisted the imposition of Spanish authority
well into the latter half of the nineteenth century. Finally,
in 1876, exploiting the advantages of steamboats, the
Spaniards captured Jolo, the capital of the Sultanate of
Sulu; three years later, by virtue of a treaty with the
Spanish government, the Sultan of Sulu acknowledged the
sovereignty of Spain, for which he was granted a yearly
salary of P2,400. Spain also promised to respect the
cultural autonomy of the Moros, but Christian missionaries
were to be left unhampered in their evangelical work within
the Sultan's realm.[103]

Such was the situation with the Sulu Moros on the eve of the American occupation. This was not the case, however, with respect to the Moros in Mindanao, especially those around Lake Lanao: The Spaniards had never been able to subdue them, and so Spanish civilization had barely affected the Moros, let alone their religion. The Americans, however, accomplished in a little over a decade what the Spaniards had been unable to achieve in three centuries. They compelled the Moros through diplomacy and force, but essentially through force, to recognize the authority of the United States and of the Philippine Commission, thereby assuring their gradual integration into Philippine political life.[104]

Like elsewhere in the Philippines, a military government was at first established over Mindanao and Sulu. In replacing the military regime, however, the Philippine Commission did not apply the regular provincial and municipal codes to the territories exclusively or predominantly inhabited by the non-Christian Filipinos. It was argued that the great cultural differences between the Moros and the Christian or Hispanized Filipinos required the adoption of such a course. In the case of the Moros, the Philippine Commission said:

> It was not deemed wise or just, except to the
> extent absolutely necessary, to impose upon
> them the system of laws and of administration
> of justice which was well adapted to the Christian
> Filipinos, but which must prove burdensome
> and odious to them. Moreover, it was under-
> stood. . . that they had a crude system of tribal
> laws and customs administered by their datos
> and priests, who were termed "panditas. "[105]

The Philippine Commission established a single provincial government for Sulu and the predominantly Moro territories of Mindanao. The province consisted of five main districts, each under a district governor: Sulu, Cotabato, Zamboanga, Lanao, and Davao.[106] The officials of the province were the governor, a secretary, a treasurer, an attorney, an engineer, and a school superintendent.

The first four officials made up the Legislative Council for
the province, which was empowered to enact rules and
regulations, or even to create local governments, subject
to confirmation by the Philippine Commission.[107] Throughout the Taft Regime, the Commission exercised exclusive
legislative power over the non-Christian provinces or
tribes, including Moro Province. Although the Philippine
Assembly resented the arrangement, the Americans remained firm on this point, contending that the Moros
themselves did not wish to be placed under a Filipino,
i.e., Christian Filipino, government.[108]

   The government of Moro Province may be described
as a paternal government, concerned primarily with
creating a minimum degree of order among the Moros and
eradicating practices that seemed repugnant to Americans,
such as slavery, piracy, arbitrary power of the datus over
their people, excessive penalties for certain offenses, etc.
By and large, however, Moro customs were respected,
and Moro customary law, subject to a few amendments,
governed "in all civil and criminal actions arising between
Moros,..."[109]

   Forbes has this to say regarding the Moro reception
to American rule and institutions:

> It was much more difficult to wind the confidence
> of the Moros and convince them of well-meaning
> than was the case of the tribal peoples [i.e.,
> Negritos, Ifugaos, Igorots, etc.] First they had
> to be assured that no ulterior designs were har-
> bored against their religion. They suspected the
> schools and in some districts it was long before
> they could be persuaded to let any of their children,
> especially the girls, attend school. They were
> quick, however, to realize the advantages of agri-
> cultural and trade schools and very appreciative
> of the service rendered by doctors and hospitals,
> ...[110]

   It may be inferred from this discussion that the impact
of American institutions upon Moro life during the Taft Era
must have been very slight. And insofar as religious

beliefs were concerned, the far-reaching developments among the Christian Filipinos were not paralleled by similar changes among the Muslim Filipinos.

TABLE 4

NUMBER OF CATHOLICS, AGLIPAYANS AND PROTESTANTS IN 1918[a]

Provinces and sub-provinces	Catholics	Aglipayans	Protestants
Abra	38,690	11,840	1,208
Agusan	25,533	9,585	246
Albay	257,852	64	776
Ambos Camarines	256,131	10,533	601
Antique	82,671	67,201	4,536
Apayao	238	170	1
Bataan	50,870	4,999	1,744
Batanes	8,209	---	5
Batangas	327,503	10,878	1,501
Benguet	7,028	124	415
Bohol	350,924	6,175	1,050
Bontoc	522	26	54
Bukidnon	6,848	86	367
Bulacan	236,486	7,638	3,959
Cagayan	149,473	30,638	2,948
Capiz	263,486	18,233	1,936
Catanduanes	63,349	1	32
Cavite	120,069	32,564	4,152
Cebu	835,192	15,042	2,435
Cotabato	2,104	1	30
Davao	41,031	563	453
Ifugao	117	8	13
Ilocos Norte	48,690	165,739	2,907
Ilocos Sur	178,264	28,573	4,714

[a] Census of 1918, Vol. II, Table No. 13, pp. 394-95. Figures based on Schedule 1.

TABLE 4 Continued

Provinces and sub-provinces	Catholics	Aglipayans	Protestants
Iloilo	392, 550	95, 772	6, 128
Isabela	80, 364	27, 483	746
Kalinga	156	2	79
Laguna	147, 353	43, 228	3, 689
Lanao	5, 964	395	222
La Union	154, 799	3, 732	1, 656
Lepanto-Amburayan	24, 798	4, 828	1, 625
Leyte	580, 156	14, 667	1, 264
Manila	157, 734	89, 554	18, 795
Marinduque	51, 693	4, 966	46
Masbate	66, 892	363	89
Mindoro	49, 436	10, 920	258
Misamis	108, 732	83, 950	1, 690
Nueva Ecija	166, 067	51, 044	8, 621
Nueva Vizcaya	12, 496	8, 872	1, 669
Occidental Negros	253, 998	132, 740	3, 519
Oriental Negros	145, 681	60, 313	4, 223
Palawan	44, 589	323	386
Pampanga	242, 791	7, 847	4, 971
Pangasinan	430, 692	124, 897	9, 498
Rizal	165, 676	51, 431	9, 157
Romblon	37, 201	27, 178	152
Samar	349, 691	10, 651	316
Siquijor	56, 639	9	107
Sorsogon	177, 106	44	552
Sulu	2, 178	11	49
Surigao	94, 716	24, 107	184
Tarlac	114, 776	49, 293	4, 070
Tayabas	196, 543	10, 005	1, 664
Zambales	24, 292	53, 997	1, 379
Zamboanga	62, 539	203	484
Total[b]	7, 751, 176	1, 413, 506	123, 362

[b] If figures based on Schedule 8 (ibid. , Table No. 38, pp. 882-95) are added to the above totals, the results would be: Catholics - 7, 790, 937; Aglipayans - 1, 417, 448; and Protestants - 124, 575. Cf. ibid. , p. 51.

TABLE 5

COMPARATIVE STRENGTH OF CATHOLICS,
AGLIPAYANS AND PROTESTANTS IN 1918[a]

Provinces and sub-provinces	Catholics	Aglipayans	Protestants
Batanes	99. 9	----	0. 1
Siquijor	99. 8	(b)	0. 2
Çatanduanes	99. 7	(b)	(b)
Albay	99. 3	(b)	0. 3
Sorsogon	99. 3	(b)	0. 3
Masbate	99. 1	0. 6	0. 1
Bohol	97. 9	1. 7	0. 1
Cebu	97. 8	1. 8	0. 3
Leyte	97. 0	2. 5	0. 2
Samar	96. 8	2. 8	0. 1
La Union	96. 4	2. 3	1. 0
Batangas	96. 3	3. 2	0. 4
Bulacan	95. 0	3. 1	1. 6
Ambos Camarines	94. 6	3. 9	0. 2
Pampanga	94. 3	3. 0	1. 9
Tayabas	92. 8	4. 7	0. 8
Marindugue	90. 9	8. 7	0. 1
Capiz	90. 1	6. 2	0. 7
Bataan	86. 8	8. 7	0. 1
Ilocos Sur	82. 0	13. 3	2. 2
Cagayan	78. 7	16. 1	1. 6
Iloilo	78. 1	19. 0	1. 2
Surigao	77. 7	19. 7	1. 2
Cavite	76. 3	20. 7	2. 7
Pangasinan	76. 1	22. 1	1. 7
Laguna	75. 4	22. 1	1. 9
Nueva Ecija	73. 1	22. 5	3. 8
Rizal	72. 4	23. 1	4. 0
Isabela	71. 2	24. 3	0. 7
Mindoro	68. 7	15. 2	0. 4

[a] Census of 1918, Vol. II, p. 50.
[b] Less than one-tenth of one (1) per cent.

TABLE 5 Continued

Provinces and sub-provinces	Catholics	Aglipayans	Protestants
Oriental Negros	67. 5	27. 9	2. 0
Tarlac	67. 0	28. 8	2. 4
Palawan	64. 9	20. 5	0. 5
Occidental Negros	64. 0	33. 5	0. 9
Agusan	63. 6	21. 5	0. 5
Romblon	57. 6	42. 1	0. 2
Manila	55. 3	31. 4	6. 6
Misamis	54. 7	42. 2	0. 9
Abra	54. 1	16. 7	1. 8
Antique	53. 4	44. 4	2. 9
Zamboanga	43. 3	0. 1	0. 4
Davao	42. 9	0. 5	0. 5
Lepanto-Amburayan	37. 1	8. 5	3. 1
Nueva Vizcaya	35. 1	24. 7	4. 7
Zambales	29. 0	64. 5	1. 7
Ilocos Norte	22. 2	75. 7	1. 3
Bukidnon	19. 6	0. 3	0. 9
Benguet	16. 2	0. 3	1. 0
Lanao	7. 5	0. 4	0. 3
Cotabato	4. 2	(b)	0. 1
Apayao	2. 6	1. 9	(b)
Bontoc	2. 0	0. 5	0. 2
Sulu	1. 3	(b)	(b)
Kalinga	1. 0	(b)	0. 6
Ifugao	0. 4	(b)	(b)
Average (Philippines)	75. 5	13. 7	1. 3

THE FILIPINOS AND AMERICAN ECONOMIC POLICY

American economic policy in the Philippines reflected America's view of what constituted her vital economic interests and, to a lesser degree, the vital economic interests of the Filipinos. Conditions in the Philippines and America's experience in dealing with economic problems also influenced the nature and content of the economic policy of the United States. Several aspects of that policy also indicated American naiveté in believing that the economic development of the Philippines, as well as some desirable changes in the economic structure, could be achieved by simply introducing American methods of free enterprise and business, enacting legislation thought to be conducive to such development, and instituting certain practices, such as homesheads and Torrens titles. Looking at the reception given to his policy by the Filipinos, their reaction ranged from complete acceptance, as in the case of free trade, to manifest opposition, as in the case of internal taxation.

Tariff Policy

The United States acquired the Philippines mainly in the interest of trade expansion, and its tariff policy was shaped accordingly.[1] Constitutional obstacles were fortunately removed by an understanding Supreme Court in the so-called Insular Cases.[2] The Supreme Court, by declaring that Congress had the power to incorporate or not to incorporate the Philippines (and Puerto Rico) within the American tariff wall, prevented the free and unlimited entry into the United States of Philippine products believed to be injurious to certain American economic interests, such as beet sugar and tobacco. It also excluded the possibility that Spanish products, and perhaps those of other foreign nations as well, might gain free entry into the United States through the Philippine backdoor. Under Article IV of the Treaty of Paris, Spanish goods brought into the Philippines were to enjoy the same treatment as

American goods for a period of ten years following the exchange of ratifications, which took place on April 11, 1909.
This agreement would have given other nations grounds for
insisting on equal treatment of their products imported into
the Philippines; to refuse this request would have embarrassed the United States at a time when she was champion-
ing the "Open Door" policy in China.[3]

The Philippine tariff. The Supreme Court decision
also worked to the advantage of the United States in another
way: it made it possible for the United States to frame a
tariff policy for the Philippine Government (actually a part
of the United States government) that enabled it to raise
revenue even from customs duties on American products.
Such revenues saved the Philippines from becoming the
"fiscal nightmare" that it had been to Spain.[4]

Outwardly, the Philippine tariff represented a faithful
observance of the Treaty of Paris and stood as proof of the
sincerity of America's pronouncements on the "Open Door"
policy. Actually, neither the Treaty of Paris not the
idealistic Open Door policy prevented American products
from entering the Philippines on a preferential basis.
This was ingeniously achieved through the reclassification
of goods in the successive Philippine tariff acts before
1909.[5] Finally, in 1909, all American products, except
rice, were admitted duty-free into the Philippines.[6] By
that time, Article IV of the Treaty of Paris had expired
and so a discriminatory tariff could be freely applied.

The movement to abolish American tariffs on Philippine sugar and tobacco. The records do not indicate early
Filipino opposition to the preferential treatment of American goods in the Philippines. Perhaps the Filipinos were
more concerned with the admission of their sugar and tobacco products into the United States on a preferential
basis through a substantial reduction, if not abolition, of
the prohibitive duties under the Dingley Law of 1897.[7] In
their campaign toward this end, the Filipinos had the support of the American administrations in Manila and in
Washington. This was, of course, perfectly understandable.
The Philippine Commission regarded the reduction of tariffs
on Philippine sugar and tobacco as an important factor in
economic revival and growth and in providing immediate

relief to the prostrate economy of the islands. Economic
collapse had followed as a direct aftermath of the Philippine Revolution and Filipino-American hostilities, the loss
of former markets for Philippine products,[8] and the successive outbreaks of cholera and rinderpest epidemics and the
prevalence of locusts.[9] In addition, greater economic
activity would mean larger internal revenues with which to
finance governmental programs. Finally, the Philippine
Commission envisioned the tariff concession as a means
of maintaining the confidence of the Filipinos in the United
States and of strengthening the bonds between "the Filipino
and American people, . . . "[10] To the Commission's pragmatic motives, President Roosevelt added considerations
of humanity, duty, and honor in pressing for a substantial
reduction of the American tariff on Philippine goods.[11]

Since so much is known of the American efforts to
secure a fair deal for Philippine sugar and tobacco during
the Taft Regime, there is no need to go into them in detail
in this work.[12] What is not generally known, although they
seem in fact only too obvious, are the efforts of the Filipinos themselves to obtain tariff concessions from the
United States.

The first American measure relating to the tariff on
Philippine goods proposed to reduce the Dingley rates by
25 per cent.[13] When this became known in Manila, the
Federalistas immediately implored Taft, then in the United
States, to obtain this "greatest reduction."[14] However,
because of opposition by American beet sugar and tobacco
interests, Congress refused to grant the 25 per cent
reduction.[15] Taft was fully aware of this fact, but he gave
an entirely different reason:

> Reluctance now to make greater reduction due
> to continuance of war and unfounded sensational
> statements concerning hostile attitude Filipino
> people and inability civil governments maintain
> law and order in pacified provinces.[16]

At any rate, the Filipinos now waged an unrelenting
campaign to demolish the larger portion of the Dingley
rates. Provincial and municipal boards, political parties,

interest groups, and, before long, the Philippine Assembly all joined efforts in demanding a better deal for Philippine sugar and tobacco in the United States. A strong argument put forward was the need for new, favored outlets, as evidenced by the following:

> With the establishment of American sovereignty ... [Philippine] sugar and tobacco lost the markets they enjoyed under the Spanish government, and it is very difficult to see how substitutes for those markets can be found unless the[ir] introduction... in the great American market can be made possible by reducing or abolishing the prohibitive rates that at present obtain.[17]

Concern for the plight of sugar and tobacco workers was used to draw the attention of the American Congress to the urgency of tariff reduction. Manila Mayor Arsenio Cruz Herrera, president of the Federal Party, told President Roosevelt that even a reduction of 50 per cent would be insufficient to help the laborers. He therefore requested that free entry be granted to "at least manufactured tobacco...."[18] In addition, the Tobacco Workers' Guild and the Labor Union of the Philippines petitioned jointly along the same lines as Herrera's cable to Roosevelt. They also cited figures to refute the claims of American tobacco growers and manufacturers that they would suffer seriously if Philippine cigars were admitted duty free.[19]

In less than a month after its inauguration on October 16, 1907, the Philippine Assembly[20] threw its weight behind scattered efforts to secure better treatment for Philippine sugar and tobacco. This was only natural. Among its members were representatives from constituencies raising mostly sugar and tobacco. It is entirely possible that some assemblymen had direct financial interests in some sugar and tobacco companies, or owed their elections to the material support of these two groups.

The Assembly's main effort on behalf of tariff reduction was the passage of Joint Resolution No. 6,[21] which became the basis of Joint Resolution No. 11 of the Philippine Legislature (May 19, 1908).[22] It is important to point out here that Quezon, then assemblyman from Tayabas (now Quezon) province, was a key figure in the passage of this resolution by the Assembly.23

By Joint Resolution No. 11, the Filipino Resident Commissioners at Washington24 were instructed to seek from Congress the free entry of 400,000 tons of sugar, 600,000 pounds of wrapper tobacco, 7,000,000 pounds of filler tobacco, and of at least 150,000,000 cigars and cigarettes. These tariff preferences were to be obtained "without special concessions" to the United States except, perhaps, the removal of Philippine duties on all agricultural and road-building machinery.25

The Filipinos and free trade. Meanwhile, at least the House of Representatives of the American Congress had not been exactly idle. In January, 1905, the Curtis Bill was introduced, providing for a 75 per cent reduction of the tariff on Philippine sugar and tobacco and for the free entry of all other goods produced wholly in the Philippines. In December of the same year, Congressman Sereno Payne, Chairman of the House Ways and Means Committee, introduced another bill providing for similar concessions as well as for reciprocal free trade after April 11, 1909 (the expiration date of the provision of the Treaty of Paris granting Spanish products the same treatment as American goods in the Philippines). Neither of these House measures, however, was enacted.26

The Payne Bill is significant in that it made a substantial reduction of duties on Philippine sugar and tobacco and the abolition of such duties at a later time contingent on the free admission of American products into the Philippines. This, as we have seen, was not entirely what the Filipinos had in mind. Even the Philippine Commission had not recommended free trade as such, although it was not opposed to free trade and had planned for it as early as 1903, on the occasion of the final drafting of the Internal Revenue Law.27 The Commission continued to assume this position as late as 1909, despite Edwards' warning a year earlier that Philippine products would never be admitted to the United States without any duties "unless we grant in turn free market for the United States goods in the Philippine Islands."28 Governor Smith explained his attitude as follows:

Commission not and has not been against free
trade with the United States, but due to the
limited resources of the government, has not
seen its way clear to recommend it.[29]

This apprehension had been voiced earlier by La
Democracia, the Progresista (formerly Federal) Party's
organ. It had most probably been inspired by Governor
Smith's views. But La Democracia also opposed free
trade, at least until April, 1909, on the ground that it
would make the United States the only market for Philippine products, with the consequence that

> Our interests would be commercially tributary
> to those of the United States, and our economic
> situation, in view of the exclusive traffic with
> that country, under the direction of strong Ameri-
> can syndicates, would lose its normal character.
> Therefore the advantages which free trade pro-
> mises would result chimerically and our prosperity
> would be more difficult to realize.[30]

In lieu of total reciprocal free trade, La Democracia
would have preferred selective reciprocity. This, in
effect, was what Joint Resolution No. 11 of the Legislature had asked for earlier and what the Manila Merchants'
Association in 1908[31] and the Second Agricultural Congress at their meeting in Iliolo in 1909 endorsed.[32]

Such was the situation when, on March 5, 1909, with
Article IV of the Treaty of Paris due to expire in a month
and a half, Congressman Payne introduced the bill which
finally became the Payne-Aldrich Tariff Act of August 5,
1909.[33] This act, together with the Philippine Tariff Act
of the same date,[34] regulated the trade relations between
the Philippines and the United States during the remainder
of the Taft Regime.[35] Before indicating the Filipino
reaction, it might be well to summarize the provisions.

1. All products and manufactures of the United
States, except rice, were to be admitted free of duty into
the Philippines provided they conformed to certain ship-
ping conditions and that there were no customs drawbacks.

2. All Philippine products shipped to the United States under similar conditions, except rice, were to be admitted duty free, with the provision that any amounts in excess of the following were to be charged the full tariff rates:

a) 300,000 gross tons of sugar,
b) 300,000 pounds of wrapper tobacco and filler tobacco mixed with more than 15 per cent wrapper tobacco,
c) 1,000,000 pounds of filler tobacco, and
d) 150,000,000 cigars.

3. The products or manufactures may contain foreign materials but not in excess of 20 per cent of their value.

Officially, the Filipino elite opposed the establishment of free trade relations.[36] This is shown by the resolutions of the Philippine Assembly,[37] as well as by the public statements of the Filipino Resident Commissioners in Washington.[38] Official statements, however, do not always reflect actual sentiments, and there are indications that the real feelings of the Filipino elite on the nature of Philippine-American trade relations during the Taft Regime and on the future political status of the Philippines were completely at variance with their official or public views.[39]

The Filipino elite gave the following reasons for opposing free trade, or the Payne Bill:

First, it "would, in the long run, be highly detrimental to the economic interests of the Filipino people."[40] By this was meant that free trade would divert Philippine sugar and tobacco from their natural outlets in neighboring Asia[41] and at the same time make the Philippines an economic dependency of the United States, which dependency, Quezon later recalled, "would create a most serious situation in Philippine economic life, especially when the time came for the granting of our independence."[42] It was further claimed that powerful economic interests alone would benefit from free trade and, still further, that "large companies from America" might eventually control Philippine commerce, industry, and especially agriculture.[43]

Second, the Filipino elite argued that free trade would
delay the attainment of Philippine independence. It was
asserted that American companies in the Philippines
reaping handsome profits from free trade might apply
pressure on the United States not to grant independence,
or at least postpone it indefinitely. The elite were willing
to concede that the Philippines stood to prosper rapidly as
a consequence of free trade, but, Quezon told the Philippine Commission, the Filipinos valued independence more
highly than economic prosperity. As the interpreter of the
sentiments of the Filipinos, therefore, the Assembly, in
Quezon's words, "opposes free trade":

> It prefers our present poverty, it prefers a slow
> prosperity which is to lead us to independence,
> rather than a rapid progress which is to make us
> renounce it perpetually. [44]

Third, and last, the elite claimed that they were
opposed to free trade because it would result in a loss of
revenue "to such an extent that it would be impossible to
sustain the burdens and services of the Insular Government
with only the remaining revenues." This argument was
supplemented by the contention that the economic condition
of the Filipinos did not permit them to pay additional taxes
to cover the huge deficit which would be created by free
trade.[45]

No one can question the overall validity of the elite's
arguments at that time; in fact, history has proven only
too well the justification of their first argument against
free trade. However, I shall attempt to prove that these
arguments were pure rhetoric on the part of both the
Assembly and the Resident Commissioners.

Shortly after the meeting between the Commission and
the Select Committee of the Assembly on March 29, 1909,
concerning the Assembly's Concurrent Resolution No.
36,[46] Forbes, then Vice Governor and soon to succeed
Smith as Governor, wrote to Edwards and to Wright; the
contents of these letters were not included in Forbes' two-
volume work published twenty years later.[47] Here is what he
told Edwards, the Chief of the Bureau of Insular Affairs:

The tariff situation was most unfortunate. Governor Smith feared the effect on our finances
and allowed himself to dwell on that to a point
which made him feel as though we ought to fight
the Payne Bill. ... In the meantime, the Assembly,
the leaders of which have tried in every way to
co-operate, did not know just what to think and
were not clear in their minds as to what the attitude of the Government really was. Quezon
introduced a resolution fighting the Payne Bill,
actuated by motives which I have as yet not been
able to fathom. Osmena was sick in bed at the
time the matter was brought up to a vote and
passed. ... It did not take me long to convince
Quezon that he had taken a dangerous course and
make him feel that he wanted to undo what had
been done but this is a thousand times more difficult that [sic] stopping it before hand. ... Quezon
told me that I could have prevented the whole
thing in two minutes if I had been in town [he
was not then in Manila, having gone to Baguio
to enjoy its healthier climate]. ... 48

Forbes' letter to Wright was almost the same as his
letter to Edwards, but he also added the following:

I came down here to see what could be done with the
deputies. I find that they feel they acted hastily, and many
of them are sorry that they took the action they did. There
would be, I am sure, very little difficulty in getting a free
trade resolution through were it not for the fact that the
Assembly has already hastily committed itself and now
wants to save its face. ... 49

We also gather the following information from Governor Smith's cablegram to the Secretary of War:

Nationalists claim that the original intent of
the resolution offered by Quezon was purely to
call the attention of the Congress to the fact
that the revenues of the Government would be

seriously affected and that the political tone of
the resolution was injected by the Progresistas.
Whatever may be the truth of the matter certain
it is that the independence part of the resolution
was offered as [an] amendment by Laguda, a
Progresista.[50]

From the foregoing, it appears, first, that Governor
Smith's fear over a loss of revenue inspired the Assembly's
resolution against free trade; second, that Quezon, the
ponente or sponsor of the resolution, omitted any reference
to independence in the original resolution; and, third, that
such an argument was added, ironically, by the Progresistas, the party supposedly pro-American and therefore less
interested in independence that the Nacionalistas.[51]

That the Assembly's opposition to free trade was not
real may also be inferred from the March 29, 1909 record
of the Select Committee's discussions with the Commission.
Since a frank exchange of views took place during the meeting, the record of the discussions should throw some light
on the actual stand of the Assembly, or at least on some of
its leaders, such as Quezon, on the issue of free trade.
Fortunately, such a record, although unpublished, is
available.[52]

A careful reading of the record of the discussions
shows that Quezon and his colleagues emerged from the
direct confrontation with the Commission evidently convinced by Smith, who — like a good proconsul — had now
become an ardent advocate of free trade,[53] and by Forbes,
who regarded himself as the hero of the occasion,[54] that
the Filipinos had everything to gain by establishing free
trade with the United States.

Smith and Forbes tried to answer the fears or arguments on which the Assembly had anchored its opposition
to free trade. Thus, while they admitted that free trade
would result in the influx of American capital, they also
maintained that Philippine agriculture would never be
controlled by American companies since the amount of
public agricultural lands which corporations could acquire
under the Public Lands Act of 1903[55] (not more than
1,024 hectares or 2,500 acres) would discourage

American capitalists from investing heavily in agriculture.
Donovan quotes Quezon on this point:

> After being informed... of the Act that limits
> the number of hectares of agricultural land that
> companies may acquire in the Philippines, my
> personal opinion,... is that there is not much
> danger of our agricultural lands falling into the
> hands of companies that might establish them-
> selves in the Philippines on the adoption of free
> trade.[56]

Smith and Forbes also countered the second of the
Assembly's arguments by stating that free trade would
enable the Filipinos to obtain their independence much
sooner because with the prosperity which was certain to
come with free trade, they would be in a position to stand
alone, at least financially. They implied, moreover, that
the United States might not grant independence if it believed that the Filipinos could not maintain their independence. While they were aware that the United States had
yet to come out officially for independence, Smith told the
Select Committee that the Filipinos must have confidence
in "America's promises not to hold the Philippines forever." Smith then pointed out that once independence had
been declared as the official policy of the United States,
American companies would adjust accordingly. For the
benefit of the Committee, Smith explained that American
experience in the Far East, at least, had been for the flag
to lead capital and not the other way around. In short,
free trade would never stand in the way of independence.
Quezon was apparently convinced, for he proceeded
to discuss the effect of free trade on the revenues of the
government. Forbes and Smith easily demolished the
argument by saying that the Filipinos could actually be
taxed a little bit more, since they were among the least
taxed people in the world. Besides, remedial action,
including financial assistance, would be requested from
Congress. As the discussions came to a close, Smith
said that the Commission would prepare a substitute resolution endorsing the Payne Bill. Quezon, speaking for

the Committee, said that the Assembly would await such
a resolution for its members to consider. We may therefore conclude that Smith and Forbes were successful in
converting Quezon and his colleagues to free trade,
assuming that they needed to be converted.

The assertion that members of the elite were not
really against free trade may be further substantiated by
pointing out that the dominant Nacionalista Party, or at
least some of its leaders, were not in favor of "immediate independence," whose attainment, the Assembly
claimed, would be jeopardized by the establishment of
free trade.[57] Yet, the Assembly persisted in its original
attitude by rejecting Commission Joint Resolution No. 8
in favor of free trade.[58] Why?

Forbes gave part of the answer when he wrote that
"the Assembly has already hastily committed itself and
now wants to save its face...."[59] Concern with amor
propio (literally "face") is a powerful determinant of
Filipino behavior or attitude. Moreover, the independence
was a popular electroal issue; standing against free trade
seemed to be the natural thing to do under the circumstances: Had the Assembly endorsed a program calculated
to make the Philippines an American economic dependency,
it would have been criticized as a body of hypocrites and
traitors by those seeking election to the Assembly, irres-
pective of their own feelings toward free trade.

Furthermore, the assemblymen probably knew that
their endorsement of free trade was not really crucial to
the passage of the Payne Bill. This, in fact, turned out to
be the case, Edwards informed Smith that insofar as
President Taft and the War Department were concerned,
the Assembly's attitude was unimportant, "especially
since views of Philippine agriculturists so vitally interested in the outcome have become known."[60] But perhaps
the most important reason why the elite were not really
against free trade was the certainty that most of them
stood to profit directly or indirectly from its establishment[61]. As we shall presently see, Philippine production
and foreign trade expanded tremendously soon after the
removal of tariff barriers on trade with the United States.

Turning now to the Resident Commissioners at

Washington, the evidence also shows that Legarda and Ocampo entertained, privately at least, views on the Payne Bill which were quite different from their public expressions on the subject. Thus, General Edwards wrote:

> Governor Smith wants to act square with his successor,... and he is fearful of losing revenue. ....
> With their ignorance of the situation over there, Osmena has cabled Ocampo expressing concern about this loss of revenue. Plainly the Nacionalistas are playing politics,.... Ocampo is thoroughly in line now, after explanations. Legarda has been in line right along, but he is a bit apprehensive on account of his gin factory, which uses rye for distillation.[63]

Legarda and Ocampo were even willing to accept a drastic reduction of the quota of 7,000,000 pounds of filler tobacco originally recommended by the Philippine Legislature.[64] Hord, then in Washington, recommended the reduction to 2,000,000 pounds, "or even 1,000,000 pounds," in order to get the support of "Griest of Pennsylvania." Hord said:

> This would also be in line with Mr. Legarda's views, and also those of Mr. Ocampo, that is, the latter's personal views although officially he claims to be under obligation to carry out the views of the Philippine legislature regarding the 3,000,000 [sic] limit.[65]

It may be suggested that Legarda and Ocampo assumed this official attitude because they owed their election to the Assembly, the more popular chamber of the Legislature, whose members were openly against free trade. If they did not voice their true feelings toward free trade, it was probably for the same reasons which we have offered to explain the real sentiments of the Assembly. So much for the attitudes of the elite.

Another way of looking at the Filipino response is through the statistics on sugar and tobacco exports to,

and Philippine imports from, the United States, all of
which figured prominently in the battle for free trade.
Table 6 below shows that in 1910, after a year of free
trade relations, the amount of sugar exported to the
United States increased by 90 per cent over 1909. The
volume of sugar exported to all other countries similarly
increased in 1911. Doubtless, the increases were due
to an unprecedented expansion of the sugar industry.
Looking at the United States' share in the sugar exports,
we note that there was a tremendous leap from 47. 2 per
cent in 1909 to a record high of 91. 2 per cent in 1911.
There were slumps in 1906, 1907, and 1913. The slump
in the last year was due to a fall in the price of sugar. [66]
The same reason accounted for the slumps in 1906 and
1907, aggravated by "a prohibitive duty. "[67]

Tables 7, 8, and 9 below indicate the response of the
tobacco industry to free trade. From these tables we
gather that in 1901, only . 02 per cent of the total tobacco
exported went to the United States, but in 1909 it reached
35. 8 per cent; in 1912, it was 37. 2 per cent. The increase
in the United States' share of the market for Philippine
cigars was even more remarkable. From a mere . 05 per
cent in 1901, it soared to 56. 56 per cent in 1910, reaching
a record high of 63. 33 per cent a year later. Cigarette
exports to the United States also showed a remarkable
rise.

There is one important fact that should be mentioned
in connection with the agricultural expansion which took
place as a consequence of free trade — the relatively
small amount of American capital invested in agriculture.[68]
Forbes believes that one reason for this was the discour-
agingly small acreage which companies were allowed to
acquire from the public lands (not more than 2, 500 acres).[69]
The more probable reason, however, was the resentment
of the Filipino elite at the intrusion of American capital,
especially in agriculture. As we have seen, such a fear
was one of the reasons put forward by the Assembly leaders for opposing the Payne Bill. Of course, the elite
were too intelligent to justify their opposition on purely
exclusivistic grounds. Opposition had to be anchored in
loftier motives, such as the fear of trusts and insistence

TABLE 6

QUANTITY OF SUGAR EXPORTED TO ALL COUNTRIES
AND TO THE UNITED STATES, 1901-1913[a]

Years Ended Dec. 31	To all Countries		To the United States	
	Metric Tons	Per cent of total Exports	Metric Tons	Per cent of total Value of Sugar
1901	56,873	10	5,226	14.4
1902	98,596	12	5,120	5.9
1903	85,308	10	29,315	34.1
1904	87,053	11	25,898	28.1
1905	108,499	15	43,591	41.4
1906	129,454	14	11,858	9.3
1907	127,917	13	10,989	9.6
1908	144,735	18	46,707	34.5
1909	129,328	16	53,073	47.2
1910	121,472	18	100,700	86.0
1911	209,044	25	187,059	91.2
1912	197,076	18	133,879	71.4
1913	157,334	15	30,717	22.2
1914	236,498	23	169,530	74.5

[a]Figures taken from Collector of Customs, Annual Report, 1921, p. 21 and idem, Annual Report, 1925, p. 71.
I have included 1914 figures to show that 1913 was an "abnormal" year.

TABLE 7

VALUE OF TOBACCO PRODUCTS EXPORTED TO ALL
COUNTRIES AND TO THE UNITED
STATES, 1901-1913[a]

Year Ending December 31	To all Countries Value	To the United States	
		Value	Per cent of total Tobacco
1901	5,263,882	984	.02
1902	3,925,248	52,544	1.33
1903	3,893,750	5,386	.14
1904	4,037,500	2,146	.05
1905	4,563,406	28,438	.62
1906	5,686,008	74,458	1.30
1907	5,454,858	49,050	.90
1908	5,652,084	37,496	.66
1909	6,649,068	1,484,054	22.32
1910	8,817,962	3,157,122	35.80
1911	7,636,162	1,840,638	24.10
1912	10,726,764	3,990,990	37.20
1913	9,933,936	3,317,510	33.40

[a]Collector of Customs, Annual Report, 1921, p. 29.

TABLE 8

QUANTITY OF CIGARS EXPORTED TO ALL COUNTRIES
AND TO THE UNITED STATES, 1901-1913[a]

Year Ending Dec. 1	To all Countries Quantity (Thousands)	To the United States Quantity (Thousands)	Per cent of total Value of Cigars
1901	238,475	72	.05
1902	117,852	698	1.11
1903	118,947	107	.19
1904	104,753	57	.10
1905	95,739	728	1.58
1906	108,635	1,690	2.95
1907	114,665	1,526	2.28
1908	115,881	1,182	1.73
1909	151,457	37,076	42.03
1910	184,407	61,526	56.56
1911	134,830	38,111	47.44
1912	190,842	90,000	63.33
1913	191,762	71,513	54.54

[a]Collector of Customs, Annual Report, 1921, p. 29.

TABLE 9

QUANTITY OF CIGARETTES EXPORTED TO ALL
COUNTRIES AND TO THE UNITED STATES, 1906-1913[a]

Year Ending Dec. 1	To all Countries Quantity (Thousands)	To the United States	
		Quantity (Thousands)	Per cent of total Cigarettes
1906	81,205	45	.09
1907	111,855	231	.44
1908	75,207	275	.80
1909	23,337	2,173	14.08
1910	35,629	8,823	39.12
1911	30,170	5,547	34.40
1912	49,310	10,968	40.36
1913	47,883	6,748	29.27

[a]Collector of Customs, Annual Report, 1921, p. 30.
Quantities for 1901-1906 not available.

that the influx of large American capital into the country was contrary to the political interests of the Filipinos.[70]

Turning now to the impact of free trade upon Philippine-American trade, we see the following expected results: Philippine imports rose more sharply than exports after 1909; by 1913, they accounted for 50 per cent of all Philippine imports. Table 10 shows the development of Philippine-American trade more clearly.

TABLE 10

PHILIPPINE TRADE WITH THE UNITED STATES[a]

Years Ended Dec. 31	Imports	Per cent of Total Imports	Exports	Per cent of Total Exports
1901	₱ 7,068,510	12	₱ 9,092,584	18
1902	8,306,348	12	22,951,896	40
1903	7,674,200	11	26,142,852	40
1904	10,197,640	17	23,309,936	40
1905	11,179,892	19	29,680,814	44
1906	8,955,772	17	23,738,578	36
1907	10,135,076	17	20,658,774	31
1908	10,203,672	17	20,901,510	32
1909	12,890,662	21	29,453,026	42
1910	40,137,084	40	34,483,450	42
1911	38,313,974	40	38,845,254	44
1912	48,618,020	39	45,764,014	41
1913	53,352,522	50	32,868,036	34

[a] Collector of Customs, Annual Report, 1925, p. 50. Does not include Hawaii and Puerto Rico.

The Filipinos and Internal Taxation

If Filipino upper class opposition to free trade was hypocritical, or at best languid, the reaction against internal taxation was real. In fact, based on available evidence, it may well be said that the initial opposition of the upper class to new internal taxes was second only in intensity to the initial resistance against the imposition of American sovereignty. In such an endeavor, the upper class could count on the support of the lower classes, to whom — as to everyone else — any new tax was bound to be unpopular and unwanted. The resistance of the elite in part explains why a comprehensive internal revenue law was enacted only on July 2, 1904, [71] and was not scheduled to go into effect fully until January, 1905. [72] This delay was in strong contrast to the Philippine Commission's haste in purchasing the friar lands, a contrast made all the more glaring since the new internal revenue law had been in preparation since the period 1901-1902. [73]

The Filipino reaction may be grasped more fully when it is recalled that when the United States took over the administration of the Philippines, it inherited a system of taxation that taxed the poor relatively more heavily than the wealthier segment of the population. [74] Any reform looking toward a more equitable system of taxation, therefore, was certain to be resisted by the upper class, whose cooperation with the United States was a necessity for the success of the Americans in the Philippines. By contrast, both Filipino upper and lower classes were only too eager to see the friars' religious and economic power removed or completely neutralized through their expulsion from the Philippines and the purchase of their estates. [75]

Filipino resistance to internal taxation also accounted for an average decrease of 50 per cent in the rates originally proposed by Commissioner Ide, then Secretary of Finance and Justice, and in the suspension of the land tax, in whole or in part, starting in 1906. [76] The attitude assumed by the leading Filipinos toward the internal revenue law was somewhat paradoxical in that they opposed a measure intended to pave the way for the establishment of free trade between the Philippines and the United States;[77] as we have tried to demonstrate in the preceding section of this chapter, this was a policy the elite by and large actually, if not enthusiastically, supported.

The Internal Revenue Law. The proposed internal revenue law was presented before the Commission for public discussion in April, 1904. Interested groups immediately registered their opposition. [78] Legarda and

Tavera, who had extensive financial interests in distilleries and cigar factories,[79] on whose products the proposed internal revenue law scheduled higher taxes than formerly, fought the measure bitterly. For obvious reasons, they did not do so in the open session of the Commission,[80] but carried out their fight through memorials with other members of the Filipino elite and through personal and confidential letters to the Secretary of War, in the hope that he would prevail upon the Philippine Commission to delay the enactment of the measure or at least reduce the tax rates. Meeting with only partial success,[81] Legarda and Tavera then resolved to fight the administration's program, and were joined by the other members of the elite. As we shall point out later, there were also other grievances against Governor Wright's administration.

In protesting against the passage of the internal revenue law, the Filipino leaders were careful to point out that they were not against any reform leading to a more just and equitable system of taxation, but that the law had been enacted at the wrong time, when the tax burdens of the people had reached "the limit of rational possibility." They also claimed that the needs of the government did not justify the new taxes created by the internal revenue law. Finally, in recommending that its execution be suspended "until the organization of the Philippine Assembly," the Filipino leaders were in fact claiming that the law had been enacted by the wrong people.[82]

It may be suggested that the latter point was a most important factor behind the opposition of the Filipino leaders, particularly the Federalistas, to the new internal revenue law. In passing the law in its final form while Tavera, Legarda, and other members of the elite were out of the country,[83] the impression was created that they were no longer considered by the administration as the leaders of the Filipinos. The effect of this action was described by a contemporary observer:

> The Filipinos,...feel slighted. Rightly or
> wrongly, they believe that they understand their
> own people and the needs of their people as well
> or better than we [i. e., Americans] do. They

resent therefore that attitude which either
ignores their ideas or overrides them in matters
of public interest.[84]

In October, 1904, Legarda visited Bulacan province,
near Manila, accompanied by John Hord, the Collector of
Internal Revenue. Writing of this trip, Legarda informed
Taft that the complaints of the Filipinos against the internal revenue law had been more numerous and more bitter
than he had been led to believe or hoped to encounter. He
therefore declared that since the law had been enacted in
spite of such objections, the following situation now existed:

> An imperialism, entirely too absolute, prevails
> here and this should not be so. I, for one, be-
> lieve that we should not be governed in this man-
> ner. It grieves me to tell you this, . . . but I note
> a great deal of restlessness in the people and
> much distrust in persons of good judgment, who
> have been conservative until now, in Manila.[85]

To Tavera, the internal revenue law was "truly imposed by a sovereign on a people who obey and pay," and
was intended to destroy the Filipino people. "From this
day," he wrote Taft, "I am living under the weight of
pessimism, apprehensions, and distrust for our future."[86]
He even went to the extent of asking President Roosevelt
to reappoint Taft as Governor of the Philippines.[87]
When Taft left the Philippines in December, 1903, to
become Roosevelt's Secretary of War, he promised the
Filipinos that he would someday return to visit them.[88]
He did return in August, 1905, together with some Senators and Representatives. While in the islands, Taft saw
and heard a great deal about the gulf between the leading
Filipinos and the administration and the feelings of some
toward Governor and Mrs. Wright.[89] He returned to the
United States somewhat "despondent" because he felt that
he might have to remove Governor Wright, Vice Governor
Ide, and possibly Forbes, then Secretary of Commerce
and Police.[90]
Wright was in fact replaced, but Ide remained as

Governor for about another year. Ide's appointment was the one Tavera and Legarda had least hoped for, if they had wanted it at all.[91] To everyone's surprise, however, Ide inaugurated a policy of extreme conciliation toward the Filipinos;[92] but he, too, was eventually replaced by General James F. Smith. Next to Taft, Smith was probably the most popular American governor during the Taft Era.[93]

It would be inaccurate to attribute this kaleidoscope of governors solely to the Filipino resistance to the internal revenue law, for there were also other internal factors which had led the Filipino elite to denounce Wright and Ide.[94] In fact, by the time Governor Ide left, Filipino opposition to the measure for which he had been respon-sible had become spasmodic, and existed mainly because of gross misconceptions about the law. Reductions in the original rates and delays in the imposition of scheduled increases in the taxes had made reconciliation easier than had seemed possible at the time the law was enacted. Furthermore, the manufacturers of liquor and cigars and cigarettes simply shifted part if not all of the indirect taxes to the consumer by increasing prices, some of which were well in excess of the stamp duties and other taxes imposed by the internal revenue law.[95] Yet, one cannot but feel that the strong opposition by the Filipino elite to the internal revenue law, at least at the outset, contributed in no small measure to Taft's decision to replace Wright and, ultimately, Ide, and to return to the "policy of attraction" or conciliating the Filipino elite, which had been the keystone of his successful administration in the Philippines.[96]

Before leaving the subject of the internal revenue law, it might be of interest to point out that it represented an institutional change that was a natural outcome of the American experience with internal taxation. Nevertheless, changes in the original draft were made to suit local conditions. For instance, an income as well as inheritance tax was deemed impractical and undesirable at that time. The need to attract capital made it necessary to eliminate proposed taxes on corporations; corporation property was taxed like individual property. Furthermore, some features of the Spanish taxation structure were retained, among them the cedula personal (poll tax), although this time it was made less onerous to the poorer people.[97]

The land tax. One of the American innovations in the field of taxation was the real estate tax, or land tax. During the period under review, it amounted to at least three-eighths and at most seven-eighths of one per cent of the assessed value of land, and was used exclusively by the provincial and municipal governments.[98] Nothing like it had been applied under Spanish rule,[99] and the revolutionary government had not succeeded in its attempts to establish a real estate tax.[100]

The land tax was due for the first time in the spring of 1902.[101] Being a new, direct tax, it immediately provoked opposition. The small landholder naturally complained that it was oppressive, especially when rinderpest later felled his carabao, swarms of locusts devoured his meagre crop, and cholera prevented him from cultivating his land, compelling him to default in his tax payments for successive years. This situation made his property liable to seizure by the authorities and to sale at public auction unless redeemed earlier.

The bitterest opposition, however, came from the caciques, the proprietors of large haciendas.[102] They protested that their properties had been overassessed, although in most cases this seemed unlikely, since collusion between the caciques or landowners in undervaluing properties certainly must have taken place.

The extent of Filipino resistance to the land tax may be seen from the following observations by Governor Wright in 1904:

> The fact is that this tax, whilst theoretically just, has been extremely difficult of administration and has been very disappointing in its results. Outside of the City of Manila the amount realized has been considerably less than a million dollars and we are continually besieged by applications for reassessment.... [103]

Wright also spoke of the forfeitures of land by the small

landowners who had been unable to pay the land tax; to him
this would be "terribly unpopular. " Recalling from Lord
Roberts' "Forty-one Years in India" that the dissatisfaction stemming from the imposition of the land tax and subsequent seizures of the small parcels of land had been one
of the causes of the Sepoy Mutiny, and since it appeared
now "as if the situation would be reproduced here, " he
and Ide, he told Taft, "are rather leaning to the opinion
that it would be well to suspend the enforcement of the
land tax" for a while.[104]

The suspension of the land tax, however, was not what
the Filipino leaders or elite wanted, perhaps recognizing
that a tax on land was after all necessary to support essential local services. What they asked instead was that the
land tax be based on the income of the property. Thus
Legarda wrote to Taft:

> Sometime ago I wrote to you sincerely expressing
> my opinon with respect to the land tax. . . that [it]
> should be changed and not suspended or abolished.
> I suggested to you that, instead of levying the tax
> on the value of land, it be levied on the income
> thereof,. . . 105

Legarda added that suspending the enforcement of the land
tax would only postpone, but not cure, "an evil which we
all lamented today,. . . "106

The implications of Legarda's proposal, which was
endorsed by the other two Filipino Commissioners,107
are obvious. The proposal would have tremendously
benefited the big landowners and rich people who wanted
to acquire more land for speculative purposes. It would
have also strengthened the hands of landlords in dealing
with their tenants, for they could then simply fire the recalcitrant among them, leave the land idle, and still pay
no tax. Of course, a small landholder would have no
choice but to cultivate his own land if only to survive; he
would, therefore, under the Legarda proposal, be unable
to escape payment of the land tax. Fortunately, the government did not totally accept Legarda's proposal, although one suspects that the main reason for retaining

land values as the primary basis of the tax was to compel hacenderos to cultivate their lands and thus promote economic prosperity.[108]

The opposition to the land tax in combination with the factors mentioned in our discussion on the Filipino reaction to the internal revenue law, fostered a situation which contributed to Governor Wright's replacement and eventually to Ide's as well. In addition, this opposition played a role in the suspension of the land tax in 1906[109] and 1907,[110] and in the revision of some assessments and the bases of such assessments. The Filipinos warm reception of the suspension was described by Governor Ide:

> The suspension of the land tax for a year coupled with the additional provision for new valuations upon a basis of cash values and annual rental values, has met with very general approval.[111]

Taft expressed satisfaction that the Philippine Commission had finally come around to easing patent discontent. "I am very glad you suspended the land tax for a year," he approvingly wrote to Governor Ide.[112]

It is all too tempting to assert that the Filipinos did nothing but show resistance to "modernization" efforts by the Americans at the beginning of the American occupation, as illustrated by their attitudes toward the internal revenue law and the land tax. The truth is that having realized that there was nothing they could do to drive the Americans away, the Filipinos tried to absorb as many of the American innovations as they possibly could. But they also found that they could get many concessions from the Americans simply by raising their voices. Thus, in the case of the land tax, the Filipinos secured its suspension and at the same time succeeded in having reimbursed to the provincial and municipal governments the total land taxes collectible in 1906 and 50 per cent of taxes due in 1907. They were also able to obtain more favorable reassessments of their landholdings.

It was not all rejection, however. As in the case of the internal revenue law, the Filipinos later came to accept the land tax as just and necessary. By 1907, all but two of the provinces had indicated that they would resume collecting the land tax in the following year.113 In just six years following its introduction, therefore, the land tax had been accepted by the Filipinos. This may be partly explained by the fact that both the large proprietor and the small landowner benefited directly from the land tax, which went to support the public schools and maintain roads and bridges. The hacendero was dependent on these latter facilities to open up his estates for cultivation and bring his products to distribution centers.

The Filipinos and American Agrarian Policy

From the beginning, the Americans set out to strengthen the system of landownership introduced earlier by the Spaniards.114 They instituted a systematic procedure for landowners to secure clear documentary Torrens titles to their holdings. They also liberalized and simplified methods through which individuals and corporations could acquire public agricultural land. Finally, they took immediate steps to purchase the friar lands and allot some of them to their cultivators. What was the Filipino response to these measures instituted, according to Forbes, in the interest of "better citizenship, economic progress, and contentment" on their part?115

Let us first consider the attempt to enable landowners to obtain titles to their real estate. For this purpose, the Philippine Commission passed a law on November 6, 1902, which provided for the granting of government-guaranteed titles after landowners had satisfied requirements as to surveys and proofs of ownership.116 Anticipating numerous applications and attendant controversies, the Commission also established the Court of Land Registration.117 Application for the grant of a Torrens title was not obligatory.

The second annual report of the Court of Land Registration makes the claim that the provisions of the law "are being more rapidly availed of than has usually been the case in other countries where the system has been introduced."118 However, we find the Philippine Commission informing the Secretary of War in 1910 that the Court of

Land Registration had succeeded in granting only 3,902 titles out of a possible 2,300,000 in more than seven years.[119] Moreover, according to Forbes, who was Governor-General at the time, most of these titles "comprised almost wholly large private properties and lands purchased by the government."[120] The government now proposed to take a bold step by having a cadastral survey of the entire Philippines made, and it prepared a law to enable it to undertake such a task.[121] The proposed cadastral law, however, was not passed by the Assembly until February, 1913, a few months before the Taft Era came to a close. According to Forbes, the delay in the Assembly's action on the proposed law had been due to "opposition by lawyers and surveyors in private practice and by large landed proprietros."[122] Even with the passage of the cadastral law, a rapid provision of titles was not assured, for the law as passed did not provide for more judges of the Court of Land Registration; finally, in 1914, the Court itself was abolished and its functions transferred to the already overworked Courts of First Instance.[123]

It is therefore clear that the Filipinos did not respond enthusiastically to the efforts of the Americans to enable them to acquire the most valid proof of real estate ownership — the Torrens title, backed by a government guarantee. This may have been due to the novelty of the whole endeavor, apart from the fact that the lowly peasant probably did not see any correlation between a title and his annual yield, although he probably sensed the tax implications of a more accurate land survey. This latter reason perhaps best accounts for the opposition of the owners of huge estates, not to mention the possibility that an honest survey might reveal that they had been usurping other individuals' properties or squatting on part of the public domain. It will be seen that the early Filipino response to the methods of acquiring agricultural lands from the public domain was not much more enthusiastic.

When the United States acquired the Philippines from Spain, it became the owner of the vast public lands of the country. The Taft Commission estimated these to be approximately 27,694,500 hectares (68,405,515 acres), out of a total estimated amount of land of 29,694,500 hectares (73, 345, 415 acres). [124] The Philippine Organic Act of 1902 authorized the Philippine Commission to classify the public lands and to provide for the homesteading, purchase, and lease by individuals and corporations of public agricultural lands, [125] whose approximate area was estimated at 6, 642, 571 hectares (16, 413, 831 acres). [126] The Organic Act also authorized the issuance of free patents conveying titles to portions of the public lands to Filipinos who had cultivated and occupied such public lands before August 13, 1898. The Act limited the amount of land to be acquired by individuals through prescription or occupation, homestead settlement, or purchase to sixteen hectares, or forty acres. Corporations could, however, acquire or lease not more than 1, 024 hectares, or 2, 500 acres. [127]

In compliance with the above mandate, the Philippine Commission passed the Public Land Act on October 7, 1903; [128] it went into full effect on July 26, 1904. [129] Next to the application for free patents, the cheapest, if not the easiest, method of acquiring forty acres of public agricultural land was by establishing a homestead. The requirements appeared relatively simple: continuous residence on the homestead and its cultivation for five consecutive years following the filing of an application and agreement as to non-alienation or non-encumbrance of the homestead or any portion thereof before the issuance of the patent, and payment of a nominal fee of ₱20. 00 in five equal annual installments.

Yet, as the figures shown on Table 11 below indicate, the number of homestead applications filed was exceedingly low, especially when account is taken of the fact that the Filipino peasant probably owned on the average just about one hectare (2. 471 acres) of arable land in 1903. [130]

Claims of private parties, protests, nonpayment of fees and, perhaps most important of all, the lack of enthusiasm and interest on the part of the agrarian population, accounted for the low number of applications filed and still lower figure for applications approved. [131] With regard to the farmer's lack of interest, the following comment is very appropriate:

The framers of the homestead law took it for
granted that the agricultural people of the Philippines were accustomed to settle on isolated farms
and live in dwellings far removed from their
neighbors. They ignored the very patent fact
that the Philippine farmer does not live on the
land he tills and cannot be persuaded to do so.
The folly of this assumption has been abundantly
proved during the years that the homestead law
has been on the books by the very few entries that
have been made under it.[132]

TABLE 11

NUMBER OF HOMESTEAD APPLICATIONS FILED,
APPROVED, AND PATENTED, 1904-1913[a]

Year	No. of applications filed	No. of applications approved	No. of applications patented
1904	69	---	---
1905	354	52	---
1906	1,543	332	---
1907	2,643	889	---
1908	2,023	1,495	---
1909	1,463	858	---
1910	2,210	1,129	1
1911	2,995	1,445	1
1912	3,706	1,941	27
1913	4,962	2,014	106
Total	21,968	10,155	135

[a]Census of 1918, ΓI, 881.

Fewer applications still were filed and approved for the
purchase of public agricultural lands. During the period
1904-1913, inclusive, only 1,103 applications, almost
entirely by individuals, were filed; of these only 200 were
approved. Seven lucky applicants were issued patents

during a nine-year period! [133] The same reasons which
limited the number of homestead applications approved
and patents issued were operative in the case of the applications filed for the purchase of public agricultural
lands.[134]

Let us now turn to the friar lands, which comprised
about 400,000 acres and with some 60,000 tenants on them
at the beginning of the American occupation.[135] We recall
that the purchase of these haciendas was one of the most
important policies adopted by the United States in an
effort to reconcile the Filipinos rapidly to American
sovereignty.[136] We recall further that the unprecendented
1902 Taft Mission to the Vatican returned practically
empty-handed because the Popse would not agree to the
withdrawal of the friars from the Philippines and to the
final consummation of the sale of their estates in Rome.[137]
The Vatican felt, perhaps not inappropriately, that such a
transaction ought to be made in the Philippines, since the
objects of the "business deal" (as Roosevelt put it) were
there. But it meant unnecessary delays, hard bargaining,
and prolonged Filipino agitation, including, perhaps, the
Aglipayan Schism.[138]

Patience, however, bore fruit, and before Taft left
the Philippine governorship in December, 1903, an agreement was finally reached on the purchase of the friar
estates for 6,930,462.70 dollars (U.S. currency). [139] The
Philippine Commission subsequently passed the Friar
Lands Act,[140] which prescribed, among other provisions,
the conditions for the sale and lease of the friar estates,
with preference to be given to the present tenants who,
according to Taft, "numbered some sixty of seventy
thousand persons."[141]

The cultivated portions of the friar estates amounted
to approximately 145,940 acres.[142] As of 1910 (July 1),
63,185 acres had been sold and another 82,755 acres
leased, with the lessees enjoying the preferential right to
buy their leaseholds.[143] The cultivated parts of the friar
estates were therefore readily disposed of. But these
constituted less than one-half of the estates, and the government was no more successful in attracting individual
farmers to purchase and settle on the unoccupied friar

lands than it had been with the public lands. Farmers were unresponsive primarily because the friar lands were expensive as compared to the practically free lands of the public domain. This was so because the government meant to recover the purchase money and the interest on the bonds which it had issued in the United States.

As it was, only the traditional landowning class and corporations could have bought the vacant friar estates, and, possibly, some of the tenanted ones through suberfuge. Therefore, to give added incentive, the Philippine Legislature enacted legislation exempting the friar lands from the area limitations of the public land act.[144]

The simple and relatively cost-free method of acquiring farms from the public domain and the sale of the cultivated portions of the friar estates to their tenants constituted attempts by the American regime during the Taft Era to broaden the base of independent landownership in the Philippines. These efforts were only partially successful. The Filipinos did not react as expected to the homestead program, and far fewer still cared to buy public agricultural lands. The breakup of the cultivated sectors of the friar lands and their sale to their cultivators appeared to be the most successful measure in the development of independent farmers. Unfortunately, the friars were not the only landlords on the eve of the American occupation: collectively, Filipino landlords probably owned more land than the friars. However, while American agrarian policy may have been aimed at developing a body of independent landowners, it did not propose to do so through the purchase of private haciendas other than those owned by the friars, which were then apportioned at cost to their cultivators. The purchase of the friar lands had been undertaken for compelling political and religious motives, rather than because of commitment to a policy of agrarian reform.

THE FILIPINOS AND THE FUTURE
POLITICAL STATUS OF THE PHILIPPINES

When the Taft Era started, there was at least one sizable group among the Filipino elite which immediately advocated statehood within the United States, rather than independence, as the future political status of the Philippines. For a while, this group appeared to be stronger and more popular than the groups advocating independence. By the middle of the Taft Era, however, the entire Filipino elite had openly embraced a program of political independence. From then on the United States came under constant pressure to re-examine its official policy, endorse Philippine independence, and introduce changes in the structure and personnel of the Philippine government to make it conform with such changes in policy.

Americans and Philippine Independence, 1901 - 1913

A brief review of American policy and attitudes toward Philippine independence constitutes a natural springboard for our discussion of Filipino views on the future political status of their country.[1] American policy was officially expressed in the Philippine Bill of 1902, although it was first indicated as early as December, 1898, when President McKinley instructed General Otis to follow a policy of "benevolent assimilation." The policy was further refined in the Letter of Instructions of April 7, 1900, and then expanded in the Philippine Bill of 1902; its goal was the progressive extension of self-government to the Filipinos as they became better qualified to accept the responsibility, and the securing to them of all the basic freedoms except the right of trial by jury and the right to bear arms.[2] That policy did not promise independence although Taft himself admitted "it necessarily involves in its ultimate conclusion... the ultimate independence" of the Philippines.[3]

For the period under review, beginning with President McKinley, it will be of interest to examine the

attitudes on Philippine independence of American presidents. There are unconfirmed reports that McKinley contemplated ultimate independence for the Philippines, but
on the basis of his statements on Philippine policy, it is
more likely that he did not.[4]

President Roosevelt, as his earlier letters suggest,
was favorably inclined toward Philippine independence
from the beginning of the American occupation of the
islands,[5] but he did not reveal this attitude officially until
1908. Even then he did so in a carefully guarded way, and
only because he thought that independence was the course
set for the Filipinos, though not promised to them, by the
Philippine Bill of 1902.[6] In 1907, Roosevelt did come
very close to announcing officially a policy of Philippine
independence. The occasion was Taft's visit to the islands
for the inauguration of the Philippine Assembly. In one of
his "Dear Will" letters to Taft, written before the latter's
departure, Roosevelt said:

> The Philippines form our heel of Achilles. They
> are all that makes the situation with Japan danger-
> ous. I think that in some way and with some
> phraseology that you think wise you should state
> to them that if they handle themselves wisely in
> their legislative assembly we shall at the earliest
> possible moment give them a nearly complete
> independence.[7]

Probably because he was assured by Japanese officials
that there was nothing "dangerous" between Japan and the
United States, Taft felt no need to promise independence
as President Roosevelt had suggested.[8] But here was evidence of the tendency to reverse completely American
policy toward Philippine independence when American
interests, as conceived by their leaders, were not being
served by the continued occupation of the Philippines.
This meant, in effect, that the Americans had no compunc-
tions about disregarding their earlier claims that the Filipinos were incapable of, or unfit for, self-government or
independence,[9] if and when American interests demanded
such a course.

Taft never thought that the United States should rule the Philippines forever, but he was more firmly opposed to an official American commitment to independence than Roosevelt. Taft's ideas were shared with relatives and intimate friends; the letter he wrote to a fellow member of the bar while Secretary of War probably best expressed his position on Philippine independence:

> The policy of the Administration is the indefinite retention of the Philippine Islands.... The policy rests on the conviction that the people are not now capable of self-government, and will not be for a long time; certainly not for a generation, and probably not for a longer time than that, and that until they are ready for self-government it would be a violation of trust for the United States to abandon the islands.
>
> . . . .
>
> Should the Philippine people, when fit for self-government demand independence, I should be strongly in favor of giving it to them, and I have no doubt that the American people of the next generation would be of the same opinon.[10]

Taft continued to advance the same views during his four years in the White House. And, since in addition to being the President of the United States he could claim personal knowledge of Philippine affairs, his words naturally carried a great deal of weight.[11]

What is interesting to point out is that both Roosevelt and Taft favored ultimate independence as the culmination of American policy, yet neither came out for it unequivocally. Their reason was that it would be less than useful to the present Filipino leaders to be promised an independence which they had no chance of enjoying in their lifetime, since it would take a generation or possibly two to prepare for self-government. According to Roosevelt and Taft, raising such an expectation would only result in useless agitation for its immediate fulfillment, a situation that would be disastrous to the development of a large body of conservatives among the educated Filipinos.[12]

If independence was in fact the inevitable consequence of
the Philippine Bill of 1902, as Roosevelt and Taft had
repeatedly affirmed, then their failure to come out for it
unequivocally was, in retrospect, shortsighted and unwise.
This policy exposed them to charges of hypocrisy. It
tempered Filipino appreciation of American efforts and
achievements, which were substantial during the Taft
Regime. Continued Filipino agitation for an American
declaration of a policy of independence led to a demand not
only for independence, but for an "absolute," "complete,"
and "immediate" independence as well. This situation
made it impossible for those Filipino leaders who would
have preferred an indefinite postponement of independence
— in view of the material benefits the Philippines was enjoying under American rule — to accept any proposal for
future Philippine-American relations that did not include
a promise of independence. Filipino criticism of the Taft-
Roosevelt policy, much of it brutally harsh, also needlessly
recurred to bedevil Filipino-American relations during the
Taft Regime. Finally, American equivocation spawned
secret, insurrectionary societies, some of which were
nothing but fronts for swindlers and opportunists. We
shall attempt to elaborate on these points in the following
pages.

The Federal Party

The first Philippine political party organized under
American rule, the Federal Party (Partido Federal), was
officially established with Taft's blessings and encourage-
ment[13] on December 23, 1900.[14] Its establishment was,
according to Taft, the direct result of President McKinley's
re-election in November, 1900.[15] At the time of its organization, it consisted of the so-called Autonomists, who had
endorsed the Hay Plan proposed by the Schurman Commission in 1899, [16] and of former officials and military officers
of the Malolos Republic who had either surrendered voluntarily or had been captured after the republican capital had
fallen into American hands. In general, the members of
the Federal Party were the wealthy and educated Filipinos,
who had more to lose in a prolonged war against the United

States and who felt that the interests of the Philippines —
or at any rate their own interests — demanded that all
opposition to American sovereignty be ended.

In addition to coming out openly for peace and acceptance of American rule, the original platform of the Federal Party also expressed the aspiration of its founders
that the Philippines would eventually be admitted as one of
the states of the United States.[17] Three of the most prominent members of the Federal Party also made the following announcement:

> Peace being secured, all the efforts of the party
> will be directed toward the Americanization of
> the Filipinos and the spread of the English lan-
> guage, so that by this medium the American
> spirit may be infused, its principles, political
> usages, and grand civilization adopted, and the
> redemption of the Filipino people be radical and
> complete.[18]

In less than a month following its establishment, Governor Taft could inform Secretary of War Elihu Root that
the growth of the Partido Federal had been very "wonder-
ful."[19] By June, 1901, the party had 290 provincial and
local committees and about 150,000 members.[20] The
rapid growth of the Federal Party's and its control of
Philippine elections before 1907[21] were due to the favors
and protection extended to it by the American government,
particularly Taft, and, above all, to the clever manipula-
tion of the ilustrados. In addition, Taft's policy of confining the major political appointments to Federalistas drew
most of the Filipino elite to the Federal Party. Tavera,
Legarda, Luzuriaga, Arellano, the first provincial governors, the mayor of Manila, and many others, were members of the Federal Party. As Taft said in 1902, the fact
that a man was a Federalista "was always a good recommendation for him for appointment" to any political
office.[22]

The Sedition Law of 1901 also enabled the members
of the Federal Party to establish themselves as the leaders
of the Filipinos and to obtain implicit acceptance of their

political program.[23] Although the law was technically no
longer operative after the official termination of hostilities
on July 4, 1902, when President Roosevelt issued his
amnesty proclamation,[24] Governors Taft and Wright continued to discourage the organization of all political parties which advocated independence — even if in a peaceful
manner. This administrative partiality deprived the
opponents of the Federalistas of an early opportunity to
reach the vast majority of the people. The situation came
to an end in 1906, but in the meantime the Federalistas
had profited from their unchallenged position.

By that time, however, the Federalistas had already
given up their impractical plank and were now working for
independence. Several factors lay behind this development,
among them the following: the disenchantment of the
Federalistas with Governors Wright and Ide;[25] the end of
the policy of confining important governmental appointments
to members of the Federal Party, which had been one of
the main attractions to membership in the party;[26] the
realization that Americans did not like the idea of the
Philippines becoming a state of the Union;[27] and, most
important of all, the discovery that the program of independence had enormous appeal to the electorate. Looking
ahead to the elections for the Philippine Assembly, the
Federalistas, like any other group of politicians, decided
to continue in the popular favor by coming out openly for
independence before it was too late. Thus, at the convention of the party on June 20, 1904, the following far-
reaching resolution was discussed:

> In so far as refers to the final and definite poli-
> tical status of the country, the party expects and
> desires that, in due time, the government of the
> Philippines may be an independent republican
> government, maintaining, if necessary, such
> political relations to the government of the United
> States as both countries may adopt by mutual
> agreement.[28]

Although this resolution was not formally adopted, because Governor Wright would not allow it,[29] it was evident

that the old platform was no longer acceptable. In December, 1904, Juan Sumulong, soon to become the vice-president of the party under a new name, wrote in an American magazine that the aspiration of the Filipino people was independence, "as soon as it is possible, according to the Nationalists, and after a probationary period, according to the Evolutionists [i. e. , Federalists]. "30 Finally, in May, 1905, the Federal Party adopted the above-quoted resolution, Tavera claiming to be the sole objector. 31 Even then, his objection seemed to have been based on the fact that the party still continued to use its old name, when its program was no longer the same. This was taken care of in January, 1907, when the name Partido Federal was replaced by the more evocative Partido Nacional Progresista.32 In explaining this development to Taft, Tavera said that the old Federal Party, as "you know it here,...is dead, and should I, at this time attempt to resurrect it, I could not gather around me more than a few adherents. "33 Legarda probably gave the best reason for the total repudiation of the Federal Party when he wrote:

> It must be kept in mind,...that if this government is to proceed within the bounds of reason, there is not at present any person or entity of any class whatsoever, no matter how popular or great he may be, who can prevent public sentiment from favoring Philippine independence,...34

Thus, as early as 1905, the American government saw its supporters openly embracing independence instead of closer political relations with the United States as the basis of the future status of the Philippines. There is no evidence that the American authorities resented the change when it finally came; in fact, they seemed to have welcomed it.35 This was not the case, however, with respect to the rise of the Nacionalista Party as the major political party in the Philippines.

The Nacionalista Party

The Sedition Law compelled die-hard advocates of independence to conceal their aims while waiting for a more favorable moment to organize themselves. Upon the official termination of the Philippine-American War on July 4, 1902, several nationalists approached Governor Taft for permission to organize political parties based on a platform of independence. Taft, however, convinced them not to proceed with their plans, which, in his view, expressed opposition to the government; law enforcement agencies might misinterpret their peaceful intentions, with consequent embarrassment to themselves.[36] Instead, Taft counseled the nationalists to forget politics for the next two years and concentrate on the economic development of the country.[37] Governor Wright was of the same opinion; the spirit of the Sedition Law was all too evident. In view of the discouraging attitude of the authorities, the Partido Independista and Partido Democrata could not be launched. The nationalists could only organize the innocuous Comite de Interes Filipinos, a civic league whose "main object was the establishment of a permanent committee in the United States to look after Philippine interests."[38] In 1906, however, the elections to the Philippine Assembly approached, the ban on the organization of radical parties was lifted. Almost immediately, the Partido Independista Immediatista, the Partido Urgentista and the Comite de la Union Nacional sprang up.[39]

The Independistas demanded "immediate" independence by peaceful means, and were most disposed to co-operate with the government. The Unionistas also believed in "immediate" independence, but were less disposed to co-operate with the authorities. Furthermore, they desired that the United States should definitely state its future political policy toward the Philippines. The Urgentistas constituted the radical wing of the nationalists. According to Governor Smith, they believed "in immediate independence at once if not sooner, by peaceful means if they can but by violence if they must."[40]

Politics, it is said, makes strange bedfellows, and Philippine politics of the early American period was no

exception. Thus, the Urgentistas and the Unionistas fused
with each other to become the Union Nacionalista, which
in turn merged with the Partido Independista on March 12,
1907, to form a single party.[41] This party was the direct
ancestor of the present Nacionalista Party in contemporary
Philippine politics. Among its leaders were Sergio Osmena,
Manuel L. Quezon, Alberto Barretto, Rafael del Pan,
Galicano Apacible, Pablo Ocampo, Felipe Agoncillo,
Rafael Palma, and Fernando and Leon Ma. Guerrerro.[42]
   The new party declared that its aim was "the immediate independence of the Philippine Islands... under a democratic government. "[43] It asserted that this goal was not
only the natural right of the Filipinos but also something
which they "desire and are ready to receive at any moment, " as shown by their past struggles for freedom.
Probably in answer to American claims that the United
States was in the Philippines for the benefit of the Filipinos and knew what was best for them, the Nacionalistas
expressed it as their "firm conviction that the peace,
order, progress and happiness" of the Filipino people
could be realized only by themselves because "nobody
knows the needs of a country better than its own people,
or can better apply to them the most adequate remedy. "
The platform concluded with the promise that the Nacionalistas would accomplish their objective without resort to
violence.
   Nacionalista ascendancy. Shortly before the organization of the Philippine Assembly in 1907, therefore, two
major political parties, both openly advocating independence, had finally emerged. Taking the results of the
elections as an index, it is obvious that by the middle of
the Taft Regime the nationalists had become the new
leaders of the Filipinos, as shown in Table 12.
   The Americans, however, were slow in admitting
that a real change in leadership had taken place. They
regarded the results of the first elections to the Assembly on July 30, 1907, as an inconclusive index of the
relative strength of the political parties. Instead, greater
significance was attached to the results of the first popular provincial elections held on November 5, 1907,[44] in
which 161,697 votes had been case. This was 69,525

TABLE 12

RESULTS OF ELECTIONS TO THE PHILIPPINE
ASSEMBLY, 1907, 1909, AND 1912[a]

Party	Number of votes			Number of seats		
	1907	1909	1912	1907	1909	1912
Nacionalista	34,277	92,996	124,753	58	62	62
Progresista	23,234	38,588	37,842	16	17	16
Others[b]	38,385	61,391	71,241	6	2	3
Total[c]				80	81	81

[a]Figures obtained from Philippine Commission Reports: 1907, Pt. 1, p. 203; 1909, p. 47; 1912, pp. 47–49.

[b]That is, Liguero, Inmediatista, Catholic, and Independent. Scattering votes not included.

[c]Cf. Table 2 (supra, p. 66) for total registration, total votes cast, percentages in relation to population.

more votes than had been cast for the members of the Assembly, so the Commission regarded the provincial elections as more reflective of the popular will. The Nacionalistas had obtained sixteen of the gubernatorial posts, and the Progresistas fifteen, but the Philippine Commission still could not believe that the Nacionalistas had become the dominant party, as may be seen from its amusing analysis of the provincial returns:

> Of 161,697 votes cast 44,288 were for the candidates of the Nacionalista Party, 38,153 for those of the Progresista Party, 17,458 for those who stood on an independent platform, 1,563 for Independista candidates, 2,983 scattering, and 1,351 for candidates whose party affiliations were unknown. Adding to the Nacionalista Party vote the entire Independista, half the scattering, and half the unknown would give a vote of 48,018 as the strength of those holding radical views. Adding to the 38,153 Progresista votes the 17,458 independent would give 55,611 as the number of views as to the political policy now pursued in the Philippines.[45]

The Commission's explanation was probably intended for Taft's benefit and to allay fears that the election of a Nacionalista majority to the Assembly meant that radicalism was widespread among the Filipinos, indicating a potentially explosive situation and, therefore, a failure of the Taft-Roosevelt policy.[46] It must be remembered that Taft was soon to succeed Roosevelt as President of the United States; as one of the principal architects of the Philippine policy of the United States, nothing would have been more pleasing to him than to be able to inform the American people that, according to the Philippine Commission, everything was well in the Philippines.

This may well have been the case, considering that the Nacionalistas included among their ranks many conservatives, including Sergio Osmena, the Speaker of the Assembly.[47] But the analysis sounded inadequate, if not childish, and was bound to give the impression that the

United States did not really wish to grant independence to
the Philippines. Such a belief was strengthened by the
slow pace of Filipinization at the higher levels of administration and by the fact that most of the few available
political appointments continued to be held by Progresistas,
who could no longer claim to be the strongest political
group in the country.[48]

The continued adherence by the United States to its
original policy, in spite of obviously changing political
conditions, was in part responsible for the more radical
temper of the Second Philippine Assembly.[49] Governor
Forbes warned the Secretary of War in November, 1910,
that the harmonious relationship between the Commission
and the Assembly might not be maintained any longer:

> The Assembly are getting a little out of hand.
> There are a number of turbulent spirits there
> and Osmena is clever enough politician to put
> himself in the forefront of the popular movement
> in order to hold his power.[50]

The anticipated split between the Assembly and the Commission finally occurred in early 1911. The most important
reasons for the disagreement were as follows: the proposed
repeal of the sedition act and the flag law;[51] the proposal by
the Assembly for a joint resolution to Congress for permission for the Filipino people to frame their own constitution; and the Assembly's insistence on the exclusive prerogative to elect the Resident Commissioners and to
initiate appropriation bills, neither of which had been conferred upon it by the Philippine Bill of 1902.[52]

The Progresistas and "immediate" independence. The
evident popularity of a more radical position on independence
which, we submit, was inspired by the firm refusal of the
United States to declare openly for Philippine independence,
had a strong influence upon the Progresistas after the
second elections to the Assembly. Although they had received general increase of more than 50 per cent in popular
votes over the previous election, their total vote was
54,408 less than that of the Nacionalistas, whereas in 1907
the difference between them had been only 11,043.

Furthermore, they had only seventeen members in the
Assembly, compared to the Nacionalistas' sixty-two. In
the expectation of a better showing in the next elections,
Assemblyman Agustin Montinola of Negros proposed to
amend the platform of the Progresista Party by "introducing the idea of 'immediate independence'. "[53] Although
Montinola's proposal was not accepted, to meet its supporters halfway a resolution was adopted petitioning "the
American Congress to declare that the United States will
grant independence to the Filipinos and that her sovereignty
over here will not be permanent. "[54] The Partido Progresista had heretofore not officially taken such a stand.[55] It
was in compliance with the party's resolution that Resident
Commissioner Legarda joined his colleague, Manuel
Quezon, in addressing a long letter-memorial to the
Secretary of War in 1910, recommending, among other
steps, "the definite declaration by Congress of the purpose
of the United States in those Islands, " i. e. , the Philippines.[56]

In their letter-memorial to the Secretary of War on
April 25, 1910, the Resident Commissioners practically
repeated comments that Tavera had made several months
earlier. "To live trustfully in the supposed generosity of
the people of the United States, " Tavera wrote in February, 1910, "does not appear to me a very dignified
position. "[57] He therefore urged that the United States
should declare immediately its intention to recognize
Philippine independence; to Tavera, the date was immateri-
al. This was one time "Mr. Federalista" had practically
executed a complete reversal of position.

According to Tavera, the "antagonism between Americans and Filipinos has been increasing, " and even the one-
time pro-Americanistas had become disillusioned with the
government. The former friends and supporters of the
government, he regretted to report, "are increasing the
ranks of those who did not trust, and from the beginning
were without confidence. " Tavera believed that such a
situation was not due to "bad government":

It is simply this persistence in not saying in a
clear and frank manner that some day independence

will be given. Naturally, upon seeing that there
is a desire to elude making this declaration, it
is understood that they do not wish to promise
that which they do not wish to concede. This is
the source of the mistrust. . . . [58]

When Governor Forbes was asked for comment on the
letter-memorial, he replied: "In regard to the growing
lack of confidence in the administration, that I admit. "[59]
The mounting lack of confidence naturally inspired adverse
criticism of, and opposition to, Governor Forbes' administration, a situation the Secretary of War could not fail to
notice during his visit to the Philippines in 1910. [60] The
enmity increased during the remining years of the Taft
Regime and was not lost on Professor Ford, President
Wilson's special investigator, who made the following observation in his report: "It is a deplorable fact that the
people of the Philippines seem unappreciative of our efforts
and resentful of our domination, . . . "[61] Ford ventured to
state that an underlying cause of these trends in Philippine-
American relations could be traced to the refusal of the
Republican administration to grant even self-government
to the Filipinos, coupled with the Filipinos' belief that they
"would have achieved independence before now but for
American intervention, and this opinion is not confined to
Filipinos. "[62]
        In its issue of September 22, 1910, El Ideal, a Nacion-
alista paper, characterized American policy of withholding
a definite promise of independence "a vicious policy. " In
any case, it added that such a promise, even if made with
a specific date for its redemption, would no longer be
enough, since independence "is considered necessary
now. "[63] La Vanguardia[64] also expressed concern over
American policy, contending that the longer the Americans
stayed in the Philippines, the harder it would be for them
to get out. However, it found solace in its belief that
"nothing is eternal in this world, " and that Philippine
independence would surely come with a Democratic victory
in the United States.[65]
        Such statements as these were bound to build up expec-
tations for immediate independence, and may have led La

Vanguardia a year later to conclude mistakenly that President Wilson's election in 1912 meant a rejection by the American people of "Taft and Roosevelt's policy." In its view, "because of its international character," the Philippine problem had been one of the main issues in the presidential elections.66 The conclusion would have been correct had the premise been correct, too. Unfortunately, the Philippine policy of the United States hardly figured in the campaign.67 However, La Vanguardia was probably accurately reflecting popular expectations when it also declared that Philippine "institutions," i. e., the government, would change with Wilson's elevation to the American presidency. For this reason, La Vanguardia said:

> We Filipinos have received the news of the
> triumph of the genial Governor of New Jersey
> with more rejoicing than the Americans. He
> will preside over our triumphal entrace into
> the Promised Land after redeeming us from the
> long captivity to which the imperial Pharoahs
> [have] reduced us. 68

Wilson's election did produce a general feeling of jubilation in the Philippines.69 "The mass of the natives, of course, have seemed to be highly elated," General J. Franklin Bell, Commanding General of the American Forces in the Philippines, wrote Governor Forbes.70 Public celebrations were held in various parts of the country, and on these occasions speeches were made and congratulatory petitions "unanimously" adopted to be sent to the President-elect. The Philippine Assembly unanimously passed a resolution congratulating Wilson and expressing the wish of its members that his administration would recognize Philippine independence, "in accordance with reiterated petitions of the Philippine Assembly."71 Certainly, there was at least a reasonable expectation of more self-government and perhaps even the prospect of a definite promise to recognize Philippine independence; at best, there was the possibility that independence would be granted within a few years. These inferences, based on the official attitude of the Democratic Party since the beginning of

American rule in the Philippines, suddenly assumed
greater validity when President-elect Wilson declared in
his Staunton speech: "The Philippines are at present our
frontier but I hope we presently are to deprive ourselves
of that frontier. "[72]

Private sentiments toward independence. If the above
views in fact represented official attitudes of the Filipinos
— particularly the elite — by the end of the Taft Regime,
what can be said about their personal sentiments on the
question of independence? It would be impossible to re-
create a reasonably accurate picture of such private sentiments, since the Filipinos do not usually keep private
diaries; at least, I have not come across or heard about a
single one by the prominent Filipinos of the Taft Era.
However, it may be argued that many, if not all, of the
Filipinos of substance, including Quezon and Osmena, held
personal views which were the opposite of their public
declarations on independence.[73]

To advance such a view, especially with reference to
Quezon and Osmena, would seem to be iconoclasm of the
first order: The careers of these Filipino statesmen —
before, during, and long after the Taft Era — were devoted
to the cause of Philippine freedom.[74] Certainly, their
records of public service would appear to be much more
impressive evidence of their real sentiments on the question of Philippine independence than all the letters or
memoranda indicating that they may have believed otherwise. But letters and memoranda, however inconspicuous,
are invaluable sources of historical data, and the ones we
have lead us to suspect that at some time in their careers,
Quezon and Osmena believed that independence, particularly
immediate independence, was not in the best interest of the
Philippines.

In attempting to show that Quezon and Osmena were
against Philippine independence, at least during the Taft
Era, I am by no means doing so with the intention of ques-
tioning their credentials as Filipino patriots or nationalists,
or of denting their images as Filipino statesmen. It comes
merely as part of an endeavor to examine and arrive at a
probable explanation for the Filipino response to American
policy on Philippine independence during the Taft Regime.

The materials we have consist of books and published
documents, which understandably do not mention names,[75]
and unpublished documents, which name only Quezon and
Osmena. The latter were singled out probably because of
their influence in Philippine affairs at that time. This is
perfectly understandable; historical records preserve for
posterity only the words and actions of those who play
leading roles in history.

All our sources were written by Americans who were
officials involved in the events they described. We should
therefore be cautioned against accepting their writings un-
questioningly, although in view of the integrity of the
authors, one cannot very well ignore all that they say.
However, because their reports need to be corroborated
by Filipino and non-official sources, assuming that these
exist, the conclusions one is likely to draw from these
materials must necessarily be tentative.

Let us at least start with one official document, Secretary Dickinson's Special Report (1910). After insinuating
that Filipino demonstrations for "immediate independence"
during his Philippine trip had been "rigged," Dickinson
nevertheless admitted:

> There is no doubt that as far as publicly expressed,
> the general desire of the Filipinos is for what they
> denominate "immediate independence," [but]... I
> became convinced from reliable evidence that
> many of the most substantial men, while not openly
> opposing the demands publicly voiced, would re-
> gard such a consummation with consternation. [76]

Secretary Dickinson, however, did not say whether the
"substantial men" would prefer independence at some
future time.

Turning to our manuscript sources, we have at the
outset Bandholtz' letters to Taft and Allen[77] and Carpenter's letters to Edwards,[78] all implying that the Nacionalistas were not as radical as they had been represented,
and that Osmena in particular was an "ultra-conservative."
One gets the impression from Bandholtz and Carpenter,
however, that both the Progresistas and the Nacionalistas

were in favor of independence, at least in the future.

On the other hand, Forbes, writing at about the same time, claimed that the Nacionalistas in general were not for independence. According to him:

> The most prominent leaders in what is called
> the Nationalists, the successful party, are some
> of them, very particular friends of mine, and I
> have asked them what their idea is in case they
> win — whether they are going to make any move
> to get independence — and they practically ad-
> mitted to me that it was really a catchway of
> getting votes; that what they wanted was office,
> not independence;... 79

Later in 1907, Forbes wrote that Quezon had informed him about a meeting of Nacionalista assemblymen, "held the night before" whereby a proposal to petition the United States for independence had been overwhelmingly defeated by a vote of 52 to 4.80 Forbes naturally interpreted this to mean that the Nacionalistas were not really for independ- ence. Three years later, when he was already Governor- General, Forbes wrote that "the vast majority of Filipinos want independence, whether Nationalists or Progresists, and I am satisfied that it should be so. "81

Before proceeding any further with our presentation of unpublished materials, it might be well to point out that in the 1910 elections for Congress, the Democrats obtained a majority in the House of Representatives. This was good news to Filipino independistas, especially since Represen- tative William A. Jones of Virginia, a rabid opponent of the Roosevelt-Taft policy, had secured the chairmanship of the House Committee on Insular Affairs, the committee responsible for Philippine affairs in the lower house of the American Congress. In March, 1912, Jones introduced the first of several bills that carried his name. This first Jones Bill provided for Philippine independence by 1921.82 Although the House itself failed to pass the bill in 1912, it was taken for granted that the bill would be enacted into law the following year,83 an expectation which was in fact reasonable because the American people had elected with

Wilson a Democratic Congress as well. Philippine independence, therefore, appeared closer than ever before.
This short digression will enable us to appreciate more
fully the following additional material on the attitudes of
the Filipino leaders toward independence.

In the same letter in which he spoke of general Filipino rejoicing over the victory of the Democratic Party,
General Bell also wrote that the "saner, wiser" Filipino
elements were "doing some tall thinking right now for fear
independence might come immediately." He made such an
observation, he said, on the basis of conversations with
"a few who have come to consult me" in confidence on
whether there was any possibility of independence being
granted. Among them was Quezon, on whose part Bell
claimed he could already observe, with unusual clarity,
"some signs of hedging."[84]

Forbes was more direct. At the height of the discussion on the final Jones Bill in 1916, he wrote former
President Roosevelt that he knew "too well the feeling of
the Filipinos toward independence to be very greatly impressed by their demand for it."[85] He went on to assert
that "the politicians who howl loudest don't want it and
have so told me," but that they howled just the same
"because it is a vote getter."[86] After stating that Quezon
had been working secretly in Washington against independence (about which more presently), Forbes went on to
describe what had happened the day he left the Philippine
governorship in 1913:

> No less a person than the Speaker of the Assembly
> [i.e., Osmena] told me that the Filipinos wanted
> independence only while it seemed to be getting
> farther off and the minute it began to get near they
> would begin to get very much frightened.

Forbes explained that "I have never, in his interests,
published these sentiments of his."[87] Thus Forbes reiterated what he had written in 1907, in spite of his having
informed Taft in 1910 that the Nacionalistas and Progresistas were for independence. Perhaps, in his letter to
Roosevelt, Forbes meant that what the Filipinos did not

want at that time was "immediate" independence. [88]

The most extensive unpublished records of Quezon's personal sentiments on independence which I came across are the memoranda of his conversations held from December, 1913 to January, 1914, with General Frank McIntyre, who had succeeded General Clarence Edwards as Chief of the Bureau of Insular Affairs of the War Department in 1912. We may be justified in considering that these memoranda[89] reflect Quezon's attitude during the latter part of the Taft Era, in view of the proximity of the dates during which the conversations took place. In any case, they confirm what Bell had earlier suspected, or detected, and agree with Forbes' later assertion that Quezon had secretly been working against the Jones Bill.

On the basis of McIntyre's memoranda, Quezon appears to have been opposed to immediate independence, as well as to fixing a specific date when independence would be granted. One can also conclude that he believed it would be a mistake for President Wilson ever to contemplate such a policy. But in order to present as faithfully as possible what Quezon said, it might be better to include copious excerpts from McIntyre's memoranda.[90] They are so lucid that any further explanation is unnecessary:

> He [Quezon] said that he was prepared to advocate a new organic act [which] would settle the question of the relations between the Philippine Islands and the United States for at least 25 years,... He said that there would perhaps be a little more difficulty in getting an agreement to this now then there would have been a few years ago, in that independence now had acquired an attractive sound to the ear of the Filipinos.
> He expressed his fears of independence in the near future, basing his fears largely on the conduct of Japan. He said that on this trip for the first time he became convinced that the Japanese had designs on the Philippine Islands; ... He said, however, that before he could advocate anything short of independence or short of what he had been talking for heretofore, he

would like to feel that it would meet the approval
of the administration. . . .

I asked him if he had explained this view to
Mr. Osmena. He said that he had, and that he
thought Osmena would be all right.

I asked him if he had spoken of it to Governor
Harrison. He said: "My God, no. I think he believes in independence. He thinks he can turn us
loose in about four years, " and he repeated:
"He believes in it. "[91]

During their conversations in early January, [92] Quezon
dwelt at length on the need for definite legislation that would
put an end to Filipino agitation for immediate independence.
He also said that he believed many Southern Democrats,
including Congressman Jones, were motivated by selfish
interests in endorsing a policy of immediate independence,
caring not a whit about the consequences of such a policy:

He [Quezon] said that he had seen Mr. Jones in
Baltimore and subsequently here in the city
[i. e. , Washington, D. C.] and that Mr. Jones
told him that he was preparing a bill which would
grant absolute independence to the Philippines
within three years, and that he was afraid that
he had impressed Mr. Jones unfavorably in
standing out against that. [93]

On January 13, Quezon left McIntyre his notes which
contained his ideas on the features of the bill he had in
mind, and which he planned to submit to Secretary Garrison and President Wilson; he asked McIntyre's assistance
in preparing such a bill. On the basis of these notes, and
after subsequent discussions with Quezon, McIntyre prepared a bill providing for an almost entirely autonomous
government of the Philippines. A section on independence
was subsequently added. It provided for a census to be
taken in 1915 and every tenth year thereafter. Whenever
such a census should indicate that 75 per cent of the male
adults could read and write in any language, or 60 per cent
of such male adults could read and write "intelligently"

the English language, and if a condition of general and complete peace existed in the Philippines, the President of the United States would, upon the request of the Philippine Legislature, initiate the steps leading to the eventual withdrawal of American sovereignty and the recognition of the complete and absolute independence of the Philippines. As to what Quezon actually thought of such a provision, McIntyre had this to say:

> He explained, on practically each call, that...
> [it] did not appeal to him; that he would rather
> that there would be no such Section, but that
> he believed that it would appeal to the President
> in view of his expression in favor of ultimate
> independence, and would [also] appeal to the
> more extreme Filipinos, as well as to those
> people in the United States who had taken so
> strong a position in favor of independence.

Quezon was convinced, however, that the literacy requirements would never be reached within the lifetime of the present generation, and so he was satisfied with the section as prepared by McIntyre.

It is clear from this discussion that at least the two foremost leaders of the Filipino elite — Quezon and Osmena — did not really desire immediate independence, or even want to have a date fixed for the future recognition of Philippine independence. What they wanted was for the United States to make an authoritative declaration that it would ultimately recognize Philippine independence, and accompany this declaration with the grant of more substantial powers to a Philippine government composed almost entirely of Filipinos.

The evidence also suggests that American reluctance to come out officially for independence, even when the Federalistas had discarded their impractical program of statehood within the United States, engendered greater radicalism and popularized the issue. As a result, the demand to set a date for independence became almost inseparable from the demand for independence itself. Because of this fact, the political parties had to be openly committed to a policy of independence, preferably "immediate independence," regardless of their leaders' real sentiments on the issue: To have acted otherwise would have meant defeat at the polls.[94] Taking these considerations into account, therefore, how may the real attitudes of the elite, or at least of some of its members, be explained?

Mention has been made of the alleged fear of Japan. This may well have been one reason. Japanese activities in Korea and Manchuria must have been regarded as ominous by the Filipino leaders, particularly Quezon. Of course, Japanese plans for expansion in Southeast Asia still belonged to the future; but we must presume that Quezon was probably thinking of that future, too.[95] The relative weight of this factor in determining the position of the Filipino leaders, however, must await the outcome of further research.

Forbes makes generous references to the elite's alleged fear of an outbreak of anarchy following an American withdrawal.[96] Attractive as this argument may appear, it could not have been significant. It is based on the assumption that anarchy had prevailed during the short-lived Philippine Republic. We now know, however, that conditions in Aguinaldo's realm were far from chaotic,[97] a fact which the Filipino elite did not question when they joined the revolutionary government in 1898-1899.[98] After more than a decade of American rule which had emphasized moderation and restraint, and severely suppressed fanatical outbreaks among the superstitious, illiterate, and discontented populace in the provinces, there was certainly less reason in 1913-1914 to be apprehensive about the possible eruption of anarchy than in 1898-1899.[99] This being the case, we must dismiss the fear of anarchy as a reason for the elite's attitude toward immediate independence.

Elliott claims that many businessmen and other propertied individuals were not in favor of immediate independence "if it is to mean an oligarchical republic under the control of the men who have established themselves as leaders during the last few years."[100] This reason is questionable. Since the beginning of American rule, the propertied classes (caciques and ilustrados) had in general been the Filipino elements in control of the government.

Of course, not every businessman, hacendero, or ilustrado could be in the government to look directly after his interests, but interlocking relationships among Filipinos in general, and among members of the same class in particular — such as the compadre system — enabled those outside the government to protect and enhance their economic and social interests. On the contrary, nothing would have been more welcome to the Filipino upper class than to have been in charge of their less affluent and generally illiterate countrymen. They would certainly have established an oligarchical government in which they held the positions of leadership, just as they had done during the later phase of the Philippine Revolution.[101]

We must look elsewhere for the probable reasons behind the sentiments of the nationalist-elite. It may be advanced as a general statement that they were entirely willing to sacrifice "immediate" independence to some indeterminate future date because most of their aspirations were being realized under American rule.[102] Looking back at the demands of the Propagandists before the Revolution,[103] we see that the elite in general desired the following: status and the protection of their economic interests; the grant of civil liberties; the separation of Church and State, or at least the expulsion of the friars and confiscation of their estates; and the reform of the bureaucracy to make it a more efficient instrument for the promotion of certain goals, viz., better educational facilities, better roads, etc. Obviously, these aspirations meant that the elite would have a controlling voice in the government. However, independence was not one of their aspirations, nor was it originally contemplated as a means to an end.

The American regime accommodated many of the demands of the elite.[104] A secular government was established in which they were accorded a greater role than in any other colonial regime in Asia. A modern civil service system was also set up. Furthermore, the American regime devoted itself to the educational and, to a lesser extent, the material progress of the country. The friar lands were acquired and the vast public lands were practically reserved for the Filipinos. Most important of all, free trade had not only increased the revenues of the government but also brought about a tremendous expansion of the sugar and tobacco industries; the elite profited immensely from such an expansion.[105] While it can be argued that a great many of these goals could have been attained under an independent republic, the elite entertained no illusions that free trade would probably cease immediately upon the grant of independence.[106]

Seditious Movements

A discussion of the Filipino reaction to the Taft Regime's policy of indefinite retention of the Philippines would be incomplete if it did not include a brief section on the Filipinos' attempts to change that policy through the use of force, or the threat to use force. These attempts included lingering guerrilla movements by remnants of General Aguinaldo's army and conspiracies by hard core nationalists. The guerrilla activities were essentially the work of the lower classes of Filipino society, which is understandable since the bulk of General Aguinaldo's army had been recruited from those elements. Substantial numbers of the upper class were directly involved in some conspiracies during the early years of the Taft Regime, but as the Americans slowly allowed them to participate in the government, their connection with such plots became more tenuous, or, at least, less conspicuous. Thereafter, only irreconcilables such as Ricarte cared to organize seditious plots.

History has not been very kind to those Filipinos who deviated from the less risky program of peaceful change embraced by most of their countrymen. They have simply been called "ladrones" (literally, bandits) and opportunist-agitators masquerading as true nationalists.[107] While too much generosity would be tantamount to making heroes out of confirmed outlaws, fanatics, and opportunists, some of whom had led a life of plunder or leisure at the expense of the credulous masses even before the American occupation,[108] it would be a mistake to regard all extra-legal opposition to the government as devoid of a nationalistic purpose. In 1903, Taft himself recognized that "ladronism" had political overtones, and even implied that it had

a relationship to the attitude of many educated Filipinos
who disliked his conservative attitude toward Philippine
independence. Part of his revealing letter to Root on this
point reads as follows:

> I thought it worthwhile to put on record in a
> correspondence which I do not intend to publish,
> the exact situation with respect to the ladrones,
> ... There are some local conspiracies among
> the more educated classes which may be called
> amateur. There was one in Vigan and another
> in Pampanga and there are doubtless societies
> of a seditious character in Manila, in which the
> members play at insurrection but accomplish
> nothing.[109]

Among the more well-known "ladrones" were Macario
Sakay and his followers;[110] of the seditious movements,
the Ricarte Movement and "Dimas-Alang" and "Makabuhay"
stand out. We shall now discuss briefly each of these activities or movements.

Sakay and the "Filipino Republic." Sakay, a former
barber from Tondo, Manila, had been a member of the
Katipunan and of the army of the revolutionary government.
He was captured during the early days of the Filipino-
American War, but soon tried to revive the Katipunan in
Manila, for which he was tried and sentenced to jail under
the Sedition Law. He was released upon the proclamation
of amnesty in July, 1902, and subsequently took the oath of
allegiance to the United States. Still a radical, however,
he again resorted to his Katipunan activities and finally fled
to the mountains in 1903 to take command of guerrillas in
the Rizal-Cavite-Laguna-Batangas area. From there,
Sakay proclaimed the establishment of a "Filipino Republic" with himself as Supreme President.[111]

The extent of Sakay's movement may be gauged from
the magnitude of the operations launched against him and
his aides by the government. In 1905-1906, several thousands of Constabulary troops, Scouts, and even American
troops were committed, necessitating the suspension of
the writ of habeas corpus in Cavite and Batangas.[112]

He and his aides finally surrendered on July 17, 1906. [113]
That Sakay wanted Philippine independence immediately
and that he at least influenced the United States to modify
its conservative policy on this question cannot be doubted.
The fact that his surrender had been effected through the
intercession of Dr. Dominador Gomez, a rabid nationalist, [114] strengthens this view. [115]

We recall that the Philippine Bill of 1902 had provided
for the organization of the Philippine Assembly two years
after the publication of the census if a condition of general
and complete peace had prevailed during those two years.
The census was published in March, 1905. If a distinctly
political movement was tying down thousands of troops,
the Philippine Commission might not see its way clear to
issuing the certificate of peace which was required before
the President of the United States could issue a call for the
elections to the Assembly. That would mean a delay of
the exercise of greater governmental powers by the Filipinos. While we can only surmise at what Dr. Gomez may
have promised or told Sakay, it is entirely plausible that
he did everything to induce Sakay to surrender, especially
since a large amount of money was involved. [116]

We may be sure that Dr. Gomez represented himself
as an emissary of Colonel Bandholtz, [117] which he was, and
of Governor Ide, which he probably was not, and promised
a lot of things. It is certain that one of these was that the
Philippine Assembly would be organized as scheduled if he
gave himself up, in spite of disorders elsewhere. Since
Sakay wanted more than the limited autonomy under the
Philippine Bill, Gomez must have told him that Governor
Ide had authorized him to say that he would recommend
ultimate independence as official policy, provided that
Sakay surrendered immediately. Finally, Gomez undoubtedly assured Sakay that he and his men would not be indicted for rebellion or other crimes, or, if tried and found
guilty, would be granted executive clemency.

The Philippine Assembly was organized in 1907, and
Dr. Gomez became a celebrity which earned him election
to the Assembly. Nevertheless, the United States did not
change its stand on Philippine independence during the
Taft Regime. In addition, Sakay and his men were indicted

not for sedition but for brigandage,[118] adding insult to
injury. Worse still, Sakay and Lucio de Vega, one of his
generals, were not granted clemency and were accordingly
hanged on September 13, 1907.[119] These were of course
the imponderables over which Sakay had no control the
moment he gave himself up. But, in all likelihood, his
motives were pure.

The Ricarte Movement. The so-called Ricarte Movement developed from the attempts by General Artemio
Ricarte and his lieutenants to incite the people to rebellion
during the period 1903-1914. Ricarte was a former school
teacher who joined the Katipunan and later became one of
its leaders. In March, 1897, upon the replacement of the
Katipunan by a revolutionary government under General
Aguinaldo, Ricarte became Captain-General of the new
organization. He stayed in the Philippines during the
period following the Pact of Biyak-na-Bato, rejoined
Aguinaldo in 1898, and commanded troops during the early
phase of the Filipino-American War. In July, 1900, he
slipped through the American lines and went to Manila to
stir up opposition to the American authorities, but he was
detected and caught. Upon his refusal to take the oath of
allegiance, he was deported to Guam in January, 1901, together with many other "irreconcilables," among them
the celebrated Mabini. He and Mabini were brought back
to the Philippines in February, 1903. Mabini decided to
take the oath of allegiance, but Ricarte did not, whereupon
he was deported for the second time, this time to Hong
Kong. While there, he infused life into the moribund Hong
Kong Junta of Filipino nationalists. With Manuel Ruiz
"Prin," Ricarte established a committee called the Universal Filipino Democratic Republic, with "Prin" as
president and Ricarte as vice president. This association
gave an aura of legitimacy to Ricarte's subsequent
activities.

Ricarte returned to the Philippines in December,
1903.[120] Fortunately, no one at the pier recognized him
when he disembarked as a stowaway at Manila. He immediately got in touch with his former comrades-in-arms.
Probably to his surprise, most of them advised him to give
himself up, on the ground that fulfillment of Filipino

aspirations was assured, even if somewhat more slowly than he would desire. Refusing to believe that the people were no longer interested in rebellion, he issued a proclamation announcing that he had returned. He exhorted his countrymen to take up arms against the United States. Attacking almost everyone of his former co-revolucionarios as having sold out to the Americans and giving a low estimate of the value of their political parties, he proclaimed that "there is no [other] way, beloved brothers, than arms and patriotism" for achieving Philippine independence. 121

Ricarte traveled outside Manila, attempting to establish contact with Felipe Salvador and Macario Sakay. Sakay, however, rebuffed him as a pretender. After all, Sakay was already President of the "Filipino Republic." Nevertheless, Ricarte's efforts were not totally fruitless. He was able to "commission" a few colonels and lesser officers of a "Revolutionary Army of the Philippines," and gave them signed blank commissions.122

Meanwhile, aware that the police and Constabulary were trailing him, he sent feelers to Governor Wright for surrender upon certain terms, but nothing came of these. He was finally captured in Bataan in April, 1904, found guilty of the crime of conspiracy and subversion by a Filipino judge, and sentenced to imprisonment for six years.123 Upon his release in 1910, he was asked to take the oath of allegiance. For the third time he refused to do so, and for the third time Ricarte was deported from the Philippines.124

General Ricarte was responsible for two major planned uprisings against the United States after his release. One was to have taken place on July 4, 1912; the other ended as the "Christmas Eve Fiasco" of 1914. Our concern here is with the Ricarte Fourth of July. Here is Watson's account of the projected uprising:

> Some weeks prior to the celebration of the Fourth of July of that year [1912], Artemio Ricarte, acting through Rufino Vicente and other local celebrities, planned to gather a large number of the members of the so-called labor unions and others of the laboring classes.... They were to

be armed with short bolos and daggers carefully
hidden in their clothing. . . . The military authorities
had planned to participate as usual in the parade. . . .
. . . .
        The plan of the Ricartistas was to wait until
the troops had lined up as usual on the Luneta to
await the formation of the rest of the parade.
At a given signal they were to rush the resting
infantry at the edge of the bolo, and having secured
the arms and ammunition, were to make their way
to the treasury. The money secured from the
vaults was to be placed abroad [sic] a steam
launch that was to be seized by its crew and taken
to Malabon which was to be the temporary headquarters of the revolutionary government.125

Unfortunately for Ricarte, the authorities had received
"tips" about the projected uprising days before July 4 and
extreme precautionary measures were taken which foiled
the attempt.126
        The "Dimas-Alang" and "Makabuhay" organizations.
Other associations or movements, some of them ostensibly
harmless but potentially dangerous, such as the "Dimas-
Alang" and "Makabuhay" organizations were also estab-
lised during this period. "Dimas-Alang" was organized
by Patricio Belen in 1910 as a sort of mutual aid society
among former Katipuneros, but its membership included
a majority of "hard working people."127 "Makabuhay"
was a more militant organization, reportedly organized by
a secret service agent of the Philippine Constabulary.128
        According to a confidential report by the Acting
Director of the Constabulary in 1912, "Dimas-Alang" had
planned an uprising against the government during the
celebrations for the "Cry of Balintawak" on August 26 of
that year,129 but premature discovery of the plot by the
Constabulary led the organizers to call off the projected
uprising.130 The Acting Director of the Constabulary,
however, warned that the government must remain con-
stantly vigilant, for in his view "there is no doubt in the
existence here of a revolutionary spirit in these benevolent
and recreational societies, . . . "131

Why, one asks, the sudden flurry of seditious movements or purported uprisings in 1912? Perhaps some
Filipino nationalists hoped to influence the outcome of the
American presidential elections in November of that year.
If so, they[132] were extremely naive, since "the Philippine
question, ... was hardly touched upon during the presidential campaign of 1912. "[133] But the planned uprisings — or
rumors of them — were one way of showing the dissatisfaction of some Filipinos with the Philippine policy of the
United States under Republican leadership from McKinley
to Taft.[134]

CONCLUSION

The Taft Regime was the first phase of the encounter between Philippine and American civilizations. In that confrontation, the Filipino elite — the traditional caciques and ilustrados on the eve of the American Occupation — were the most important single factor and emerged as the immediate beneficiaries. Their reaction limited the United States in its choice of a Philippine policy. They determined the range of institutional change; unavoidably, their attitudes tempered the reception of many an American institution which was introduced in the Philippines.

These developments took place because the cooperation of the Filipino elite meant the difference between the success or failure of the American program for the political, social, and economic reconstruction of the Philippines. If the Filipino elite did not in fact determine American actions, they nevertheless made it impossible for the United States to have a free hand with any important undertaking which did not have their endorsement or, at the very least, their tacit approval. The Filipino reaction to American rule, therefore, was essentially the reaction of the Filipino elite.

The Filipino reception to American policy was most enthusiastic, and institutional change greatest, in the educational and religious fields (except among the Muslim Filipinos, or Moros). This was so because the Filipino elite's aspirations in these areas coincided to a significant degree with what Americans were prepared to undertake in the spirit of their own institutions. Thus, the foundations of a modern, secular educational system were readily and warmly accepted. The Filipinos also welcomed the introduction of the English language, not only as a medium of communication but also as the language of public school instruction. The principles of religious freedom and separation of church and state found a congenial home in the Philippines, and only the Catholic hierarchy seemed to lament the government's purchase of the extensive friar estates.

In other areas of American policy, the Filipinos
proved more selective and resistant. The American program to democratize Philippine politics suffered from the
high qualifications for voting; only about 3 per cent of the
entire population were eligible to vote. The result was
the creation of an essentially oligarchical government, i. e.,
one controlled by the Filipino upper class or elite. The
original goal of administrative decentralization was abandoned almost at the very start; and slowly, the lower units
of government were subjected to the same centralizing
tendency which had been a hallmark of the Spanish regime.
To be sure, the Filipinos readily adopted American political forms — such as the Assembly and the party system —
but in operation they reflected, inescapably, the conditions
of Philippine life and the experience of the Filipino elite
more than the characteristics of comparable American
political institutions.

The Taft Regime, however, left at least one indelible
imprint in the field of government: a modern civil service
system that was not only more efficient and dedicated to
public service than anything like it in the Philippines before
but even more "forward-looking" than some of the civil
service systems in the United States at the time.[1] The
American influence on the Philippine judicial system, at
least in the higher courts, was also significant.

From the viewpoint of Philippine institutions, American influence was perhaps weakest in the economic and
social aspects of Philippine life, except for education.
This resulted partly from the absence of concrete American plans along these lines, partly from the opposition of
the Filipino elite, and partly from the conservatism of the
people themselves, which in turn was due to their relative
isolation from the main currents of change. The Americans
succeeded in partially modernizing the tax structure, but
that was practically all that they did achieve in the economic
sphere. Their efforts to create a body of independent farmers were limited to the breakup of the friar haciendas
(and even then only in part) and to the liberalization of procedures for obtaining lands from the public domain; to
these measures the Filipino farmer was almost totally in-
different because he was not used to living on his own

farm, which the law required him to do in order to obtain
a homestead. A more positive effort might have been
made by purchasing other haciendas owned by non-friar
landlords and apportioning them at cost to their tenants.
But even if contemplated, in all likelihood such a policy
would have been strongly resisted by the Filipino elite.

Since the friar estates were not the only haciendas
and the homestead program had at best only a limited success, the social structure in the rural areas of the Philippines remained practically unchanged during the Taft
Regime. The traditional caciques, therefore, remained
as the dominant social, political, and economic group in
the villages and rural towns. The Americans intended the
public schools to serve as a means of counteracting
caciquism; the policy was a glaring display of naiveté.
The American policy of free trade further entrenched the
Filipino elite in Philippine society, just as it also dictated that Philippine economic development should take
place mainly along agricultural lines.

Previously, our knowledge of the reaction of the Filipino elite to the establishment of free trade relations between the United States and the Philippines was limited to
the record of the position of the Philippine Assembly and
the Filipino Resident Commissioners in Washington, which
was one of opposition. Forbes had insinuated that that
position "was not representative of all the intelligent
opinion in the Islands. "[2] We now know from newly opened
records and from a contextual analysis that the elite
actually welcomed free trade, and that the main reason for
their public opposition was to warn Americans that they
would resent the intrusion of huge American investments
in the Phillipines, especially investments in agriculture.
Thus, the Filipino elite got free trade from which many of
them profited immensely, and at the same time kept
Philippine agriculture practically to themselves.

The Americans inaugurated their regime in the
Philippines by destroying an independent republic. And,
until 1906, they also suppressed the overt expression of
any desire for independence which, though not widespread
in 1896, had become a generalized sentiment during the
second phase of the Philippine Revolution, especially among

the elite. There was understandable resentment on the
part of the Filipinos at this cold-blooded disregard of
their right to self-determination; it was heightened by the
prevailing Filipino view that recognition of Philippine
independence had been the primary basis of Filipino-
American collaboration in the war against Spain. Filipino
resentment was manifested in lingering guerrilla activities
against the United States, in the pre-Assembly attempts of
the Filipino elite to organize independista parties, and in a
few conspiracies, such as the Ricarte Movement, organized
in an attempt to influence the conservative Roosevelt-Taft
policy toward Philippine independence.

While the Americans did not officially endorse a
policy of independence during the Taft Regime, they nevertheless adopted a policy of extreme conciliation, brought
many of the elite into the government, and took positive
measures to meet their other aspirations. Such a policy,
coupled with the continuing material blessings of free
trade, had a sobering effect on the real sentiments of the
elite toward Philippine independence, although in public
they continued to express their opposition to American
rule. The record suggests that as the Taft Era wore on,
some of the leaders of the dominant and openly more
radical party — the Nacionalista Party — began to equi-
vocate on the issue of independence. And by the end of
the Taft Regime, what they seemed to desire was not
independence, let alone "immediate independence, " but
an autonomous and Filipinized government under the protection of the United States. In this respect, the reaction
of the Filipino political elite — or at any rate of Quezon
and Osmena — foreshadowed their later reaction to the
prospects of Philippine independence: according to a most
recent and thorough study, that reaction was one of fear
and anxiety.[3]

APPENDIX

APPENDIX

EXCERPTS FROM PRESIDENT WILLIAM McKINLEY'S LETTER OF INSTRUCTIONS TO THE TAFT COMMISSION, APRIL 7, 1900[a]

. . . .

The commissioners... will meet and act as a board, and the Hon. William H. Taft is designated as president of the board.... The commission will... report to the Secretary of War, and all their action will be subject to your approval and control.

You will instruct the commission to proceed to the city of Manila, where they will make their principal office,... Without hampering them by too specific instruction, they should in general be enjoined, after making themselves familiar with the conditions and needs of the country, to devote their attention in the first instance to the establishment of municipal governments, in which the natives of the islands, both in the cities and in the rural communities, shall be afforded the opportunity to manage their own local affairs to the fullest extent of which they are capable, and subject to the least degree of supervision and control which a careful study of their capacities and observation of the workings of native control show to be consistent with the maintenance of law, order, and loyalty.

The next subject in order of importance should be the organization of government in the larger administrative

---

[a]The full text is in Annual Reports of the War Department...1900, Vol. I: Report of the Secretary of War, Pt. 1, Appendix B, pp. 72-76. For the background of the Letter of Instructions, see supra, pp. 37-38. The instructions were addressed to the Secretary of War, the Hon. Elihu Root, who in turn transmitted them to the Commission. Besides W. H. Taft, the other members of the Commission were: Dean C. Worcester, Luke E. Wright, Henry C. Ide, and Bernard Moses.

divisions, corresponding to counties, departments, or provinces, ... Whenever the commission is of the opinion that the condition of affairs in the islands is such that the central administration may safely be transferred from military to civil control, they will report that conclusion to you, with their recommendations as to the form of central government to be established for the purpose of taking over the control.

Beginning with the 1st day of September, 1900, the authority to exercise, subject to my approval, through the Secretary of War, that part of the power of government in the Philippine Islands which is of a legislative nature is to be transferred from the military governor of the islands to this commission, ... under such rules and regulations as you shall prescribe, until the establishment of the civil central government, ... or until Congress shall otherwise provide.

Exercise of this legislative authority will include the making of rules and orders, having the effect of law, for the raising of revenue by taxes, customs, duties, and imposts; the appropriation and expenditure of public funds of the islands; the establishment of an educational system throughout the islands; the establishment of a system to secure an efficient civil service; the organization and establishment of courts; the organization and establishment of municipal and departmental governments, and all other matters of a civil nature for which the military governor is now competent to provide by rules or orders of a legislative character.

The commission will also have power during the same period to appoint to office such officers under the judicial, educational, and civil-service systems and in the municipal and departmental governments as shall be provided for. Until the complete transfer of control the military governor will remain the chief executive head of the government of the islands, ... In the meantime the municipal and departmental governments will continue to report to the military governor and be subject to his administrative supervision and control, under your direction, ...

All legislative rules and orders, establishments of government, and appointments to office by the Commission

will take effect immediately, or at such times as they
shall designate, subject to your approval and action upon
the coming in of the commission's reports,...

. . . .

In the distribution of powers among the governments
organized by the commission the presumption is always
to be in favor of the smaller subdivision, so that all the
powers which can properly be exercised by the municipal
government shall be vested in that government, and all
the powers of a more general character which can be
exercised by the departmental government shall be vested
in that government, and so that in the governmental system which is the result of the process the central government of the islands, following the example of the distribution of the powers between the States and the National
Government of the United States, shall have no direct
administration except of matters of purely general concern, and shall have only such supervision and control
over local governments as may be necessary to secure
and enforce faithful and efficient administration by local
officers.

The many different degrees of civilization and varie-
ties of custom and capacity among the people of the different islands preclude very definite instruction as to the
part which the people shall take in the selection of their
own officers; but these general rules are to be observed:
That in all cases the municipal officers, who administer
the local affairs of the people, are to be selected by the
people, and that wherever officers of more extended
jurisdiction are to be selected in any way, natives of the
islands are to be preferred, and if they can be found competent and willing to perform the duties, they are to receive the offices in preference to any others.

It will be necessary to fill some offices for the present
with Americans which after a time may well be filled by
natives of the islands. As soon as practicable a system
for ascertaining the merit and fitness of candidates for
civil office should be put in force. An indispensable
qualification for all offices and positions of trust and
authority in the islands must be absolute and unconditional
loyalty to the United States;...

In all the forms of government and administrative provisions which they are authorized to prescribe, the commission should bear in mind that the government which they are establishing is designed, not for our satisfaction or for the expression of our theoretical views, but for the happiness, peace, and prosperity of the people of the Philippine Islands, and the measures adopted should be made to conform to their customs, their habits, and even their prejudices, to the fullest extent consistent with the accomplishment of the indispensable requisites of just and effective government.

At the same time the commission should bear in mind, and the people of the islands should be made plainly to understand, that there are certain great principles of government which have been made the basis of our governmental system which we deem essential to the rule of law and the maintenance of individual freedom, and of which they have, unfortunately, been denied the experience possessed by us; that there are also certain practical rules of government which we have found to be essential to the preservation of these great principles of liberty and law, and that these principles and these rules of government must be established and maintained in their islands for the sake of their liberty and happiness, however much they may conflict with the customs or laws of procedure with which they are familiar.

It is evident that the most enlightened thought of the Philippine Islands fully appreciates the importance of these principles and rules, and they will inevitably within a short time command universal assent. Upon every division and branch of the government of the Philippines, therefore, must be imposed these inviolable rules:

That no person shall be deprived of life, liberty, or property without due process of law; that private property shall not be taken for public use without just compensation; that in all criminal prosecutions the accused shall enjoy the right to a speedy and public trial, to be informed of the nature and cause of the accusation, to be confronted with the witnesses against him, to have compulsory process for obtaining witnesses in his favor, and to have the assistance of counsel for his defense; that excessive bail

shall not be required, nor excessive fines imposed, nor
cruel and unusual punishment inflicted; that no person
shall be put twice in jeopardy for the same offense, or be
compelled in any criminal case to be a witness against
himself; that the right to be secure against unreasonable
searches and seizures shall not be violated; that neither
slavery nor involuntary servitude shall exist except as a
punishment for crime; that no bill of attainder or ex post
facto law shall be passed; that no law shall be passed
abridging the freedom of speech or of the press, or the
rights of the people to peaceably assemble and petition
the Government for a redress of grievances; that no law
shall be made respecting an establishment of religion or
prohibiting the free exercise thereof, and that the free
exercise and enjoyment of religious profession and worship without discrimination or preference shall forever
be allowed.

It will be the duty of the commission to make a thorough investigation into the titles to the large tracts of land
held or claimed by individuals or by religious orders; into
the justice of the claims and complaints made against such
landholders by the people of the island [sic], or any part
of the people, and to seek by wise and peaceable measures
a just settlement of the controversies and redress of
wrongs which have caused strife and bloodshed in the past.
In the performance of this duty the commission is enjoined
to see that no injustice is done; to have regard for substantial rights and equity, disregarding technicalities so far as
substantial right permits, and to observe the following
rules:

That the provision of the treaty of Paris pledging the
United States to the protection of all rights of property in
the islands, and as well the principle of our own Government which prohibits the taking of private property without
due process of law, shall not be violated; that the welfare
of the people of the islands, which should be a paramount
consideration, shall be attained consistently with this rule
of property right; that if it becomes necessary for the public interest of the people of the islands to dispose of claims
to property which the commission finds to be not lawfully
acquired and held, disposition shall be made thereof by

due legal procedure, in which there shall be full opportunity for fair and impartial hearing and judgment; that if
the same public interests require the extinguishment of
property rights lawfully acquired and held, due compensation shall be made out of the public treasury therefor; that
no form of religion and no minister of religion shall be
forced upon any community or upon any citizen of the islands; that upon the other hand no minister of religion
shall be interfered with or molested in following his cal-
ling, and that the separation between state and church
shall be real, entire, and absolute.

It will be the duty of the commission to promote and
extend, and, as they find occasion, to improve, the system of education already inaugurated by the military re-
authorities. In doing this they should regard as of first
importance the extension of a system of primary education
which shall be free to all, and which shall tend to fit the
people for the duties of citizenship and for the ordinary
avocations of a civilized community. This instruction
should be given in the first instance in every part of the
islands in the language of the people. In view of the great
number of languages spoken by the different tribes, it is
especially important to the prosperity of the islands that
a common medium of communication may be established,
and it is obviously desirable that this medium should be
the English language. Especial attention should be at once
given to affording full opportunity to all the people of the
islands to acquire the use of the English language.

It may be well that the main changes which should be
made in the system of taxation and in the body of the laws
under which the people are governed, except such changes
as have already been made by the military government,
should be relegated to the civil government which is to be
established under the auspices of the commission. It will,
however, be the duty of the commission to inquire dili-
gently as to whether there are any further changes which
ought not to be delayed; and if so, they are authorized to
make such changes, subject to your approval. In doing so
they are to bear in mind that taxes which tend to penalize
or repress industry and enterprise are to be avoided; that
provisions for taxation should be simple, so that they may

be understood by the people; that they should affect the fewest practicable subjects of taxation which will serve for the general distribution of the burden.

The main body of the laws which regulate the rights and obligations of the people should be maintained with as little interference as possible. Changes made should be mainly in procedure, and in the criminal laws to secure speedy and impartial trials and at the same time effective administration and respect for individual rights.

In dealing with the uncivilized tribes of the islands the commission should adopt the same course followed by Congress in permitting the tribes of our North American Indians to maintain their tribal organization and government, and under which many of those tribes are now living in peace and contentment, surrounded by a civilization to which they are unable or unwilling to conform. Such tribal governments should, however, be subjected to wise and firm regulation; and, without undue or petty interference, constant and active effort should be exercised to prevent barbarous practices and introduce civilized customs.

Upon all officers and employees of the United States, both civil and military, should be impressed a sense of the duty to observe not merely the material but the personal and social rights of the people of the islands, and to treat them with the same courtesy and respect for their personal dignity which the people of the United States are accustomed to require from each other.

The articles of capitulation of the city of Manila on the 13th of August, 1898, concluded with these words:

"This city, its inhabitants, its churches and religious worship, its educational establishments, and its private property of all descriptions are placed under the special safeguard of the faith and honor of the American army."

I believe that this pledge has been faithfully kept. As high and sacred an obligation rests upon the Government of the United States to give protection for property and life, civil and religious freedom, and wise, firm, and unselfish guidance in the paths of peace and prosperity to all the people of the Philippine Islands. I charge this commission to labor for the full performance of this obligation, which concerns the honor and conscience of their country, in the firm hope that through their labors all the inhabitants of the Philippine Islands may come to look back with gratitude to the day when God gave victory to American arms at Manila and set their land under the sovereignty and the protection of the people of the United States.

WILLIAM McKINLEY

NOTES

Chapter I

1. The reader may be directed to the following, though not the only, recent works: H. Wayne Morgan, William McKinley and His America (Syracuse: Syracuse University Press, 1963), Ch. XVIII; Margaret Leech, In The Days of McKinley (New York: Harper and Brothers, 1959), Ch. 14; Louis J. Hallé, Dream and Reality: Aspects of American Foreign Policy (New York: Harper and Brothers, 1959); Samuel Flagg Bemis, A Diplomatic History of the United States (4th ed. ; New York: Henry Holt and Company, 1955), Ch. XVI; Richard Hofstadter, "Manifest Destiny and the Philippines, " America In Crisis, ed. Daniel Aaron (New York: Alfred A. Knopf, 1952), Ch. VIII; Garel A. Grunder and William E. Livezey, The Philippines and the United States (Norman: University of Oklahoma Press, 1951), Ch. II; and Honesto A. Villanueva, "The Diplomacy of the Spanish-American War, " published serially in The Philippine Social Sciences and Humanities Review, XIV-XV (1949-1951). Cited hereafter simply as PSSHR.

2. Hay to Day, October 28, 1898, in U.S. , Dept. of State, Foreign Relations of the United States, 1898 (Washington: U.S. Government Printing Office, 1862-), p. 937. An earlier telegram dated October 26, 1898 (ibid., p. 935), was not sent, claims Prof. Leopold after an examination of the original in the U.S. National Archives. "The instruction on which the commission acted, " he says, "was the longer telegram of October 28,... " Richard W. Leopold, "The Foreign Relations Series: A Centennial Estimate, " The Mississippi Valley Historical Review, XLIX (March, 1963), 598, n. 11.

3. The text of the Treaty of Paris is in U.S. , Statutes at Large, XXX, 1754-1762. Henceforth, U.S. , Statutes.

4. An excellent study on the Filipino response to Spanish rule has already been made. See John Leddy Phelan, The Hispanization of the Philippines: Spanish Aims and Filipino Responses, 1565-1700 (Madison, Wis. : The University of Wisconsin Press, 1959). Dr. Phelan's work is the product of "an effort to combine sound

historical practices with some anthropological techniques.
Ibid. , p. viii.
    5. These works will be mentioned in the course of
our presentation.

Chapter II

    1. See Phelan, op. cit.
    2. Cesar Adib Majul, The Political and Constitutional
Ideas of the Philippine Revolution ("PSSHR, " Vol. XXII,
Nos. 1-2; Quezon City: University of the Philippines,
1957), p. 15.
    3. The exceptions were the sultanates, or "supra-
barangay" organizations, among the Muslims in Mindanao
and Sulu. Phelan, op. cit., pp. 15-17.
    4. A convenient summary of the political system un-
der Spain is Edward Gaylord Bourne, "Historical Introduction, " ed. Emma Helen Blair and James Alexander
Robertson, The Philippine Islands, 1493-1898 (55 vols. ;
Cleveland, Chic: The Arthur H. Clark Company, 1903-
1909), I, 49-56. An excellent and detailed analysis is
Onofre D. Corpuz,The Bureaucracy in the Philippines
(Manila: University of the Philippines, 1957), Chs. II-VI.
See also Phelan, op. cit., Ch. IX.
    5. The less peaceful provinces, found mostly outside
of Luzon, were administered by corregidores, who were
generally, if not always, military personnel. See Corpuz,
op. cit., p. 92.
    6. [U. S. , Philippine Commission], Report of the
Philippine Commission to the President (4 vols. ; Washington: U. S. Government Printing Office, 1900-1901),
I, 122. This is the report of the Schurman Commission
and will be cited hereafter as such. See also U. S. , Congress, Senate, Reports of the Taft Philippine Commission,
56th Cong. , 2d Sess. , 1901, Senate Doc. 112, Exhibit J.
Cited hereafter as Taft Commission Report.
    7. Bourne, loc. cit. , p. 56. The Spanish parish
priest was, among others, the local inspector of primary
schools, president of the local boards of charities, health,
urban taxation and prison; he was censor of the municipal
budget, attested to the correctness of the taxes, or

cedulas; and had to be present during the elections of
municipal officials. The parish priest of the provincial
capital was also a member of the provincial board. See
the testimony of Fr. Juan Villegas, Superior of the Fran-
ciscan Order in the Philippines, before the Taft Commission, in U. S., Congress, Senate, Lands Held for
Ecclesiastical or Religious Uses in the Philippine Islands,
56th Cong., 2d Sess., 1901, Senate Doc. 190, pp. 63-71.
Cited hereafter as Lands Held for Ecclesiastical Uses.
At the central level, the Archbishop of Manila was President of the Board of Authorities, the highest advisory
body to the Governor-General. The Archbishop and the
superiors of the religious orders were also members of
a larger advisory body, the Council of Administration. In
addition, the friars controlled the Permanent Commission
on Censorship. See Schurman Commission Report, Vol.
I, p. 75, and Corpuz, op. cit., p. 136.

8. Cesar Adib Majul, Mabini and the Philippine
Revolution (Quezon City: University of the Philippines,
1960), p. 350.

9. James A. LeRoy, Philippine Life in Town and
Country (New York: G. P. Putnam's Sons, 1905), p. 119.
Phelan, op. cit., pp. 31-32, gives a brief background of
the special dispensation.

10. The friars refused visitation by bishops on the
ground that it was contrary to the rule of their orders.

11. Throughout this study, "to secularize" or
"secularization" will refer to the replacement of regular
priests by secular priests as administrators of the parishes of the Roman Catholic Church.

12. LeRoy gives the following data on the state of
secularization in the late nineteenth century: "In 1870,
of the 792 Philippine parishes, excluding the ten mission
parishes of the Jesuits, the friars were in charge of 611,
and secular priests, nearly all natives, of 181. The contention that in general only the poorer, less productive
parishes were assigned to native priests is borne out by
the fact that the average number of parishioners in their
181 parishes was 4500, while in the friars' parishes the
average was well beyond 6000.... The number of native
priests, coadjutors and all, was about 600 in 1898; but

the number of their parishes did not increase, and they
remained to the last mainly the coadjutors of the friar
priests in the larger parishes. " James A. LeRoy, The
Americans in the Philippines (2 vols. ; Boston: The
Houghton Mifflin Company, 1914), I, 60-61, citing primary
sources.

13. It was the belief of many Filipinos that the friars
had usurped the properties of Filipinos. This may have
been true in some instances, but it was also true that the
friars came to own some of their estates through legitimate land grants by the Spanish Crown, purchases, and
donations by private individuals. It is also possible that
these estates developed from the encomiendas they had
received from the Spanish Crown, although technically
speaking the encomienda was not a land grant but simply
the right to collect tributes, or taxes, from the natives
within a certain jurisdiction. See my article entitled
"Was the Philippine Encomienda a Land Grant?, " Historical Bulletin, VII (March, 1963), 34-51.

14. Taft Commission Report, p. 27, and U. S. ,
Philippine Commission, Fourth Annual Report of the
Philippine Commission, 1903 (Washington, D. C. : U. S.
Government Printing Office, 1904), Pt. 1, p. 202. A more
or less accurate survey undertaken between 1901 and 1903
showed that the friar lands aggregated 422, 337. 29 acres.
Ibid. , p. 303. As we shall point out later in this study,
these estates were purchased by the government in 1903
for about 7, 500, 000 dollars (U. S.). Assuming that this
sum was equally divided among the three orders (which
was not so since the Recollects owned only two-thirds of
the amount of land held by either the Dominicans or
Augustinians), an Augustinian friar recently commented
that after three hundred years of evangelical labor in the
Philippines, of untold sufferings and sacrifices, etc. , in
the end the net worth of each of these religious corporations amounted to only two and a half million dollars! To
him, they should have gotten more haciendas. P. Isacio
R. Rodriguez, O. S. A. , Gregorio Aglipay y los origenes
de la Iglesia Filipina Independiente (1898-1917) (2 vols. ;
Madrid: Departamento de Misionologia Espanola, 1960),
I, 53-54.

15. Majul, Mabini, pp. 50-51. LeRoy (Americans in the Philippines, I, 18) briefly discusses agrarian troubles in areas where most of the friar estates were located. See also his Philippine Life, pp. 157-58.

16. This is attested to by the increase in the number of public primary schools from 1,016 in 1877 to 1,943 in 1892, fifteen years later. See Evergisto Bazaco, O.P., History of Education in the Philippines, Vol. I: Spanish Period — 1565-1898 (Manila: University of Santo Tomas Press, 1939), p. 254.

17. Schools were also to be established in some large barrios distant from the town proper (poblacion), provided they had at least 500 inhabitants. See ibid., p. 253.

18. That is, Spanish. Heretofore, instruction in the parish or parochial schools had been conducted in the native languages or dialects. Ibid., pp. 65 and 72.

19. Quoted in Jorge R. Coquia, The Legal Status of the Church in the Philippines (Washington: The Catholic University of America Press, 1950), p. 117. Italics are Coquia's.

20. For Dr. Rizal's attitude toward the friars, see his novels: The Social Cancer (Manila: Philippine Education Company, 1912) and The Reign of Greed (Manila: Philippine Education Company, 1912), both translated by Charles E. Derbyshire. The titles of del Pilar's works alone suggest his scorn for the friars: La Soberania monacal en Filipinas (Barcelona: Imp. de F. Fossas, 1888) and La Frailocracia filipina (Barcelona: Imp. de F. Fossas, 1899). Lopez-Jaena himself wrote a parody on the friars entitled Fray Botod. See also his Discursos y articulos varios (Manila: Bureau of Printing, 1951).

21. Taft Commission Report, p. 23. For the grievances of the revolutionists against the friars, see Teodoro A. Agoncillo, The Revolt of the Masses: The Story of Bonifacio and the Katipunan ("PSSHR," Vol. XXI, Nos. 1-4; Quezon City: University of the Philippines, 1956), pp. 152-54.

22. Phelan, op. cit., p. 15.

23. Wickberg places the Spanish mestizos in the same class as the Spaniards. E. Wickberg, "The Chinese Mestizo in Philippine History," Journal of

Southeast Asian History, V (March, 1964), 63.
      24. LeRoy, Philippine Life, pp. 173-74. See also
Karl J. Pelzer, Pioneer Settlement in the Asiatic Tropics:
Studies in Land Utilization and Agricultural Colonization
in Southeastern Asia (New York: American Geographical
Society, 1945), p. 89.
      25. LeRoy, Philippine Life, p. 176.
      26. Pelzer, op. cit.
      27. Majul, Mabini, p. 64.
      28. LeRoy claims (Philippine Life, pp. 36-40) that
the mestizo-ilustrados were Spanish mestizos. Wickberg
(loc. cit.), however, has recently demonstrated with con-
vincing thoroughness that these were actually Chinese
mestizos, i. e., of mixed Chinese and Filipino parentage.
      29. LeRoy, Philippine Life, pp. 71-2.
      30. For details, see Carl C. Plehn, "Taxation in
the Philippines," The Philippine Social Science Review,
XIII (February, 1941), 79-117. Cited hereafter as PSSR.
See also John S. Hord, Internal Taxation in the Philippines
("Johns Hopkins University: Studies in Historical and
Political Science," Series XXV, No. 1; Baltimore: The
Johns Hopkins Press, 1907), pp. 7-11. Hord was the
first American Collector of Internal Revenue of the
Philippines.
      31. This was probably part of the Spanish efforts to
stimulate agriculture.
      32. A Peso (₱) was equivalent to U. S. fifty cents.
      33. Plehn, loc. cit., p. 89, citing the Royal Cedula
of 1884.
      34. Such as those derived from customs duties, gov-
ernment lottery, mint charges, royalties on forest products, and the Chinese poll tax. Cf. Hord, op. cit., p. 10.
      35. Corpuz, op. cit., p. 140.
      36. The Philippine tariff under Spain is discussed by
Plehn, loc. cit., pp. 101-10. There is no detailed study
on the nature of Philippine export trade with Spain. Our
single source has only one short paragraph on the subject.
See Pedro E. Abelarde, American Tariff Policy Towards
the Philippines, 1898-1946 (Morningside Heights, N. Y.:
King's Crown Press, 1947), p. 10. Abelarde claims that
sugar was not admitted free of duty because it paid a

large internal tax, but the latter did not seem to be a customs duty per se.

37. Recommended background studies on the Revolution are Agoncillo, op. cit., Chs. I-III; Majul, Mabini, Ch. I; and LeRoy, Americans in the Philippines, II, Chs. I-II.

38. Majul, Mabini, p. 8.

39. LeRoy, Americans in the Philippines, I, 63.

40. Majul, Mabini, p. 9.

41. The literature on the revolution continues to increase. Among important works are the following: Agoncillo's Revolt of the Masses and his later study, Malolos: The Crisis of the Republic ("PSSHR," Vol. XXV, Nos. 1-4; Quezon City: University of the Philippines, 1960); Majul, Mabini; Teodoro M. Kalaw, The Philippine Revolution (Manila: Manila Book Company, 1925); Gregorio F. Zaide, The Philippine Revolution (Manila: Modern Book Company, 1954). See also LeRoy, Americans in the Philippines, I, Ch. III

42. Majul, Mabini, p. 10.

43. For the attitude of the Filipino upper class as a whole towards the Katipunan, including Antonio Luna's denunciation of it, see Agoncillo, Revolt, pp. 109-13.

44. The Pact of Biyak-na-Bato actually consisted of three complementary agreements signed on December 14 and 15, 1897, by which the revolutionists led by General Emilio Aguinaldo agreed to lay down their arms. In return the Spanish government promised to pay ₱ 1,700,000 (Mex.). Of this amount, ₱ 800,000 was to go to those in arms and ₱ 700,000 to non-combatants who had suffered as a direct consequence of military operations. General Aguinaldo was to be given ₱ 400,000 upon his departure for Hong Kong, the other half to be paid in two equal installments when certain conditions had been met. No stipulations were made regarding the indemnity to non-combatants.

It was also claimed by Pedro A. Paterno, who negotiated the pact or agreements, and General Aguinaldo that Governor-General Miguel Primo de Rivera had also promised certain reforms, among them the expulsion of the friars or the dissolution of their monasteries — at least — Filipino representation in the Spanish Cortes, and the grant of individual civil liberties. None of these reforms were enumerated in the agreements, but it was argued that since reforms could only be granted by the Spanish Crown, Rivera had insisted that no such promise of reforms be incorporated into the agreements.

In any case, General Aguinaldo got the ₱ 400,000 which he deposited upon arrival in Hong Kong at the end of December, 1897, and the revolutionary leaders remaining at Biyak-na-Bato, including Paterno, received another ₱ 200,000. No reforms were granted by the Spaniards, and the renewal of the revolution had become a fact by March, 1898. For details, see Agoncillo, Malolos, pp. 25-77, and Leandro H. Fernandez, The Philippine Republic ("Columbia University: Studies in History, Economics and Public Law," Vol. CXXII, No. 1; New York: Columbia University Press, 1926), pp. 35-44.

45. Its consitution is hardly referred to as the Constitution of the Philippine Republic, but is known generally as the Malolos Constitution.

46. The government established by General Aguinaldo passed through these stages: (1) the Dictatorial Government, May 24-June 23, 1898; (2) the Revolutionary Government, June 23, 1898-January 21, 1899 to 1901. Agoncillo, Malolos, pp. 217, 233, 389. For convenience, however, I shall invariably use revolutionary, Philippine, or Malolos government to refer to any or to all of these stages in the life of the government established by General Aguinaldo.

47. Unfortunately for many ilustrados, the Spaniards suspected them just the same for complicity in the revolution and incarcerated and tortured them in the dungeons of Fort Santiago, releasing them only after handsome bribes had been paid to their captors and tormentors. On top of that the ilustrados were re-arrested, tortured once more, and forced to pay yet more sums of money to be released. See Agoncillo, Revolt, pp. 162-63.

48. Rounseville Wildman, the American consul in Hong Kong, was the purchasing agent. Agoncillo, Malolos, pp. 127-28. He failed to deliver the second consignment, and did not make a refund to Aguinaldo either.

49. The following, by U. S. Consul-General E. Spen-

cer Pratt in Singapore to General Aguinaldo, is very
apropos: "You need not have any worry about America.
The American Congress and President have just made a
solemn declaration [the Teller Resolution] disclaiming any
desire to possess Cuba and promising to leave the country
to the Cubans after having driven away the Spaniards and
pacified the country. Cuba is at our door while the Philippines is 10,000 miles away." Quoted in ibid., p. 125.

50. Copious extracts of General Aguinaldo's circular,
by which he also officially dissolved the Katipunan, are
given in ibid., pp. 241-42.

51. Decree of the Revolutionary Government, dated
June 18, 1898, in Majul, Mabini, p. 178, and Agoncillo,
Malolos, p. 228. Those entitled to vote were also re-
quired to be "friendly to Philippine independence."

52. Majul (Mabini, p. 183) gives a short table showing the limited number of electors in relation to the population in actual cases where elections were held. From the
table, we learn that only about one-half of one per cent of
the population in each of the five towns actually voted.

53. Of the 32 known elected members of the Malolos
Congress, 14 were lawyers, 5 physicians, 1 a businessman, 1 a pharmacist, 1 an educator, 1 simply an A. B.,
1 a publisher, and 1 a priest. Seven were listed as being
without any degree or occupation; it is reasonable to
assume, however, that in all probability most of these
were also ilustrados. See The Malolos Congress (Manila:
Philippines Historical Committee, 1963). This is a
"souvenir brochure" containing capsule biographies and,
where available, pictures of the 92 signers of the Malolos
Constitution.

54. Felipe G. Calderon, Mis memorias sobre la
Revolución Filipina. Segunda etapa. (Manila: Imp. de
El Renacimiento, 1907), p. 239, as quoted in Agoncillo,
Malolos, p. 308.

55. Forty-three friars were killed during the revolution, and the revolutionary government held another 403 as
prisoners, including the Bishop of Nueva Segovia (Vigan).
Taft Commission Report, p. 23.

56. Aguinaldo to Gen. Elwell S. Otis, American
Military Commander, November 13, 1898, quoted in

Agoncillo, Malolos, pp. 249-50 and Leon Wolff, <u>Little</u>
<u>Brown Brother: How the United States Purchased and</u>
<u>Pacified the Philippine Islands at the Century's Turn</u>
(Garden City, N. Y. : Doubleday and Company, Inc. , 1961),
p. 142.

    57. Agoncillo, <u>Malolos</u>, p. 249, citing Aguinaldo to
Otis, November 10, <u>1898</u>. Both of Aguinaldo's letters
were penned by Mabini, then Aguinaldo's chief adviser.

    58. I have used the following sources for the history
of the National Church: Juan A. Rivera, "The Aglipayan
Movement, " <u>PSSR</u>, IX (December, 1937), 301-6; Majul,
<u>Mabini</u>, pp. 408-27; Pedro S. de Achutegui, S. J. , and
<u>Miguel</u> A. Bernad, S. J. , <u>Religious Revolution in the</u>
Philippines: The Life and Church of Gregorio Aglipay,
<u>1860-1960</u>, Vol. I: From Aglipay's Birth to his Death,
<u>1860-1840</u> (Manila: Ateneo de Manila, 1960), esp. chap.
<u>VI</u>; Rodriguez, <u>op. cit.</u>, I, 174-92; and Sister Maria Dorita
Clifford, "Aglipayanism As a Political Movement, " (un-
published Ph. D. dissertation, Dept. of History, St. Louis
University, 1960), chap. III. A microfilmed copy of
Sister Maria Dorita's work is at the Yale Library.

    59. During the second phase of the revolution, Fr.
Aglipay, an Ilocano priest, had been appointed by General
Aguialdo as Vicar General, first of the revolutionary army,
and later of the revolutionary government. He was also
appointed by the Bishop of Nueva Segovia as Ecclesiastical
Governor of the diocese but imprisonment prevented him
from taking care of the affairs of the bishopric. When the
Archbishop of Manila heard about Fr. Aglipay's positions
in the revolutionary government and his circulars urging
the Filipino clergy to support the revolution, he immediately excommunicated Aglipay. Achutegui and Bernad,
<u>op. cit.</u>, <u>passim.</u>

    60. Clifford, <u>op. cit.</u>, p. 161, also believes that the
proposed concordat was also a diplomatic trump card, for
had such a concordat been negotiated with the Vatican,
which had a diplomatic standing, the revolutionary government would then have acquired a status in international
law at precisely the moment when the American and Spanish Peace Commissioners were meeting at Paris to conclude a treaty of peace. This may well have been the

case, although Mabini's latest biographer (Majul, op. cit.)
is silent on this point.

61. For the Philippine Independent Church, see
infra, pp. 97-107.

62. I have used the English version of the Malolos
Constitution as given in Agoncillo, Malolos, Appendix D.

63. Quoted in Majul, Mabini, p. 47.

64. Ibid. , p. 49.

65. Cf. Encarnacion Alzona, A History of Education
in the Philippines, 1565-1930 (1st ed. ; Manila: University
of the Philippines Press, 1932), pp. 177-186.

66. Agoncillo, Malolos, pp. 250-51.

67. Majul, Political and Constitutional Ideas, p. 186.

68. Ibid.

69. See supra, n. 20 of this chapter.

70. Cartas sobre la Revolución: (1897-1900) (Manila:
Bureau of Printing, 1932).

71. For a convenient summary of the teachings of the
Katipunan, see Agoncillo, Revolt, pp. 76-97, and Majul,
Political and Constitutional Ideas, p. 29 et passim.

72. In addition to the Malolos Constitution of 1899
(loc. cit.), there were also the Biyak-na-Bato Constitution
of 1897 (PSSR, III [August, 1930], 78-82). Mabini's Constitutional Program of 1898 (ibid. , IV [October, 1932],
315-44), the proposed Constitution of the Island of Negros
of 1899 (Schurman Commission Report, Vol. I, Exhibit V),
and the Constitution Prepared by Certain Eminent Filipinos for the Schurman Commission in 1899 (ibid. , Exhibit
VI). See also the First Manifesto of the Hong Kong Junta
of April, 1898, in Murat Halstead, The Story of the Philippines (Chicago: Our Possessions Publishing Co. , 1898),
pp. 294-303.

73. Malolos Constitution, Art. 57. The constitution
prepared by prominent Filipinos for the Schurman Commission went even further by proposing a federal system:
Each region was to enjoy "complete olegislative, governmental, and administrative autonomy, having power to
dictate its own political constitution peculiar to itself, . . . "
(Art. III). This was probably an attempt to please the
Americans and therefore less reflective of Filipino aspirations than the Malolos Constitution.

74. Art. 82, Sec. 4.

75. For the debates and votings on the Calderon draft and the amendment, see Agoncillo, Malolos, pp. 198-306.

76. Art. 100.

77. Majul, Political and Constitutional Ideas, p. 14.

78. LeRoy, "The Philippines, 1860-1898 — Some Comment and Bibliographical Notes," in Blair and Robertson, op. cit. , LII, 206.

Chapter III

1. For Filipino diplomatic efforts, see Agoncillo, Malolos, pp. 310-30 and 355-68; Fernandez, op. cit. , pp. 115-29; and Honesto A. Villanueva, "A Chapter of Filipino Diplomacy," PSSHR, XVII (June, 1952), 103-78. Dr. Villanueva prints several documents heretofore unpublished.

2. We recall that General Aguinaldo left for Hong Kong on December 27, 1897. He sailed for Singapore in April, 1898, to avoid appearing in a law suit filed against him by Isabelo Artacho, his former Secretary of the Interior, for his share of the ₱400,000. General Aguinaldo had two conferences with Consul-General Pratt, which paved the way for his return to the Philippines. He hurried back to Hong Kong, but Dewey had already sailed for Manila Bay. While waiting for another opportunity to return to Manila, Aguinaldo met with the other Filipino exiles in Hong Kong, reconciling with Artacho. He also met with U. S. Consul Wildman, who agreed to act as Aguinaldo's purchasing agent for arms. On May 19, 1898, Aguinaldo finally sailed for the Philippines on board the S. S. McCulloch, a revenue cutter attached to Dewey's squadron. Agoncillo, Malolos, pp. 122-23; Fernandez, op. cit. , p. 52.

3. Since 1962, we have been celebrating our independence day on June 12 instead of July 4.

4. For pertinent correspondence, see U. S. , Adjutant General's Office, Correspondence Relating to the War Wtih Spain. . . from April 15, 1898 to July 30, 1902 (2 vols. ; Washington, D. C. : U. S. Government Printing Office, 1902), II, passim. Cited hereafter as USAGO, Correspondence. Aguinaldo had been addressed simply as

Commanding General, Philippine Revolutionary Forces.

5. The "capture" of Manila was preceded by a secret agreement between Dewey and the Spanish authorities for the surrender of the city after a token resistance, on the condition that no Filipino forces were to enter Intramuros, or the Walled City, which then constituted the heart of Manila. See Nathan Sargent, comp., Admiral Dewey and the Manila Campaign, (Washington, D. C., Naval Historical Foundation, 1947), pp. 77 ff.; Agoncillo, Malolos, pp. 186-93; LeRoy, Americans in the Philippines; and George Dewey, Autobiography (New York: Charles Scribner's Sons, 1913), pp. 269-75.

6. Fernandez, op. cit., pp. 93-94.

7. Morgan, op. cit., p. 437, calls Otis "a stuffy martinet." Cf. Wolff, op. cit., pp. 141-42 and 149-52.

8. McKinley to Otis, December 21, 1898, USAGO, Correspondence, II, 719.

9. Ibid., II, 873.

10. The full text of President McKinley's Instructions to the Schurman Commission, dated January 20, 1899, is in Schurman Commission Report, Vol. I, Exhibit II. The members of the Commission were Jacob Gould Schurman (President) and Charles Denby, Dean C. Worcester, Dewey, and Otis (members). Cf. Jacob Gould Schurman, Philippine Affairs: A Retrospect and Outlook (New York: Charles Scribner's Sons, 1902), esp. pp. 2-7.

11. See the minutes of meetings of the Aguinaldo and Otis Commissions in January, 1899, generously printed in Agoncillo, Malolos, pp. 438-49, and the findings of the Schurman Commission in its Report, Vol. I, esp. Ch. II of Part IV. While discounting Filipino aspirations for independence, the Commission nevertheless indicated that the Filipinos wanted a protectorate.

12. Hay to Schurman, May 5, 1899, Schurman Commission Report, I, 9. Probably because the Treaty of Paris had yet to be ratified when the Commission was established, it was instructed to report to the Secretary of State, unlike the Taft Commission which, as we shall presently see, reported to the Secretary of War.

13. Ibid.

14. Ibid., pp. 6-7.

15. Agoncillo, Malolos, pp. 516-18. The conservatives in the Malolos Republic had decided to accept the Hay Plan, but General Antonio Luna, an irreconcilable like Mabini, arrested a commission which was to have informed the Schurman Commission of the desires of the Pedro A. Paterno-Felipe Buencamino Cabinet.

16. Schurman Commission Report, I, 185.

17. As paraphrased by Leech, op. cit. , p. 408.

18. Schurman Commission Report, I, 90.

19. Ibid. Italics mine.

20. McKinley to the Secretary of War, April 7, 1900, in U. S. , War Department, Annual Reports for the Fiscal Year Ended June 30, 1900, Vol. I: Report of the Secretary of War (Washington, D. C. , U. S. Government Printing Office, 1900), Pt. 1, Appendix B. Cited hereafter as SecWar, Report.

21. Taft to Charles P. Taft, June 12, 1900, in Ralph Eldin Minger, "Taft, MacArthur, and the Establishment of Civil Government in the Philippines, " The Ohio Historical Quarterly, LXX (October, 1961), 314. Italics mine. The Taft Commission, consisting of Taft, Luke E. Wright, Henry C. Ide, Dean C. Worcester, and Bernard Moses, arrived in the Philippines on June 3, 1900.

22. Taft to Secretary of War Elihu Root, June 12, 1900, Personal, in Wm. Howard Taft Papers (Library of Congress, Washington, D. C.). Cited hereafter as Taft Papers. A microfilmed copy of the entire Taft-Root personal correspondence during Taft's tenure in the Philippines, 1900-1903, in the Taft Papers, is in the Yale Sterling Memorial Library.

23. Taft Commission Report, p. 35.

24. The Democratic Party platform for 1900 promised an immediate declaration of American purpose to grant the Filipinos independence, and William Jennings Bryan, the Democratic presidential candidate, promised that, if victorious, he would immediately convene the American Congress to enact a law making the Philippines an American protectorate. Maximo M. Kalaw, The Development of Philippine Politics (1872-1920) (Manila: Oriental Commercial Company, Inc. , [1926]), p. 249.

25. Taft to Root, December 14, 1900, Taft Papers.

26. This is the American term for the Filipino-American War, and is based on the fact that the Philippine Republic of 1899 was never recognized by any power.

27. Taft to Root, loc. cit.

28. Idem, February 24, 1901, Taft Papers. For a corroboration from a military officer, see General Joseph Wheeler to President McKinley, January 1, 1900, in William McKinley Papers, Microfilms, Series 1, Reel 9. I have used the microfilmed copy of the McKinley Papers at the Yale Sterling Memorial Library.

29. The Commission undertook three provincial tours in 1901. An account of each of these trips is given by Taft in lengthy, chatty personal letters to Root on February 24, 1901; March 17, 1901; April 3, 1901; August 25, 1901; and September 2, 1901, all in the Taft Papers. See also D. R. Williams, The Odyssey of the Philippine Commission (Chicago: A. C. McClurg and Co., 1913), Chaps. IX-XIII. Williams was a private secretary to one of the Commissioners.

30. More about the Partido Federal in Chapter VIII.

31. Taft to Root, March 17, 1901, Taft Papers. Cf. Williams, op. cit., pp. 136-37.

32. Taft to Roosevelt, May 12, 1901, Taft Papers.

33. Morgan, op. cit., pp. 432-33.

34. See also ibid., pp. 442-43, and Minger, loc. cit., for the Taft-MacArthur controversy over the replacement of the military regime.

35. General Arthur MacArthur, father of the late General of the Army Douglas MacArthur, succeeded General Otis as Military Governor in June, 1900. He resigned in 1901.

36. Root to McKinley, January 24, 1901, in Taft Commission Report, p. 7.

37. U. S., Statutes, XXXI, 895. The "Spooner Amendment" ratified all acts of the President in administering the Philippines under his war powers and also empowered him to proceed further with the organization of the Philippine government until Congress could formulate policy.

38. U. S., War Department, Five Years of the War Department... 1899-1903, as shown in the Annual Reports

of the Secretary of War (Washington, D. C. , U. S. Government Printing Office, [1904?]) p. 208. The military
probably enjoyed one last laugh at the eagerness of the
Commission to take over when in less than two weeks, the
provinces of Cebu, Batangas and Bohol had to be returned
to military rule, no doubt for more intensive pacification
by force. SecWar, Reports, 1901 (3 vols.), I, Pt. 1, p.
15. This is the Report of the Philippine Commission, 1901,
and will henceforth be cited as such.

    39. For the text of the order, see Five Years of the
War Department, p. 257.

    40. Ibid. , p. 258.

    41. Reverend Charles W. Briggs to Reverend Henry
C. Mabie, Secretary of the American Baptist Missionary
Union, in The Boston Transcript, April 7, 1902. Clipping
forwarded by Mabie to John Hay, in U. S. National Archives,
Record Group 350: Records of the former Bureau of Insular
Affairs Relating to the Philippines - Selected Documents,
1898-1946, File Number 364, Incls. 29 and 30. Since all
materials in the U. S. National Archives used in this study
belong to Record Group 350, all subsequent citations will
simply be as follows: NA, 364 (or other, for file number),
30 (or other, for inclosure number).

    For a guide to a bulk of these records of materials,
see Kenneth Munden, comp. , Records of the Bureau of
Insular Affairs Relating to the Philippine Islands, 1898-
1935: A List of Selected File (Special List No. 2) (Washington, D. C. , The National Archives, 1942).

    42. For the first reports of these governors, many of
whom were American military officers, see U. S. , Congress, Senate, Committee on the Philippines, Hearings,
Affairs in the Philippine Islands, 57th Cong. , 1st Sess. ,
1902, Senate Doc. 331, Pt. 1, pp. 190-214; 349-62; 429-
504. Cited hereafter simply as Senate Doc. 331. The
report of the governor of Rizal province is in SecWar,
Reports, 1902, Vol. X: Report of the Philippine Commission (Washington, D. C. U. S. Government Printing Office,
1903), Pt. 1, Exhibit B. Hereafter Philippine Commission
Report.

    For an assessment of the military government, see
Charles Burke Elliott, The Philippines: To the End of the

Military Regime (Indianapolis: The Bobbs-Merrill Company, 1916).

43.   Public No. 235, in U. S. Statutes, XXX, 691-712. Technically speaking, the Philippines Bill was the foundation of American policy until it was superseded by the Jones Law in 1916, Public 240, in ibid. , XXXIX, 545.

44.   For American tariff policy, laid down in 1902 and 1909, see Chapter VII, infra, pp. 121-126.

45.   Schurman Commission Report, I, 82.

46.   Ibid. , p. 120. Italics mine. This was the primary motive behing the Commission's having recommended the adoption of the Hay Plan.

47.   Ibid. , p. 84.

48.   The Schurman Commission's four-volume Report consisted, first, of a study of the political history and government of the Philippines on the eve of the American Occupation. This portion of the Report was based largely on government decrees, some of which were never carried out. In some respects, therefore, the description of the government was not very realistic. The exposition on the aspirations of the Filipinos was based on interviews with leading residents of Manila — like Cayetano Arellano, Jose Albert and Felipe Calderon — with a few foreign residents and, to a lesser extent, with a commission from the Philippine Republic. It was also based on several constitutional programmes of the Filipinos, including one prepared specifically at the Commission's request. The Commission's treatment of the friar question is one of the weakest points of the Report; the Commission did not investigate the charges or grievances of the Filipinos against the friars, although it made recommendations which were later adopted, of which more will be said in the latter part of this chapter. Finally, the Commission's Report included treatises on Philippine geography, agriculture, resources, etc. , prepared by the Jesuits.

49.   On this point, the Taft Commission was to make further investigations and make recommendations to the Secretary of War. See Letter of Instructions.

50.   W. Cameron Forbes, The Philippine Islands (2 vols. ; Boston: Houghton Mifflin Company, 1928), II, 160. See also Crunder and Livezey, op. cit. , p. 63.

51. Philip C. Jessup, Elihu Root (2 vols.; New York: Dodd, Mead and Company, 1938), I, 345.

52. A newly published work on Philippine-American relations only somewhat inconspicuously mentions the Letter of Instructions. George E. Taylor, The Philippines and the United States: Problems of Partnership (New York; Council on Foreign Relations, 1964), p. 61.

53. Forbes claims (op. cit., I, 130, n. 2) that in 1912 Taft had told him that it was "probably" Ide who made the suggestion regarding the Commission's control of the purse strings. Henry F. Pringle used Forbes' account for his treatment of the background of the Instructions. The Life and Times of William Howard Taft (2 vols.; New York: Farra and Rinehart, Inc., 1939), I, 182. Dean C. Worcester, unfortunately, is silent on this point. The Philippines: Past and Present, ed. [Joseph] Halston Hayden (2 vols.; new ed.; New York: The Macmillan Company, 1930).

I am inclined to believe what Taft wrote to LeRoy, if only because he was closer to the event in 1905 than in 1912. It is also possible that Forbes misquoted Taft. The importance of the power to appropriate money as a leverage against the Military Governor, who was to continue as executive for some time, was probably uppermost in Taft's mind.

54. Taft to LeRoy, December 1, 1905, Personal, Taft Papers. A typewritten copy of the Instructions is in the McKinley Papers, Microfilm, Series 1, Reel 9. See Appendix for the text.

55. Supra, p. 30. See also Taft to Root, March 17, 1901, loc. cit.

56. See Appendix of this study.

57. See Leech, op. cit., p. 408; Morgan, op. cit., p. 436; and supra, p. 29.

58. Supra, p. 28.

59. Schurman Commission Report, I, 111 and 121.

60. Ibid., p. 111.

61. Philippine Commission Report, 1901, Pt. 1, p. 21.

62. Ibid., p. 22.

63. Taft to Lodge, October 21, 1901, Taft Papers.

64. Senate Doc. 331, Pt. 1, p. 333.

65. Wright to Clarence Edwards, February 20, 1902, in Clarence R. Edwards Papers (Massachusetts Historical Society, Boston, Massachusetts). Hereafter cited simply as Edwards Papers. Colonel Edwards was then Chief of the Bureau of Insular Affairs of the War Department.

66. So claims Representative Henry A. Cooper, Chairman of House Committee on Insular Affairs and co-sponsor of the Philippine Bill, in a confidential letter to Taft, dated September 27, 1902, in the Taft Papers.

67. Taft to Lodge, March 26, 1902, in Elihu Root Papers (Library of Congress, Washington, D. C.). Cited hereafter as Root Papers.

68. U. S., Bureau of the Census, Census of the Philippine Islands taken under the Direction of the Philippine Commission in the Year 1903 (4 vols.; Washington: U. S. Government Printing Office, 1905). Cited hereafter as Census of 1903.

69. For a brief discussion on the Assembly as a political institution, see infra, pp. 61-65.

70. "I can well remember," Secretary of War Taft told the members of the First Philippine Assembly in 1907, "when that section [on the Assembly] was drafted in the private office of Mr. Root in his house in Washington. Only he and I were present. I urged the wisdom of the concession and he yielded to my arguments and the section as then drafted differed but little from the form it has to-day. It was embodied in a bill presented to the House and passed by the House, was considered by the Senate, was stricken out in the Senate, and was only restored after a conference, the Senators in the conference consenting to its insertion with great reluctance. I had urged its adoption upon both committees, and, as the then governor of the islands, had to assume a responsibility as guarantor in respect to it which I have never sought to disavow." Excerpt from "Address Before the Inaugural Session of the Philippine Assembly," October 16, 1907, in Philippine Commission Report, 1907, Pt. 1, p. 224. See also P. I., Legislature, Philippine Commission, Journal of the Philippine Commission, 1st Leg., Inaug. Sess., 1907, p. 30. Hereafter cited as Commission Journal.

71. Philippine Commission Report, 1901, Pt. 1, pp. 22-23.

72. Taft to Lodge, October 21, 1901, loc. cit.

73. Although the Philippines was represented in the Spanish Cortes in 1810-1813, 1820-1823, and 1834-1837, the delegates were all Spaniards, who could not by any means claim to represent Filipino (i. e., native) interests. And even if they had represented Filipino interests, such representation was withdrawn in 1837.

For the best discussion on the representation of the Philippines in the Spanish Cortes, see Gregorio Y. Yabes, "The Philippine Representation in the Spanish Cortes," PSSR, VIII (February, 1936), 36-67 and (June, 1936), 140-60. See also Roberto A. Regala, "The Development of Representation in the Philippines," Philippine Law Journal, X (September, 1931), 81-88; and James Alexander Robertson, "The Evolution of Representation in the Philippine Islands," The Journal of Race Development, VI, (October, 1915), 160-61.

74. The Resident Commissioners' salaries and other expenses were borne by the Philippine treasury, but they enjoyed the franking privileges of members of Congress. Originally, they served for two years; this was increased to four by law of February 15, 1911 (U. S., Statutes, XXXVI, 910), with the additional stipulation that they were to remain in office "until their successors shall have been duly elected and qualified."

The Resident Commissioners who served during the Taft Era were: Honorable Benito Legarda (1907-1911); Honorable Pablo Ocampo (1907-1909); Honorable Manuel Luis Quezon (1909-1916); and Honorable Manuel Barnshaw (1912-1917). See Forbes, op. cit., II, 140, n. 2.) Legarda served longer than his first colleague, Ocampo, because the Assembly and the Commission could not agree on a common replacement, or for that matter as to whether he should be replaced at all. The Commission was for Legarda, but the Assembly was not.

75. For Quezon's appraisal of his activities as a Resident Commissioner, see his autobiography, entitled The Good Fight (New York: D. Appleton-Century Company, Inc., 1946), pp. 117-30. Quezon later became the first Senate President of the Jones Law Legislature in 1916 and also the first President of the Philippine Common-

wealth in 1935. He held the latter position until his death
at Saranac, New York, on August 1, 1944.

76. For a discussion of the Northwest Ordinance of
July 13, 1787, and its bearing upon the Philippine policy
of the United States, see Nicolas Zafra, "The Northwest
Territory and the Ordinance of 1787," PSSR, XIII (February, 1941), 1-29.

Out of the Northwest Territory emerged the present
states of Ohio, Indiana, Illinois, Michigan, Wisconsin,
and a portion of Minnesota.

77. Philippine Commission Report, 1902, Pt. 1, p. 5.

78. One of the limitations on the Assembly's powers
and prerogatives as the lower and more popular chamber
of a democratic legislature was its lack of power to with-
hold appropriations, which neutralized the chamber's
potentiality as a leverage for extracting concessions from
the government. The Philippine Bill provided for the
automatic re-enactment of the budget of the current year
should the Legislature (i. e. , Commission and Assembly)
fail to enact one for the next year. "I think this last provision necessary," wrote Taft, "to prevent a choking of
the government by people unused to legislative power and
drunk with the thought that they could hold the government
up. " Taft to Lodge, October 21, 1901, loc. cit. , and Taft
to Root, September 26, 1901, Taft Papers. Taft's original
proposal for the Assembly provided for the enactment by
the Commission of the budget should the Assembly fail to
pass one.

79. General Smith arrived in the Philippines with the
First California Volunteers as Colonel in 1898. After
successful work as Military Governor of Negros and Collector of Customs of Manila, he was discharged from the
Army as Brigadier-General in June, 1901, and appointed
as an associate justice of the Philippine Supreme Court.
He became a member of the Commission and Secretary of
Public Instruction in 1903 and in September, 1906, was
appointed Governor-General of the Philippines, serving
in the latter capacity until he resigned in November, 1909,
to become a Judge of the United States Court of Customs
Appeal, Washington, D. C. Forbes, op. cit. , II, 411 n.

80. In this respect, Smith was like his fellow army

officers who believed in pacification by the Krag rifle (the
standard arm of the United States Army from 1892 to 1898,
i.e., a military rather than civil government).

81. Smith to Taft, October 7, 1907, Edwards Papers.
Italics mine. However, Worcester, who served as Secretary of Interior from 1901 to 1913, believes that the early
concession of the Assembly was a mistake, since it had
failed to gain the good-will and cooperation of many members of the elite. Worcester-Hayden, op. cit., pp. 545-46.
We must accept Worcester's words with caution. He
was writing in 1913, after five years as probably the
"ugliest" American to the Nacionalistas because of his
suits against El Renacimiento, for which he was awarded
₱25,000 in damages and the owner and editor convicted.

82. Juan Sumulong, "The Philippine Problem From
A Filipino Standpoint," The North American Review,
CLXXIX (December, 1904), 862.

83. For the policy of the Malolos Government regarding the friars and their lands, see supra, pp. 19-22.

84. For the Faribault Plan, see infra, p. 78.

85. Cf. Clifford, op. cit., p. 316.

86. U.S., War Department, Report of Major General
E.S. Otis....On Military Operations and Civil Affairs in
the Philippine Islands, 1899 (Washington, D.C., U.S.
Government Printing Office, 1899), pp. 22-28. See also
Wolff, op. cit., p. 142 and Agoncillo, Malolos, p. 248.

87. Article VIII of the treaty reads as follows: "And
it is hereby declared that the relinquishment, or cession
[of the Philippines], can not in any respect impair the
property or rights which by law beong to the peaceful possession of property of all kinds, of...ecclesiastical or
civic bodies,...having legal capacity to acquire and possess property in the aforesaid territories, renounced, or
ceded, or of private individuals, of whatsoever nationality
such individuals may be." Italics mine.

88. Schurman Commission Report, Vol. I, pp. 130-
36. The Commission did not even bother to investigate
the charges lodged by the Filipinos against the friars.

89. Ibid., p. 131.

90. Ibid.

91. Ibid.

92. Italics mine. For Root's Instructions, see the Appendix of this study.

93. "In the assignment of subjects" among the Commissioners, Taft wrote, "the most delicate matter of the whole lot — the friar question — has fallen to me. I made the assignment myself so that I have no reason to complain of it. " Taft to Horace Taft, September 8, 1900, quoted in Pringle, op. cit. , I, 221. Taft probably wanted to establish right away his popularity among the Filipino elite, knowing that this was one question in which they had an absorbing interest, for he seems to have made up his mind even before the hearings began that the friars would have to go. This is shown by his letter to Mrs. Wm. H. Taft seven days after arriving in Manila: "If there is one fact that is settled by all the evidence [sic] it is that these friars will be killed if they go back [to their parishes] and some other provision must be made for the spiritual control of the inhabitants. " Taft to Mrs. Taft, June 10, 1900, in ibid. , I, 177-78. Italics mine.

94. See Lands Held for Ecclesiastical Uses.

95. Taft Commission Report, p. 30. Cf. Catholic Chaplain E. J. Vattman to John Ireland, Archbishop of St. Paul, Minn. , December 31, 1902, original in NA, 1318-11. Father Vattman, after a rather extensive trip through the Visayan Islands, confirmed the findings of the Taft Commission.

96. Taft to Mrs. Bellany Storer, December 4, 1900, transmitting a copy of the hearings, as yet unpublished, quoted in John T. Farrell, "Background of the 1902 Taft Mission to Rome--I, " The Catholic Historical Review, XXXVI (April, 1950), 25. This is a well-documented article.

97. Taft Commission Report, p. 30. But see Vattman, loc. cit. , who claims that American priests would be unwelcome, for, in his words, "the hatred of the people, or shall I say of the native Priests, towards all Friars, good and evil alike, is intense. . . . For that reason it will be a long time before any Friars, no matter of what nationality, will be welcomed by the Priest and people of the Philippines. " Italics mine.

98. Ibid. , p. 29.

99. Ibid. , p. 31. The Commission could never admit that the Filipinos were also against Americans because they were opposing their aspirations for independence.

100. Ibid. , p. 32.

101. Philippine Commission Report, 1901, Pt. 1, p. 25.

102. Taft To Root, September 26, 1901, loc. cit. See also my comment above, p. 90, n. 99.

103. Frederick J. Zwierlein, Theodore Roosevelt and Catholics, 1882-1919 (Rochester, N.Y.: Printed for the Reverend Victor T. Suren by the Art Print Shop, 1956), p. 35.

104. See infra, p. 99 and n. 14.

105. Papal Secretary Mariano Cardinal Rampolla to Archbishop Ireland, May 23, 1901, in James H. Moynihan, The Life of Archbishop John Ireland (New York: Harp and Brothers, 1953), p. 180.

106. Farrell, I, loc. cit. , pp. 6-7. Mrs. Maria Storer, wife of American Minister Bellamy Storer, was a very close friend of Taft and Roosevelt; her nephew later married Roosevelt's daughter, Alice Roosevelt. At the time, Mrs. Storer was trying to get a red hat for Archbishop Ireland and was also serving as Taft's unofficial go-between with the Vatican over Church questions in the Philippines.

107. Zwierlein, op. cit. , p. 40.

108. Roosevelt to Root, December 7, 1901, in The Letters of Theodore Roosevelt, ed. Elting Morison et al. , (8 vols. ; Cambridge, Mass. : Harvard University Press, 1951-1954), III, 189. Cited hereafter as Roosevelt Letters.

109. Taft left the Philippines in late December, 1901, to recuperate from a serious illness and operations. Pringle, op. cit. , I, 214-18.

110. Zwierlein, op. cit. , p. 43; Pringle, op. cit. , I, 225-26.

111. It is in the Taft Papers.

112. Smith was included in the mission because Roosevelt thought that, being a Catholic, he might be useful. Then a member of the Philippine Supreme Court, Smith later became Governor-General (1906-1909). Cf.

supra, n. 79 of this chapter. A biography of General Smith
is in preparation. Interview with Mrs. Lillian Smith Berg,
General Smith's granddaughter, July 6, 964, Tacoma,
Washington.

113. Zwierlein, op. cit. , p. 43; Moynihan, op. cit. , p.
183; Farrell, II, loc. cit. , p. 14.

114. Roosevelt to St. Clair McKelway, April 1, 1902,
in Roosevelt Letters, III, 251.

115. Cf. Pringle, op. cit. , I, 228, wherein the year
appears as 1901! This is evidently a misprint.

116. Root to Taft, May 9, 1902, Taft Papers. This
letter contains the instructions to the Taft Mission.

117. Taft to Root, July 22, 1902, Taft Papers. This
is an unofficial, supplementary account of the Rome negotiations.

118. See infra, p. 113, and p. 151.

Chapter IV

1. Julius Pratt, America's Colonial Experiment: How
the United States Governed, And in Part Gave Away A
Colonial Empire (New York: Prentice-Hall, Inc. , 1950),
p. 200.

2. "The visitor to the Philippines, " wrote a Harvard
professor who visited the Philippines in 1909, "is impressed with the feeling that the Americans in the island
are all engaged in a great missionary enterprise; that they
are setting themselves to the problme of elevating a people;
that they are spending energy, money and governmental
force for the benefit of /the Filipino/ people. . . . " Albert
Bushnell Hart, The Obvious Orient (New York: D. Appleton
and Company, 1911), p. 269. See also Joseph Ralston
Hayden, The Philippines: Study in National Development
(New York: The Macmillan Company, 1955), pp. 575-76.

3. Charles Burke Elliott, The Philippines: To The
End of the Commission Government — A Study in Tropical
Democracy (Indianapolis: The Bobbs-Merrill Company,
1917), p. 401. Hereafter, this second volume on the
Philippines by Elliott will simply be cited as Elliott, Com-
mission Government.

4. I have discussed this point more fully in Chapter
VIII of this work.

5. Taft to John N. Blair, March 16, 1905, NA, 364-73 [Copy]. Cf. infra, p. 155.

6. Taft made this point very clear in his letter to the Rt. Rev. William Lawrence, Episcopal Bishop of Massachusetts, when he wrote: "When we shall have made a successful government, when we shall have developed and educated the people, when we shall have created an independent opinion... [and] if America follows her duty.... I do not think that the Filipino people will [ever] desire to sever the bonds between us and them. " Taft to Lawrence, February 16, 1904, Taft Papers. See also General Arthur MacArthur's remarks in his report for 1901, to the effect that "in due time, and beyond any question, if beneficent republican institutions are permitted to operate in full force, the Filipino people will become warmly attached to the United States by a sense of self-interest and gratitude. " U. S. , War Department, Annual Reports of the War Department For the Year Ended June 30, 1901. Vol I, Pt. 4: Report of the Lieutenant-General Commanding the Army (Washington, D. C. , U. S. Government Printing Office, 1901), Pt. 2, p. 98, [hereafter, MacArthur, Report].

7. U. S. , War Department, Special Report of Wm. H. Taft to the President on the Philippines (Washington, D. C. , U. S. Government Printing Office, 1908), p. 74. Hereafter cited simply as Taft, Special Report.

8. This made American policy different from those of earlier colonial powers, which had emphasized economic development, and was deprecated by Alleyne Ireland as "putting the cart before the horse. " The Far Eastern Tropics: Studies in the Administration of Tropical Dependencies (Boston: Houghton Mifflin and Company, 1905), p. 205.

9. See Pratt, op. cit. , pp. 157-64.

10. Cf. Corpus, op. cit. , p. 161.

11. Taft Commission Report, p. 15. It is obvious that Root and Taft were not completely satisfied with the findings and recommendations of the Schurman Commission: see supra, pp. 35-6.

12. Ibid. For a fuller presentation of social conditions, see Philippine Commission Report, 1901, Pt. 1, pp. 19-21. See also, Taft to Lodge, March 21, 1903, Taft Papers.

13. _Philippine Commission Report_, 1901, Pt. 1, p. 19. Italics mine.

14. _Ibid._, pp. 20-21.

15. "All of us will recognize sooner or later," wrote the Director of the Philippine Constabulary as early as 1903, "that the tendency of the administration of these islands will be towards a centralized policy, curtailing rather than extending the liberal concessions made towards local self-government." Henry T. Allen to General John A. Johnson, April 9, 1903, in Henry T. Allen Papers (Library of Congress, Washington, D.C.) Cited hereafter as Allen Papers.

16. _Op. cit._, p. 268. Hayden served as Vice-Governor of the Philippines (1933-1935) and was professor of political science at the University of Michigan. His work is still regarded as the most comprehensive and scholarly single volume on Philippine political and social development under American rule. It is rather weak, however, on the Filipino response; that was not, of course, the theme of his study. Although Hayden's conclusions and generalizations apply to the entire period of the American impact, some of them are directly relevant to the Taft Era.

17. The Municipal Code, Act No. 82, Philippine Commission, January 31, 1901. Act Nos. 1-1800 were enacted exclusively by the Philippine Commission, and Act Nos. 1801-2287 were enacted by it and the Philippine Assembly, during the Taft Era. The latter became the lower chamber of the Philippine Legislature on October 16, 1907. See P.I., Philippine Commission [after 1907, Philippine Legislature], _Public Laws Passed by the Philippine Commission [and Legislature]_ (9 vols.; Manila: Bureau of Public Printing, 1903-1915). Those exclusively enacted by the Philippine Commission may also be found in the _Annual Reports of the War Department_ (1901-1907).

18. _Philippine Commission Report_, 1901, Pt. 1, p. 20.

19. Act No. 83 (Provincial Code), Philippine Commission, February 6, 1901, as amended by Act No. 1545, Philippine Commission, October 20, 1906.

20. Taft to Root, February 8, 1901, Root Papers.

21. It is only fair to state here that the enhancement of the provincial governor's position, if not his powers, was not left unattended by the superior authorities. In 1905, following his first trip to the Philippines as Secretary of War, Taft called Governor-General Wright's attention to a matter of the "utmost importance," namely, the increase in the salary of the provincial governor to equal, at least, the salary of the provincial treasurer because, to quote Taft, "for political purposes the position of Governor is so important that he ought to feel that he is the chief officer in his province, and nothing tends so much to make him feel so as the fact that he has a larger salary than the other officials. Taft also endorsed the plan to make the Senior Inspectors of the Constabulary "harmonize with the provincial governors." Taft to Wright, September 2, 1905, Taft Papers. For the latter plan, see also Allen's Memorandum to the Chiefs of Constabulary Districts, emphasizing the role of Constabulary officers as "political agents" as more important than their functions as military officers. Allen to Taft, September 5, 1905, Taft Papers [copy.]

22. Among the methods used by the Executive Bureau to control local governments were: (1) disciplinary authority over local officials; (2) administrative review of provincial acts; (3) control over provincial budgets and limits of loans provincial and municipal governments could float; (4) supervision of property valuation for taxation purposes; and (5) administrative control, since November 1, 1905, over provincial treasurers. Hayden, op. cit., pp. 271-73. The Insular Treasurer controlled the provincial treasurers before November 1, 1905.

23. LeRoy, Philippine Life, p. 199.

24. Philippine Commission Report, 1901, Pt. 1, p. 32.

25. Senate Doc. 331, Pt. 1, p. 61.

26. A few Americans were originally appointed and later elected as provincial governors. The reports of the provincial governors, except the first (see supra, Chapter III, n. 42), are appended to the annual reports of the Executive Secretary to the Governor-General, and are included in the yearly Reports of the Philippine Commission.

27. See, for instance, Commissioner W. Cameron Forbes to H. L. Higginson, February 13, 1905, in W.

Cameron Forbes Papers (The Houghton Library of Harvard University, Cambridge, Massachusetts). Cited hereafter as Forbes Papers. See also Taft, Special Report, pp. 31-37.

28. Philippine Commission Report, 1908, Pt. 1, p. 418.

29. Ibid. , p. 341.

30. Philippine Commission Report, 1907, Pt. 1, p. 293.

31. Ibid. , p. 287.

32. Ibid. , p. 271.

33. A highly critical judgment on the record of provincial and municipal governments during the Taft Era is given by D. R. Williams in his The United States and the Philippines (Garden City, N.Y.: Doubleday, Page and Company, 1924), p. 137: "Possibly the best illustration of the disillusion suffered by our authorities in their early estimate of Filipino governmental capacity, is found in the Municipal Code and Provincial Government Acts. Taking these laws as first enacted, and then studying the amendments successively added thereto, it will be found how, with further experience, the unpreparedness of the people for the measure of local control originally bestowed became apparent, and how various powers were gradually withdrawn and vested in the central government and in responsible American heads of departments. This action resulted not only from the ignorance and inexperience of the masses, . . . but from a prevailing disposition of the dominant few to. . . use their authority for personal rather than public ends. " Williams liked the Filipinos but did not think they were entitled to an early independence, and his critical remarks must be seen in that context. Thus, he wrote Edwards in 1911 of a work he had completed, the last chapter of which might help "counteract independence agitation in the United States. " Would the Chief of the Bureau of Insular Affairs please help get the work published by a "reputable" publisher? Edwards, however, politely and wisely declined to do so. Williams to Edwards, November 1, 1911, and Edwards to Williams, January 24, 1912, both in NA, 3849-47.

Williams' book (Odyssey, op. cit.) was eventually

published in 1913, but was considerably milder in tone than
his later book. Significantly, his later book was published
in 1924, at the height of Governor-General Leonard Wood's
controversy with the Filipino leaders, particularly Quezon,
who renewed the agitation for independence if only to end
Wood's regime.

Williams, by the way, was Secretary of the Philippine
Commission in 1901 and was appointed associate judge of
the Court of Land Registration in 1903, but resigned in
1905 to engage in private practice in Manila. Forbes, op.
cit., II, 382, n. 1.

34. The three Filipinos became members of the Commission on September 1, 1901. Taft had wanted an earlier
date, but Wright and Ide were hesitant on the ground that
necessary interpretation might delay action on important
legislation, such as the civil and criminal codes. Taft to
Root, June 25, 1901, Taft Papers.

35. Same to same, April 12, 1901, loc. cit. Taft's
original proposal for five, later reduced to four, Filipino
members of the Commission did not meet with the other
Commissioners' approval, particularly Wright and Moses'.
The result was that only three Filipinos were appointed to
the Commission. Idem, April 3, 1901, and June 25, 1901,
loc. cit. See also, Pringle, op. cit., I, 205.

36. "I... know that [Forbes], Wright, and Ide constitute a majority of the Commission...," Taft told his wife
after his first Philippine visit as Secretary of War in 1905.
This is rather odd since there were eight members of the
Commission! Taft to Mrs. Wm. H. Taft, September 24,
1905, Taft Papers.

37. See supra, p. 141-42 and 144-46.

38. For the role of political elites in nation-building,
see Karl W. Deutsch, Nationalism and Social Communication: An Inquiry into the Foundations of Nationality (Cambridge, Mass.: Technology Press, and New York: John
Wiley and Sons, 1953).

39. Moro Province (consisting of Sulu, Cotabato,
Davao, Lanao, and Zamboanga) and other provinces which
contained a majority of other non-Christian Filipinos, were
organized as special provinces over which the Philippine
Commission exercised exclusive lawmaking prerogatives

throughout the Taft Regime.

40. For a list of the members of the First Philippine Assembly, see Philippine Commission Report, 1907, Pt. 1, pp. 50-51.

41. Public No. 376, U. S. , Statutes, XXXVI, 910.

42. In 1911 the date was changed to October 16.

43. See James A. Robertson, "The Extraordinary Session of the Philippine Legislature and the Work of the Philippine Assembly, " American Political Science Review, IX (November, 1910), 516-36.

44. See P. I. , Legislature, Philippine Assembly, Diario de sesiones de la Asamblea Filipina (11 vols. to 1916, when it became the House of Representatives of the Jones Law Legislature). Henceforth, cited simply as Diario de sesiones, Vol. I, etc.

The Philippine Commission kept a record of its own proceedings in English and Spanish. There are nine volumes of the Commission Journal until 1916, when the Commission was replaced by the Philippine Senate, an all-Filipino body, by the Jones Law Legislature.

45. Regala, loc. cit. , p. 65.

46. Gregorio Nieva, "The Philippine Assembly, " in M. M. Norton (ed.), Builders of a Nation: A Series of Biographical Sketches (Manila: n. p. , [1914], p. 84. Mr. Nieva later became a member of the Second Philippine Assembly (1910-1912).

47. See Table 12, infra, p. 162.

48. Hayden (op. cit. , p. 170, et seq.) gives a more or less detailed discussion of most of these factors.

49. See infra, pp. 168-72.

50. Hayden, op. cit. , p. 173.

51. Ibid. , p. 172.

52. Secretary of War Taft was responsible for this policy, when he said in a speech at the Army and Navy Club in Manila on October 19, 1907: ''I am going to make an order. . . that the Governor-General shall be first and the Speaker of the House [Assembly] shall be second. '' Quoted in Forbes, op. cit. , II, 92, n. 2.

53. Even before the organization of the Assembly, Governor Smith showed every indication of conciliating the Nacionalistas by not confining important appointments to

the Progresistas (old Federalistas). To do otherwise, he
said, ''would only serve to alienate the friendship of many
good men who had by force of circumstances allied themselves with the extremists and that the personal influence
of members of the Commission with many members of the
Assembly would be lost, ... '' Smith to Commissioner
Morgan W. Shuster, May 20, 1907, Confidential, Edwards
Papers.

54.   Elliott, Commission Government, p. 125. Note
also the following entry in Elliott's ''Diary'' when he was
a Commissioner and Secretary of Commerce and Police:
''The fact is that the Govgen takes all his policies, so far
as handling the natives is concerned, from [Executive
Secretary Frank H.] Carpenter, who is certainly an expert
so far as getting certain immediate results goes. [Forbes]
regards the policy of extreme conciliation as necessary
under the general plan outlined by McKinley and carried
out by Taft, ... '' (Entry for August 1, 1911), in Charles
Burke Elliott Papers (Library of Congress, Washington,
D. C.)

Forbes' own words support Elliott's: ''In closing, ''
he advised Vice-Governor Newton Gilbert when he was
preparing for an extended leave in the United States in
1912, ''I want to say one word about the Assembly. I may
be wrong, but I am firmly of the conviction that what Mr.
Taft speaks of as the policy of attraction is the only way
of handling the Assembly. '' Forbes to Gilbert, March 12,
1912, Personal and Confidential, Forbes Papers.

55.   I have discussed the development of Philippine
political parties more fully in connection with the issue of
independence. See infra, pp. 156-61.

56.   See infra, pp. 153-56.

57.   Legarda to Taft, April 15, 1907, Personal, Taft
Papers.   English translation.

58.   For contemporary observations on the composition of the major parties in 1906-1907, see, among others,
David J. Doherty to Taft, August 17, 1906, Taft Papers;
General Smith to Taft, September 24, 1906, loc. cit. ;
Carpenter to Edwards, September 6, 1907, Confidential,
loc. cit. ; and Col. H.H. Bandholtz to Allen, May 16, 1907,
loc. cit., and same to Taft, December 5, 1906, loc. cit.

59. Onofre D. Corpuz, "Western Colonisation and the Filipino Response," Journal of Southeast Asian History, III (March, 1962), 13.

60. The most conspicuous recent examples of this "party mobility" in Philippine politics are the defections of the late Ramon Magsaysay from the Liberal Party to the Nacionalista Party in 1953 to become the latter's successful presidential candidate that year, and of Senate President Ferdinand Marcos, also from the Liberal Party, to become the Nacionalista Party presidential candidate this year. Magsaysay was Secretary of Defense in the Liberal administration of President Elpidio Quirino before he became a Nacionalista; Marcos was, until late last year, the president of the Liberal Party and had been instrumental in President Diosdado Macapagal's victory over then President Carlos P. Garcia of the Nacionalista Party in the elections of 1961. Vice President Emmanuel Pelaez, also now a Nacionalista, had been twice a Liberal.

61. It is only fair to point out that Taft, then Secretary of War, considered appointing Gregorio Araneta as the first Filipino secretary of an executive department as early as 1906, but he apparently wanted to do so without altering the existing 5:3 ratio of Americans and Filipinos in the Commission. He thought that Tavera ought to give way, but the latter indicated in so many words that he did not want to leave the Commission voluntarily; Legarda and Luzuriaga would have probably reacted similarly. Since Taft did not wish to antagonize any of these early pillars of American rule in the Islands, the only solution was to increase the membership of the Commission from eight to nine. A law to that effect was passed by Congress and approved on May 11, 1908. Araneta was appointed to the Philippine Commission on June 8, 1908; in less than a month he became Secretary of Finance and Justice. See Taft to Governor Ide, January 22, 1906; Taft to LeRoy, January 22, 1906; Tavera to Taft, February 9, 1906, Personal and Confidential (translation); and Ide to Taft, March 4, 1906, all in the Taft Papers. See also, Forbes, op. cit., I, 170, and U.S., Statutes, XXXV, Pt. 1, 125 (for the law increasing Commission membership).

62. Corpuz, Bureaucracy, p. 175.

63. Ibid. , p. 165.

64. Ibid. , p. 183, prints a table showing the number of Filipinos and Americans in the service.

65. Cf. ibid. , p. 170.

66. Hayden, op. cit. , p. 94.

67. The classified civil service appointments in theory applied to appointments from Bureau Chiefs down, but in practice, positions from bureau chief up, and judge-ships, were filled up by the Governo-General with the advice and consent of the Commission (Corpuz, Bureaucracy, pp. 163, 165-67). Where Filipinos were appointed to any of these positions, like Araneta as Attorney-General (not a cabinet post), political considerations were probably determinative. The mayorship of Manila was a good example of a purely political appointment; it was originally held by Arsenio Cruz Herrera, president of the Partido Federal, until 1905 (see Chapter VII, n. 89.)

68. Forbes, op. cit. , I, 315.

69. Cf. Eugene A. Gilmore, "The Development of Law in the Philippines, " Iowa Law Review, XVI (June, 1931), 465-79.

70. Root to Judge W. W. Howe, September 11, 1899, in Jessup, op. cit. , I, 346. "It seems to me too clear, " the author of the Letter of Instructions wrote, ". . . that we should start with the statutes which have already been adapted to the insular life, and modify them only where it appears to be necessary to conform to our fundamental ideas of justice. " See also the Letter of Instructions.

71. Taft wrote: "With a few notable exceptions, there is not a [single] Filipino lawyer who could be trusted to resist the temptation of a bribe were he raised to the bench, . . . " Taft to Senator John C. Spooner, September 3, 1900, Taft Papers.

72. Taft to Hollister, May 26, 1901, loc. cit. "What is more, " Taft added, "the Filipino judges do not know what work is. They get down at eleven o'clock in the morning and stay for an hour or two and then go home and never come back in the afternoon at all. "

73. P. I. , Department of Finance and Justice, Third Annual Report of the Secretary of Finance and Justice to the Philippine Commission (Manila: Bureau of Public

Printing, 1904), p. 12. Cited hereafter as P. I. Finance
and Justice, Report (followed by last year covered by
report.)

74. Ibid. , 1903, p. 17.
75. Ibid. , 1904, p. 13.
76. Philippine Commission Report, 1901, Pt. 1,
p. 86.
77. Ibid. , p. 87.
78. See Act No. 190 of the Philippine Commission,
August 7, 1901, and ibid. , p. 86. English never became
the official language of the courts during the Taft Era.
See infra, pp. 88-89.
79. Taft to Roosevelt, June 23, 1901, Taft Papers.
80. Philippine Commission Report, 1901, Pt. 1,
p. 84.
81. Corpuz, Bureaucracy, p. 162.
82. Exclusive jurisdiction over civil cases involving
amounts up to one hundred dollars and concurrent jurisdiction with Courts of First Instance with cases involving over
one hundred dollars but less then three hundred dollars.
In criminal cases, jurisdiction extended to those where the
penalty was not more than six months in jail or a fine of
one hundred dollars. Forbes, op. cit. , I, 312.
83. Until 1911, the tenure of justices of the peace
was two years; thereafter, it was "during good behavior. "
Ibid. , I, 313.
84. See Otis Report: 1899, pp. 146-47.
85. Philippine Commission Report, 1901, Pt. 1,
p. 77.
86. Chief Justice Arellano gave the following observation in 1905: "Even among that class of persons in these
Islands who are fairly well educated, I do not believe that
we could expect them to have the stability of judgment
which would be necessary for them to pass fairly and
justly upon the questions that a jury would have to decide. "
[U. S. Philippine Commission], Hearings before the Secretary of War and the Congressional Party. . . . (Manila:
Bureau of Public Printing, 1905), pp. 103 and 104.
87. Observations by Mr. Dooley (New York: Harper
and Brothers, 1906), p. 119. Edited, the above reads:
"I have not considered it advisable to introduce any

fads like trial by jury of your peers into my administration.
Plain straight-forward dealing is my motto. A Filipino at
his best has only learned half his duty to mankind. He can
by tried but he can't try his fellow man. It takes him too
long. '' Philip Dunne (ed.), Mr. Dooley Remembers: The
Informal Memoirs of Finley Peter Dunne (Boston: Little,
Brown and Company, 1963), p. 294.

    88. Forbes, op. cit. , I, 307. Italics mine.

    89. Hayden, op. cit. , pp. 245-47. Hayden speaks very
highly of the performance of the early Filipino jurists and
their American colleagues in the Courts of First Instance
and the Supreme Court.

    90. Ibid. , pp. 248-49.

    91. Taft to Lodge, March 21, 1903, Taft Papers.

    92. Taft, Special Report, pp. 25, 35, and 36.

    93. Ibid. , p. 24.

Chapter V

    1. See Appendix of this work.

    2. "Our educational problems in the Philippines are
comparatively simple, " wrote a former member of the
Philippine Commission, "in fact, they are mostly financial. '' Elliott, Commission Government, p. 250.

    3. The University moved to its present campus at
Diliman, Quezon City in 1949, the present writer being
among the "Diliman pioneers. ''

    4. The transport Thomas discharged some 600
American teachers at Manila on August 23, 1901. The
experiences of some of the Thomasites have been collected
in a handy volume, entitled Tales of the American Teachers
in the Philippines, ed. Geronima T. Pecson and Maria
Racelis (Manila: Carmelo and Bauermann, Inc. , 1959).
See, in particular, the contribution by Dr. Amparo Santa-
maria Lardizabal, "Pioneer American Teachers and
Philippine Education, '' pp. 81-118. See also Mary H.
Fee, A Woman's Impressions of the Philippines (Chicago:
A. C. McClurg and Co. , 1910). Miss Fee was originally
assigned to a town in Capiz, on Panay Island, in the
Visayas.

    5. For a brief discussion of the educational system

under Spain, see supra, pp. 10-11.

6. Cf. Fr. Vattman to Archbishop Ireland, December 31, 1902, NA, 1318-11. Fr. Vattman, it will be recalled, travelled extensively in the Visayas.

7. See supra, p. 22, and p. 24.

8. Actually, it should be called "Faribault and Stillwater Plan." It was an application of Archbishop Ireland's educational ideas in the towns of Faribault and Stillwater, Minn. At the time the "Plan" was adopted by the Commission in 1901, Faribault and Stillwater had already abandoned it for almost a decade. For details, see Moynihan, op. cit., pp. 84-102. The modified "Faribault Plan" is still the basis of the public school system in the Philippines today.

9. Act No. 74 of the Philippine Commission, January 21, 1901. See also Philippine Commission Report, 1901, Pt. 1, p. 134.

10. Commission Government, p. 226.

11. "Report of the Division Superintendent of Ilocos Sur and Abra for 1903," in Philippine Commission Report, 1903, Pt. 3, p. 757.

12. Harty to Ireland, March 17, 1906, in Moynihan, op. cit., p. 208, and Harty to Governor-General Henry C. Ide, February 27, 1906, NA, 1534-51. Ide was so infuriated that he asked that Harty recall his denunciatory letter, "in the interests,... of peace and harmony between the Government... on the one side, and the Church... on the other side,... " Ide to Harty, March 2, 1906, Confidential, loc. cit. For complaints about the way the Normal School and the city schools of Manila were being operated, see an earlier letter to Archbishop Ireland by R. J. O'Hanlon, a Catholic layman, dated February 25, 1902, in Moynihan, op. cit., p. 198. Dr. David P. Barrows was then Director of Education.

13. Rooker to Roosevelt, May 9, 1904, quoted in Zwierlein, op. cit., p. 115.

14. "Report of Interview Between Rt. Rev. Thomas A. Hendrick and Major Frank McIntyre," Washington, D.C., March 10, 1908, in NA, 1318-81. The following, in longhand, appears on the first page of the 31-page typescript of the report: "These notes have not been corrected, FMI."

15. The land tax and, later, a portion of the internal revenue taxes were set aside to support the public primary, intermediate, and secondary schools in the towns and provinces. Of course the taxpayer's money helped support the teachers' and technical institutes, as well as the University of the Philippines, all non-sectarian in curricula.

16. For the advent of Protestantism in the Philippines and the rise of Aglipayanism, see infra, pp. 97ff.

17. The hierarchy may have been pleased to a certain extent when General James F. Smith, a Catholic, was named Secretary of Public Instruction in 1903. Supra, Chapter III, n. 79.

18. Elliott, Commission Government, p. 226.

19. I have briefly pointed out Archbishop Ireland's role as intermediary between the Vatican on the one hand, and the United States Government (including the Philippine Commission) on the other, over the Taft Mission to the Vatican in 1902, in Chapter III, supra, pp. 49-50. For more details, see Moynihan, op. cit., pp. 177-84.

20. For these controversies, see supra, pp. 104-6.

21. Moynihan, op. cit., p. 94.

22. This was one of the reasons why the Church hierarchy hated the Federalists. Cf. Rooker to Roosevelt, loc. cit.

23. Quoted in Philippine Commission Report, 1903, Pt. 3, p. 695. Italics mine. Barrows was then General Superintendent of Education. His title was later changed to that of Director of Education.

24. "Report of the Assistant to the General Superintendent of Education, 1903," loc. cit., p. 709.

25. "Report of the School Superintendent of Cavite, 1903," loc. cit., p. 752.

26. "Report of the Assistant to the General Superintendent of Education, 1903," loc. cit., p. 707.

27. Loc. cit., p. 707.

28. "Report of the General Superintendent of Education, 1903," loc. cit., p. 694.

29. Philippine Commission Report, 1904, Pt. 3, p. 871. Italics mine.

30. Fr. McKinnon had only an "oral," i.e., informal,

appointment from General Otis as school superintendent.
See Brother V. Edmund McDevitt, F. S. C. , The First
California's Chaplain (Fresno, Calif. : Academy Library
Guild, 1956), p. 102, quoting General Otis' cable to the
Adjutant-General in Washington.

31. Ibid. , pp. 100-101. See also Forbes, op. cit. ,
I, 410, 420-23.

32. Barrows, then superintendent of city schools in
Manila, reported in May, 1901, that only a few of the
Filipino teachers had gained any knowledge of English,
"and Spanish was the only language heard in the school
buildings. " Quoted in MacArthur's Report, 1901, p. 356.

33. Philippine Commission Report, 1901, Pt. 1,
p. 133.

34. Cf. Elliott, Commission Government, p. 250.

35. Taft Commission Report, p. 109.

36. Quoted in Elmer Ellis, Mr. Dooley's America:
A Life of Finley Peter Dunne (New York: Alfred A. Knopf,
1941), pp. 117-18.

37. Cf. Taft Commission Report, p. 110; supra,
pp. 10-11.

38. Ernest J. Frei, "The Historical Development of
the Philippine National Language, " PSSHR, XV (March,
1950), 53. Frei is, I believe, more suggestive than
definitive on this point since he did not consult the official
reports, relying primarily on secondary works.

39. P. I. , Department of Public Instruction, The First
Annual Report of the Secretary of Public Instruction to the
Philippine Commission. . . 1902 (Manila: Bureau of Public
Printing, 1902), p. 25. Cited hereafter as Dept. of
Public Instruction, Report.

40. Forbes to C. E. Perkins, April 20, 1906, Forbes
Papers. Italics mine.

41. Dept. of Public Instruction, Report, 1910, p. 10.
Italics mine. See also U. S. , War Department, Special
Report of J. M. Dickinson, Secretary of War, to The
President on the Philippines (Washington, D. C. , U. S.
Government Printing Office, 1910), p. 12. Cited hereafter
as Dickinson, Special Report.

42. See Frei, loc. cit. , pp. 55-62 and 163-66.

43. Willis was Professor of Economics and Politics

at Washington and Lee University. Ford was Woodrow
Wilson's "successor in the chair of economics and government in Princeton. " Forbes, op. cit. , II, 205.

44. For highly critical observations by English
writers on American colonial policy and practice, see Mrs.
Campbell Dauncey, An English Woman in the Philippines
(New York: E. P. Dutton and Company, 1906); and Ireland,
op. cit.

45. For the pertinent correspondence, see Moorfield
Storey Papers (Library of Congress, Washington, D. C.)

46. See Henry Parker Willis, Our Philippine Problem:
A Study of American Colonial Policy (New York: Henry
Holt and Company, 1905).

47. The originals are in NA, 364-295 and 296. The
main report (hereafter Ford, "Main Report, 1913") con-
sists of 98 typewritten pages (exclusive of appendices).
The supplementary report (hereafter Ford, "Supplementary Report, 1913") is 13 pages long and is marked "Confidential. " These reports are undated, although Forbes,
who excerpted a few passages from both, believes that
they were submitted either to President Wilson or to his
Secretary of War in September, 1913 (op. cit. , II, 205).
The Ford reports were filed with the records of the former Bureau of Insular Affairs on March 6, 1915. I have,
by the way, a microfilmed copy of each of these reports.

Frei states (loc. cit. , p. 65) that "the publication of
this report [i. e. , main report] in the United States must
have started a widespread argument,... " The truth is
that except for a few excerpts of it in Forbes (op. cit. , II,
206-8), the Ford reports have never been published!

48. Willis, op. cit. , pp. 238-39.

49. Supra, pp. 83-4.

50. Ford, "Main Report, 1913, " p. 23.

51. Corpuz, Bureaucracy, pp. 182 and 184.

52. In this case, it was Ford's own son who, as an
army officer, had formerly been stationed in San Fernando,
Pampanga.

53. Diario de sesiones, I, 288. During the discussions on the bill, originally introduced by Assemblyman
Carlos Corrales of Misamis (ibid. , p. 104), Assemblyman Vicente de Vera of Sorsogon proposed that instead of

the regional dialects, Taglog be utilized as the medium of
instruction. To him, the use of the local dialects would
only accentuate what he termed "insensible regionalism. "
He proposed Tagalog as the common medium of instruction
because it was, in his view, "the most widespread native
language throughout the Philippines. " The entire membership of the Assembly, save perhaps the assemblymen from
the Tagalog provinces, shouted "No! " and the Speaker had
to rule de Vera out of order. Ibid. , p. 288.

54. Commission Journal, II, 196-99.

55. Ford, "Main Report, 1913, " p. 28.

56. Ibid. , p. 75. Ford had two meetings with
Speaker Osmena.

57. Ibid.

58. It might be pertinent to add at this point that
since the 1950's, except at the University of the Philippines
Elementary School, the Ateneo, and a few other schools
where English is the medium of instruction, the local
languages have been the media of instruction, i. e. , Iloko
in the Ilocos provinces, Tagalog in the Tagalog areas,
etc. In this case, English and Filipino (actually Tagalog)
are taught as secondary languages.

59. Supra, p. 77.   This compromise was incorporated in the new Code of Civil Procedure of 1901.

60. Philippine Commission Report, 1912, pp. 28-29.
For the previous two-year postponements, see Forbes,
op. cit. , I, 304 and II, 444. Frei (loc. cit. , pp. 51-53)
had nothing new to add to Forbes' treatment. He did not
even use the official sources.

61. El Ideal, February 7, 1912. I have used the
English translation of the clipping in the Forbes Papers.
For a similar attitude, see La Vanguardia, April 19, 1912
(clipping and translation) and El Renacimiento, July 21,
1912 (clipping and translation) in the Forbes Papers.

62. Philippine Commission Report, 1913, p. 29.
Italics mine.

63. Among these may be mentioned El Renacimiento,
La Democracia, El Ideal, La Vanguardia, El Comercio,
El Grito del Pueblo, etc. Except for the short-lived The
Renacimiento (not to be confused with El Renacimiento,
above) in 1908, no Filipino-owned newspaper was

published in the English language during the Taft Regime.
The English papers (Manila Times, Manila Daily Bulletin,
Cablenews — later Cablenews-American —, the weekly
Philippines Free Press, etc.) were American-owned. For
a survey of the Filipino and American press in the Philip-
pines during the Taft Regime, see Jesus Z. Valenzuela,
History of Journalism in the Philippine Islands (Manila:
Published by the author, 1933), pp. 123-32; 133 et passim.
See also Carson Taylor, History of the Philippine Press
(Manila: n.p., 1927), pp. 43-44, Yale Library Micro-
films, Film B 434, No. 4.

    64. Quoted in Lardizabal, loc. cit., p. 95. See also
Fee, op. cit., pp. 77-78 and chap. 14, where she des-
cribes her acting as godmother (madrina) at a wedding.

    There were, of course, the usual exceptions to the
rule. For instance, in Mambajao, Masamis (northern
Mindanao) the American teachers were deliberately driven
out. Philippine Commission Report, 1903, Pt. 3, p. 778.
In another case, that of Lock, Romblon (Visayan Islands),
the American teachers were received with "general in-
difference and some rather prominent hostility on the part
of the people and officials." Ibid., p. 805.

    65. The hardships accompanying the pacification of
Batangas are poignantly told in The Story of the Lopez
Family, ed. Eyot Canning (Boston: J.H. West Company,
1904).

    66. Philippine Commission Report, 1903, Pt. 3, p.
735. Some American teachers did get into trouble, however, especially with government officials, due to interference in local elections. Among these were James R.
Fugate in Siquijor and Jaime McLeod in Cavite. Cases
like these make the folder on education in the James F.
Smith Papers (Washington State Historical Society,
Tacoma, Washington) bulge.

    67. The vacation normal institutes were held between
April and June of each year in Manila and in the capitals
of the provinces. They were conducted by the American
teachers in those places. Philippine Commission Report,
1902, Pt. 2, p. 930, discusses the origins of the vacation
normal institutes.

    68. Ibid., p. 878.

69. It was authorized by Act No. 854, Philippine Commission, August 26, 1903. For a summary of the provisions of the act, see Philippine Commission Report, 1903, Pt. 1, p. 60. As far as I know, no adequte study on the pensionado program has been made. Only brief discussions of it are in the Census of 1903 (Vol. III, pp. 668-69), Forbes (op. cit. , I, 457-58) and Elliott (Commission Government, p. 242). The primary official sources are in the U. S. National Archives, Record Group 350. For specific files, see Munden, op. cit. , p. 28.

70. "Report of the Superintendent of Filipino Students in the United States, ... July 1, 1904, " NA, 363-104. Cited hereafter as SFSUS, "Report. " Mr. W. A. Sutherland was the first superintendent.

71. Same, "1905, " loc. cit. , 363-157. This report includes a list of the names of the first grantees, including those in 1904.

72. There were 183 pensionados in the United States in 1907 (Philippine Commission Report, 1911, p. 167), the largest number in any single year during the Taft Era. As of June, 1913, only 11 pensionados were in the United States. See Chas. G. Walcutt, Jr. , Assistant to the Chief, Bureau of Insular Affairs, to W. J. Platka, June 26, 1913, NA, 363-249.

The appointments were good for four years, unless the degree sought could be obtained in less time. Of the original pensionados, 36 were reappointed to enable them to complete their studies in either medicine or law. This meant, therefore, that until 1907, only a few annual appointments were available to fill up the authorized quota which seems to have increased each year until 1908 through curable ailments. The creation of the University of the Philippines in 1908 greatly reduced the number of pensionados. Thus, in 1909, only one new appointment was made (Leandro H. Fernandez); 4 in 1912 and 2 in 1913. See SFSUS, "Reports (1904-1913), " File 363, Incls. 104, 153, 157, 164, 178, 181, 187, 204, 223, 148 and 251, National Archives. It might be pertinent to add that one or two pensionados are still sent to the United States annually. One of them, a man of 56, was at Yale in 1955-56.

73. Elliott, Commission Government, p. 242.

74. Some of the more outstanding among the Taft Era pensionados were the following: Jorge Bocobo, who became Secretary of Public Instruction and President of the University of the Philippines; Sotaro Baluyot, Secretary of the Interior and Senator; Francisco Delgado (who got a doctorate in law at Yale), Senator and Ambassador to the United Nations; Honoria Acosta-Sison, first Filipino lady physician; Mariano de Joya, Justice of the Supreme Court; Jose Batungbacal, author; Gregorio Paredes, artist; and Leandro H. Fernandez, historian.

75. The fact that not one of the first pensionados was placed in a Catholic school was criticized and interpreted as part of the anti-Catholic policy of the United States government, so much so that Taft, then Secretary of War, had to advise Edwards of the Insular Bureau to enjoin the superintendent of students to place the future pensionados in such a way that they may be exposed, as much as possible, to the same "moral and religious surroundings" that they have had in the islands. Taft's reason, in all likelihood based upon the arguments of the Catholics, was that in the Philippines it was alright for the pupils to study in the secular public schools because they were still subject to the moral influences of their Catholic parents "and their home church" after a few hours at school. Taft to Edwards, October 17, 1904, NA, 363-135.

76. P.I., Board of Educational Survey, A Survey of the Educational System of the Philippine Islands (Manila: Bureau of Printing, 1925), pp. 322-27. The chairman of this board was Dr. Paul Monroe of Columbia University, and its work is more popularly known as the Monroe Survey; hereafter, it will be cited as such.

77. Quoted in SFSUS, "Report, 1904," NA, 363-104. Italics mine. The date of the telegram is not given. Of the first 100 grantees, 75 were distributed among the various provinces; 25 were chosen at large by the Civil Governor (Taft). Since the former were to be chosen from the public schools, the latter were probably picked from the denominational secondary schools. Cf. Philippine Commission Report, 1903, Pt. 1, p. 60.

78. Philippine Commission Report, 1903, Pt. 1, p. 60.

79.   Taft to Edwards, October 22, 1904, NA, 364-18.
It is probably correct to say that Taft relied heavily upon
Tavera's recommendations in choosing the pensionados-
at-large.

80.   It still is today.

81.   This has led the late Professor Craig to claim
that the University of the Philippines "boasts no ancient
lineage. " Austin Craig, "History of the University of the
Philippines, " in Norton (ed.), op. cit. , p. 92.

82.   The University of the Philippines was created by
Act No. 1870, Philippine Legislature, June 18, 1908.

83.   Dept. of Public Instruction, Report, 1909, p. 12.

84.   See supra, p. 91, and Table 28 of the Monroe
Survey, p. 325.

85.   See supra, p. 22.

86.   See supra, p. 71 and p. 84.

87.   For the background of United States Philippine
policy, see supra, pp. 38-43.

88.   Monroe Survey, p. 610. The College of Liberal
Arts used to be called College of Philosophy and Letters.
In 1960, it divided into the University College (first two
years) and the College of Arts and Sciences (last two
years).

89.   Taft, Special Report, p. 26.

90.   Op. cit. , p. 24. Italics mine.

91.   Ibid.

92.   Forbes to Charles W. Eliot, August 13, 1910, in
Charles W. Eliot Papers (The Houghton Library of Harvard
University, Cambridge, Massachusetts). A copy of this
letter is also in the Forbes Papers.

93.   I have discussed this subject more fully in
Chapter VII.

Chapter VI

1.   See Letter of Instructions, April 7, 1900, which is
is given as the Appendix of this work.

2.   For further discussion on this point, see supra,
pp. 45-49.

3.   For the Taft Mission to the Vatican in 1902, see
supra, pp. 49-51.

4. See supra, pp. 78-80.

5. See supra, p. 9.

6. Cf. Agoncillo, Revolt, pp. 15-16; LeRoy, Americans in the Philippines, I, 57-59. The Spanish view of the Cavite Mutiny — that it was an insurrection — is given in a contemporary account by Fr. Casimiro Herrero, Resena que demuestra el fundamento y causas de la insurreccion del 20 de enero en Filipinas (Madrid: Imp. de Segundo Martinez, 1872), esp. pp. 87-100. Actually, it was a mere mutiny of workers at the Cavite arsenal, caused by the withdrawal of privileges which they had hitherto enjoyed.

7. See supra, p. 15 and pp. 19-20.

8. For the National Church, see supra, pp. 20-21.

9. Achutegui and Bernad, op. cit., p. 137.

10. There are now many works, to which the reader is referred, dealing exclusively with the history of the Aglipayan Church or the life of its first Supreme Bishop, Father Gregorio Aglipay y Labayan. Some of these have already been cited, but it might be convenient to mention them here again, in addition to citing those which we shall mention for the first time. Among these are the following: Rivera, ''The Aglipayan Movement, '' (1937-1938); Francis H. Wise, ''The History of the Philippine Independent Church, '' (unpublished Master's thesis, Department of History, University of the Philippines, 1954); Achutegui and Bernad, Life and Church of Gregorio Aglipay, (1960); Rodriguez, Gregorio Aglipay y los origenes de la Iglesia Filipina Independiente, (1960); Clifford, ''Aglipayanism as a Political Movement, '' (MS, 1960); and Lewis Bliss Whittemore, Struggle for Freedom: History of the Philippine Independent Church (Greenwich, Connecticut: The Seabury Press, 1961).

The monographs by Achutegui and Bernad, Rodriguez, and Clifford are imposing and broadly based, but unfortunately are written from an understandably Catholic viewpoint and are derogatory to the Aglipayan Church. Whittemore's is less solid from the standpoint of research, but its insights, clear logic, and readable style make it nonetheless valuable. Furthermore, Whittemore had the benefit of conversations and correspondence with the top dignitaries of the IFI and presents their side on some aspects of the lives of Bishop Aglipay and Don Isabelo de los Reyes, Sr. , first President of the IFI Supreme Council and its early theologian. As such, Struggle for Freedom is an attempt to correct some of Achutegui's and Bernad's conclusions. But one must be a little wary of Whittemore's sympathetic treatment of the IFI. He is an Episcopalian; and his reasons for writing the way he did may be guessed from the preface of his work, which reads in part: "The General Convention of 1961 will be asked to consider a Concordat with the Philippine Independent Church which will provide for full intercommunion with this large body of Christians with the Episcopal Church in the United States. "

11. McDevitt, op. cit. , 1. 176.

12. Whittemore, op. cit. , p. 94.

13. Quoted in McDevitt, op. cit. , p. 180.

14. For the Taft Commission's recommendations on the friars, see supra, pp. 48-49. Chapelle's view of the Commission's policy was as follows:

"That the Civil Commission of the United States of these Islands has taken, unconsciously perhaps, indirectly surely, a hostile attitude toward the Catholic Church and her interests as officially represented by your humble servant is to my certain knowledge the sincere conviction of all the conservative, wise and serious minded men, both here and in America, with whom I have had the honor to have had any relations concerning this grave fact. " Chapelle to Taft, April 13, 1901, quoted in Farrell, loc. cit. (XXXVI), p. 30.

15. It is well to point out that Fr. Aglipay was born in Ilocos Norte.

16. IFI, Proceedings of the Asamblea Magna of the Iglesia Filipina Independiente (Manila: 1918), quoted in Achutegui and Bernad, op. cit. , p. 163.

17. Ibid.

18. Whittemore, op. cit. , p. 101.

19. Ibid. , pp. 101-2. Whittemore says that such "apparent indecision" revealed Fr. Aglipay's "depth of character. "

20. De los Reyes was one of the most unusual

characters of the period. An ilustrado of varied talents,
a gifted writer, and a radical (although he was not associ-
ated with the Katipunan), he was deported and imprisoned
in Montjuich, Spain in June, 1897, for having written a
sensational memorial against the friars. He was freed
when the truce of Biyak-na-Bato was signed in December,
1897. He was a member of the Madrid Junta of Filipinos
who opposed American annexation, publishing for two
years Filipinas ante Europa. He also acted as an intermediary between the Filipino clergy and the Vatican.

Soon after his return to the Philippines on October 15,
1901, a few months following Aglipay's surrender, de los
Reyes organized the first federation of workers or labor
unions in the Philippines, the Union Obrera Democrática
in Manila. Achútegui and Bernad, op. cit., Ch. IX.

21. Ibid., p. 182.

22. Whittemore, op. cit., p. 102. For Taft's personal feelings on the Vatican's reply to the objectives of
his mission, see supra, p. 50.

23. The details are given in Achútegui and Bernad,
op. cit., pp. 182-84; Whittemore, op. cit., p. 102.

24. Quoted in Achútegui and Bernad, op. cit., p. 183.

25. Rivera, loc. cit., (IX), p. 309; Achútegui and
Bernad, op. cit., p. 184.

26. Ibid., p. 186; Whittemore, op. cit., p. 103.

27. Aglipay was then on good terms with the Jesuits
because he had effected the release of two Jesuits em-
prinsoned by the revolutionary government in 1898. Besides, the Jesuits held only a few parishes and owned no
estates, which had made the other friars the object of
Filipino hatred.

28. See Whittemore, op. cit., pp. 103-4. The Catholic side is given very briefly in Achútegui and Bernad,
op. cit., pp. 191-92, and footnote.

29. Achútegui and Bernad, op. cit., pp. 199-202.

30. Evidently, Fr. Brillantes had never for a moment
vacillated from the decision to secede from the Vatican. He
took possession of an old Church of St. James the Greater
in Bacarra, Ilocos Norte on October 1, and was consecrated
Bishop on October 19.

Clifford (op. cit., p. 353) regards Bishop Brillantes'

consecration as the real reason for Aglipay's finally casting his lot with the IFI. "The Ilocos provinces," says Clifford, "were Aglipay's own bailiwick and he had no intention of permitting even a Filipino to supersede him in religious authority...." This is not true, for Aglipay had definitely cast his lot with the IFI by early September.

31.   There were over 800 Filipino priests at the beginning of the American occupation. Of these, according to Achútegui and Bernad, only 36 (26 of them from the North) turned Aglipayan. Op. cit., p. 231. The other claims range from 100 by de los Reyes to 200 by Laubach. Frank Charles Laubach, The People of the Philippines: Their Religious Progress and Preparation for Spiritual Leadership in the Far East (New York: George H. Doran Company, 1925), p. 144. Even so, the reaction of the Filipino clergy was by and large timid, to say the least.

32.   Rivera, loc. cit., (X), pp. 17 and 18.

33.   LeRoy (Philippine Life, p. 165) says that there were at least two million Aglipayans; Forbes (op. cit., II, 61), "something like two million people;" and Stuntz, "at least 1,500,000." Homer C. Stunz, The Philippines and the Far East (Cincinnati: Jennings and Pye, 1904), pp. 491-92. Achútegui and Bernad (op. cit., p. 226) reluctantly accepts Stuntz' estimate.

34.   See Table 4 at the end of this chapter.

35.   This is exactly the position taken by Achútegui and Bernad, op. cit., p. 226.

36.   Whittemore (op. cit., p. 129) has another reason for doubting that the 1918 figure reflects the real number of Aglipayans as of 1918. He says that during the early days, Aglipayans referred to their religion as Santa Iglesia Catolica Filipina, and perhaps the census enumerator simply thought that this meant the Roman Catholic Church! This may well have been the case in a number of instances, although one must not forget that by law the census enumerator was supposed to be extremely familiar with the barrio to which he was assigned.

37.   Aguinaldo was probably referring to Frs. Gomez, Burgos, and Zamore who were martyred in 1872. Supra, p. 98.

38. El Renacimiento, October 26, 1902, English translation of clipping in the Taft Papers. Aguinaldo was ill at that time. His speech was read by a Senor Felipe Mendoza.

39. See Rodriguez, op. cit. , I, 100-108.

40. La Democracia, October 26, 1902, English translation of clipping in the Taft Papers. Italics mine. Taft, who was in the Philippines at the time the schism gained momentum because of Aglipay's acceptance of the post of Obispo Maximo of the IFI, asked for a collection of newspaper opinions on the movement.

41. Bishop D. J. Dougherty to Taft, April 19, 1904, Private and Personal, loc. cit. Italics mine.

42. Taft to Lyman Abbott, January 24, 1903, loc. cit.

43. Luke E. Wright to Theodore Roosevelt, August 15, 1904, quoted in Zwierlein, op. cit. , p. 128.

44. Testimonies like this, in addition to evidence derived from a study of the tenets, polity, and actual practices of the Aglipayan Church and the involvement of many prominent Aglipayans in both the nationalist movement and parties, have led Clifford to consider the Aglipayan Movement as "more political and nationalist... than religious. " Op. cit. , p. 400. See also Achútegui and Gernad, op. cit. , pp. 234-41.

This is true to a great extent, although one suspects that in approaching the rise of the IFI, Catholic priests and nuns start with the premise that — except for a few adventurers — the Filipinos, even if they did not love the friars, were not really against them, and that the friars were therefore merely being used as "whipping boys" by both the American regime and the Filipino nationalists, including Filipino priests. The evidence is overwhelming, however, that Filipino hatred for the friars was not mere fancy.

45. For the practices, doctrines, and teachings of the Aglipayan Church, see Achútegui and Bernad, op. cit. , chaps. XIII-XIX; Rivera, loc. cit. , chap. IV; and Whittemore, op. cit. , pp. 139-45.

46. Processions during the Holy Week are, to many rural Filipinos, the only symbols of their being Christians. I can still vividly recall such processions in my hometown

in Central Luzon during the pre-war and war years. The Catholic procession always started at dusk, when most of the barrio folks were still on their way to the poblacion, or town proper. If lucky, they might be able to catch up with the tail of the procession, or go to the church right away.

At about the time that the Catholic procession would be almost over, the Aglipayan procession would start. The barrio folks who had not yet gone around the town would then join the Aglipayan procession. It did not matter whether they had been baptized as Catholics or as Aglipayans. (Incidentally, the two churches were situated just a hundred yards or so from each other on the same side of the public plaza).

47. For a discussion of the "Philippinized" or symcretic Catholicism under Spain, see Phelan, op. cit., Chapter VI: "The 'Philippinization' of Spanish Catholicism."

48. This is the theme of Donald Anderson McGavran, "The Independent Church in the Philippines: The Story of A Spiritual Quest," Encounter (Indianapolis), XIX (Summer, 1958), 299-321. In spite of a few historical inaccuracies, Professor McGavran's analysis of the IFI as a "movement of peoples" into a new faith is very incisive and highly illuminating. At the time McGavran's article was published, he was Visiting Professor of Missions in the Divinity School of Drake University.

49. See Article VIII.

50. These were generally the leading families in the towns who had a vested interest in the anti-friar movement.

51. Achútegui and Bernad, op. cit., p. 315.

52. Ibid., pp. 315-16.

53. Taft's Proclamation of Peaceful Possession, January 10, 1903.

54. Achútegui and Bernad, op. cit., pp. 236-38.

55. 7 Phil. Reports 41 (1907). The three Filipino justices of the Court concurred with three of their four American colleagues. One American justice abstained. For a brief summary of the Barlin v. Ramirez case, see Coquia, op. cit., pp. 85-90.

56. See Roman Catholic Church v. Santos, 7 Phil.

Reports 66 (1907) and Santos v. Roman Catholic Church, 212 U. S. 463 (1909). Cited in Achútegui and Bernad, op. cit. , p. 345, n. 40. See also Coquia, op. cit. , p. 93.

57. The adjective is Whittemore's op. cit. , p. 135. "In the background, " he adds, "was the enormous pressure of the Roman Catholic Church in the United States. "

58. Achútegui and Bernad, op. cit. , p. 346.

59. Ibid.

60. This is the judgment of Whittemore, op. cit. , and of Rivera, loc. cit. , (IX), p. 316. Indeed, I believe that this is the only possible judgment, given the incalculable loss of prestige which went with the abandonment of the churches in question. It is not hard to imagine almost whole parishes becoming Catholis again, simply because their church was again a Catholic church.

61. McGavran, loc. cit.

62. Charles W. Briggs, The Progressing Philippines (Philadelphia: The Griffith and Rowland Press, 1913), p. 115.

63. Clifford, op. cit.

64. See supra, p. 79.

65. Villamor was later elected to the First Philippine Assembly from the third district of Ilocos Sur.

66. See supra, p. 102.

67. Philippine Commission Report, 1910, p. 9.

68. Charles A. Olcott, The Life of William McKinley (2 vols. ; Boston: Houghton Mifflin Company, 1916), II, 109-11, quoting from The Christian Advocate, January 22, 1903. Italics mine.

69. Alexander C. Zabriskie, Bishop Brent: Crusader for Christian Unity (Philadelphia: The Westminster Press, 1948), pp. 44-46. Brent was consecrated bishop on December 19, 1901. He arrived in the Philippines with Taft (from his Vatican Mission) on August 24, 1902.

70. The standard account on the early Protestant missions in the Philippines is Laubach, op. cit. See also Stuntz, op. cit. , and Briggs, op. cit.

71. The "assignments" are listed in Laubach, op. cit. , pp. 204 and 483-84. The Episcopalians refused to be "dictated" to with regard to missionary areas, although the bulk of their activity came to be confined to Mountain

Province, Manila, and Zamboanga. Ibid. , pp. 205 and
481; Zabriskie, op. cit. , passim.

72. Donald D. Parker, "Church and State in the
Philippines, 1896-1906, " PSSR, X (November, 1938), 360.
This article is an abstract of a dissertation of the same
title presented to the University of Chicago Divinity School
in 1936. For a similarly exaggerated view, see Briggs,
op. cit. , p. 112.

73. Based on the chart showing the growth of the
Methodist Mission, 1898-1921, in Laubach, op. cit. , p. 183.

74. See supra, p. 101.

75. "Report of Interview Between Bishop Hendrick
and Major McIntyre, March 10, 1908, " NA, 1318-81.

76. Laubach, op. cit. , esp. pp. 272-89 and 441-49,
discusses these factors in great detail.

77. For the Filipino reaction to Catholicism in the
16th and 17th centuries, see Phelan, op. cit. , chaps. V-VI.

78. According to Laubach, the Filipinos did not respond warmly to "the cold intellecturalism of Puritannical
forms of worship. " Op. cit. , p. 221. Thus, Congregationalists and Presbyterians had to swallow "their prejudices against emotional manifestations. . . . " Ibid. ,
p. 223.

79. Instead of welcoming it, the early Protestant
missionaries literally snubbed Aglipayanism because "in
ritual, it was too Roman; in theology, too rationalistic;
in ethics, too Spanish; and in politics, too independista. "
Ibid. , p. 146.

A more profound explanation is offered by Professor
McGavran (loc. cit. , pp. 314-15) as follows:

"First, because the movement of populations to
Evangelical faith was not 'missions' to the Evangelical
leadership. They were immersed in the individualistic
proces. . . .

"Second, each American Church was reproducing its
denominational pattern rather than creating a free biblical
Philippine church. . . .

"Third, between Filipinos and Americans there was
a maximum degree of mutual suspicion. . . .

"Fourth, the IFI was substantially an Asian revolt
against European domination. It was a nationalistic move-

ment tinged with religious fervor, but lacking any biblical conviction. Protestant leaders did not appreciate at all the degree to which it was able to be guided, not by superiors but by friendly equals. "

80. Laubach, op. cit. , p. 204. It was not until 1923 that Filipinos became active participants in the Union, when Dean Jorge Bocobo was elected its first Filipino president. Ibid. , p. 210.

81. Such as the famous Brent School in Baguio and the Silliman Institute at Dumaguete, Oriental Negros, now Silliman University and one of the foremost centers of higher learning in the Philippines today.

82. Among these may be mentioned Mary Johnston Hospital in Tondo, Manila and the well-known St. Luke's Hospital, formerly in Manila, now in Quezon City.

83. Laubach, op. cit. , esp. chaps. XXI-XXIX, discusses these activities in great detail. Perhaps mention should also be made of the Protestants' contribution to literature. Ibid.

84. Cf. Achútegui and Bernad, op. cit. , p. 365.

85. Chapelle arrived in the Philippines in January, 1900. For his activities and disagreement with the Taft Commission, see supra, pp. 88-89.

86. See supra, pp. 49-51.

87. From the opening sentence, as is customary, of the papal bull. The English version may be found in American Catholic Quarterly Review, XXVIII (January-October, 1903), 372-79.

88. Achútegui and Bernad, op. cit. , p. 204.

89. Ibid.

90. Although there were five dioceses, the Philippines at the time constituted a single ecclesiastical province.

91. There were Archbishop Harty of Manila, Bishop Dougherty of Nueva Segovia, Bishop Hendrick of Cebu, and Bishop Rooker of Jaro. Nueva Caceres remained vacant.

92. He was consecrated as bishop of the vacant see of Nueva Cáceros (Bicol region) on June 29, 1906. Achútegui and Bernad, op. cit. , p. 358. Father Barlin had been "nominated" by de los Reyes as a bishop of the IFI, but he refused to be "honored" by the "nomination. "

93. Philippine Commission Report, 1903, Pt. 1, p. 45. Unfortunately, I could not locate figures for later years.

94. Achútegui and Bernad, op. cit., pp. 353-55.

95. Ibid., p. 364.

96. Quoted in ibid., p. 362.

97. Ibid., p. 364.

98. The term "Moro," a corruption of the word "Moor," was applied to the Muslim Filipinos by the Spaniards.

99. Philippine Commission Report, 1904, Pt. 1, p. 5. In 1918, the Muslims were estimated to number around 443,000. See P.I., Census Office, Census of the Philippine Islands Taken...in the Year 1918 (4 vols.; Manila: Bureau of Printing, 1921), II, 51-52. Cited hereafter as Census of 1918. The latest estimates place the number of Muslims at 1,600,000. See Peter G. Gowing, Mosque and Moro: A Study of Muslims in the Philippines (Manila: Philippine Federation of Christian Churches, 1964), p. 1.

100. Cf. supra, pp. 6-7, and p. 11.

101. I haved based this very brief discussion on the political organization and religion of the Moros on Philippine Commission Report, 1904, Pt. 1, pp. 5-8; Gowing, op. cit., pp. 18, 38-39; Forbes, op. cit., II, 3; and "The Muslim Minority in the Philippines," June 11, 1962, MS, p. 2. I am grateful to Professor Benda for lending me his copy of this anonymous work.

102. This is one of the main conclusions of Dr. Phelan, op. cit., pp. 151 and 161.

103. Gowing, op. cit., p. 22.

104. For the first diplomatic efforts of the United States, which resulted in the signing of the so-called Bates Treaty with the Sultan of Sulu on August 20, 1899, based upon the latter's agreement with Spain described above, see Schurman, op. cit., pp. 16-17. By virtue of this "treaty" (full text in Forbes, op. cit., II, Appendix XIX), the Sulu Moros recognized the sovereignty of the United States in return for the latter's protection and promise not to interfere in the internal administration and customs of the Moros, and also the payment of annual subsidies to the Sultan and his datus.

For subsequent efforts to bring the Mindanao Moros and recalcitrant Sulu Moros into submission, see Richard O'Connor, Black Jack Pershing (Garden City, N. Y.: Doubleday and Company, Inc., 1961), chaps. III and IV, and Hermann Hagedorn, Leonard Wood: A Biography (2 vols.; New York: Harper and Brothers, 1931), II, chaps. I-III.

Pershing served as a captain in the military district of Mindanao and Sulu from 1901 to 1903. His brilliant campaigns against the Moros in the Lake Lanao area earned for him the unusual promotion from captain to brigadier-general. He returned to Mindanao in 1909 as the third and last governor of Moro Province during the Taft Era, remaining until 1913. Wood was the first governor of Moro Province (1903-1906). He was succeeded by General Tasker H. Bliss (1906-1909).

105. Philippine Commission Report, 1904, Pt. 1, pp. 8-9.

106. The other provinces of Mindanao were organized as follows: Misamis and Surigao, regular; Agusan and its sub-provinces of Bukidnon, special, under the jurisdiction of the Secretary of the Interior.

107. See Act No. 787 of the Philippine Commission, June 1, 1903. Pertinent provisions are summarized in Philippine Commission Report, 1904, Pt. 1, pp. 9-10.

On December 20, 1913, the Philippine Commission (under the Harrison Administration) enacted Act No. 2309. Under this act, Moro Province was changed to the Department of Mindanao and Sulu and expanded to include the province of Agusan and its sub-province of Bukidnon.

Throughout the Taft Regime, the governor of Moro Province was an American military officer, and so was the secretary. During the succeeding Harrison administration, conditions reached a point whereby it became possible to appoint a civilian governor. The first to be so appointed was Frank W. Carpenter, who for several years had served as Assistant Executive Secretary and finally Executive Secretary of the Philippine Commission. See Elliott, Commission Government, pp. 939. For a "capsule" biography of Carpenter, see Arthur B. Pier, American Apostles to the Philippines (Boston: The Beacon

Press, 1950), pp. 83-93. The title of this work probably influenced the librarian of the Yale Divinity School to order it for his unit (and has so remained there), although Bishop Charles H. Brent was, properly speaking, the only "apostle" among the dozen Americans whose short biographies appear in this handy volume.

108. Forbes, op. cit., II, 44-46, discusses this point. See also Dickinson, Special Report, p. 8. For contemporary Moro attitudes toward the Philippine Republic, see "Muslim Minority in the Philippines, " pp. 24-25 and Gowing, op. cit., pp. 23-38.

109. Philippine Commission Report, 1904, Pt. 1, p. 9.

110. Forbes, op. cit., II, 27-28. Cf. Philippine Commission Report, 1904, Pt. 1, p. 10.

Chapter VII

1. With the exception of political relations, no other aspect of Philippine-American colonial relations has received as excellent treatment as tariff relations. Although not based on on manuscript sources, the following are highly recommended: Jose S. Reyes, Legislative History of America's Economic Policy toward the Philippines ("Columbia University: Studies in History, Economics and Public Law, " Vol. CVI, No. 2; New York: Columbia Unitersity Press, 1923); Abelarde, op. cit.; Grayson L. Kirk, Philippine Independence: Motives, Problems, and Prospects (New York: Farra and Rinehart, Inc. , 1936), chpas. III-VI; and Grunder and Livezey, op. cit. , chap. VI.

2. De Lima v. Bidwell, 182 U. S. 1 (1900); Fourteen Diamond Rings, 183 U. S. 176 (1901); and Downes v. Bidwell, 182 U. S. 244 (1901).

3. Cf. Reyes, op. cit. , p. 73; Grunder and Livezey, op. cit. , p. 105. For the ''Open Door'' policy, see the useful monograph by the late Yale President A. Whitney Griswold, The Far Eastern Policy of the United States (New York: Harcourt, Brace and Company, 1938), chap. II. See also George F. Kennan, American Diplomacy, 1900-1950 (Chicago: The University of Chicago Press, 1951), pp. 21-45.

4. Phelan, op. cit., p. 93.

5. Cf. Reyes, op. cit., chap. IV; Abelarde, op. cit., passim; Grunder and Livezey, op. cit., pp. 109-10.

6. For the Philippine Tariff Act of August 5, 1909, see U. S., Statutes, XXXVI, Pt. 1, 130-78.

7. For the Dingley Law or Act of 1897, see loc. cit., XXX, Pt. 1, 203ff. Since there were no American interests which would be harmed by the free entry of Philippine copra and abaca (the famous "Manila hemp"), these products did not pay any duties. However, an export tax was levied on them in the Philippines.

8. Philippine products were admitted free of duty in Spain during the last decade of Spanish rule. Sugar, however, was charged a high internal tax. See supra, p. 14.

9. For the extent and effects of these natural scourges during the Taft Regime, see Forbes, op. cit., I, 27, n. 2; 242, and 553, n. 2.; Elliott, Commission Government, pp. 205 and 347; and the short but highly informative publication of the War Department, Bureau of Insular Affairs entitled, The Philippine Islands (Washington, D. C., U. S. Government Printing Office, 1913), pp. 27-29. This report was prepared by General Frank McIntyre, then Chief of the Bureau of Insular Affairs, and is dated March 1, 1913. Hereafter, it will be cited as The Philippine Islands, 1913.

10. Philippine Commission Report, 1901, Pt. 1, p. 28.

11. "Special Message to the Senate on H. R. 15702," Feb. 27, 1903, in James D. Richardson, A Compilation of the Messages and Papers of the Presidents (20 vols.; New York: Bureau of National Literature, Inc., [1917?], XV, 6737-39.

12. For the details, see Reyes, op. cit., esp. chap. V, and Abelarde, op. cit., chaps. II-III, passim.

13. Grunder and Livezey, op. cit., p. 107.

14. Jose Albert to Taft, March 1, 1902, NA, C-1246-17. Cablegram.

15. Reyes, op. cit., p. 90.

16. Taft to Wright, March 1, 1902, NA, C-1246-17. Cablegram intended also for Albert. While there was some truth about the attitude of many Filipinos toward American rule, this was not the reason, of course, for

Congressional refusal to reduce the Dingley rates any further. It must have been an occasion, therefore, for one of
Taft's celebrated chuckles when he received the following
reply from Albert on April 18, 1902: "Now war finished
beg reduction tariff bill...." Loc. cit., C-1246-27. The
famous General Malvar had just surrendered two days
earlier.

17. Philippine Honorary Commission to the St. Louis
Exposition to President Roosevelt, July 28, 1904, NA,
6830-3. English translation. There were forty-three
members of the Honorary Commission, about forty of
whom, including Tavera and Legarda, signed the memorial
to Roosevelt. See also the petition of Cebu provincial and
municipal officials, led by then Governor Sergio Osmena,
to the members of the Taft Party, August 15, 1905, loc.
cit., 1239-50. English translation.

18. Herrera to Roosevelt, January 1, 1904, loc. cit.,
C-519-11. Cablegram.

19. Petition to Governor Wright, January 25, 1904,
loc. cit., C-519-15. Many other similar petitions, memorials, and resolutions are in the files of the National
Archives. See, among others, C-1246-57; C-1246-71;
2202-3; and 1228-16. See also Public Hearings on the
Philippine Tariff... Held during the Month of August before
the Secretary of War and the Congressional Party [in]...
the Philippine Islands, in Senate Doc. 277, 59th Cong.,
1st Sess., 1905, Appendix. This is also available in U.S.,
Congress, House, Committee on Ways and Means, Hearings Before the Committee of Ways and Means on the
Philippine Tariff, 59th Cong., 1st Sess., 1905, Appendix.
Cited hereafter as Hearings on the Philippine Tariff, 1905.

20. For the Philippine Assembly, see supra, pp.
61-67.

21. Text in Diario de sesiones, I, 239-40, and Commission Journal, I, 137-38. It was unanimously adopted
by the Assembly on December 19, 1907.

22. Text in Commission Journal, III, 265-66.

23. See the record of the Assembly's proceedings on
the resolution, Diario de sesiones, I, 240-44. Quezon
was also instrumental in the Assembly's passage of Commission Joint Resolution No. 2, which became Joint

Resolution No. 2, which became Joint Resolution No. 6 of the Philippine Legislature after the Commission had accepted the Assembly's amendments on January 14, 1908 (Commission Journal, I, 188-89), authorizing John S. Hord, Insular Collector of Internal Revenue, to proceed to Washington as the government's expert advocate before Congress.

24. For the Resident Commissioners at Washington, D. C. , see supra, pp. 41-43.

25. The Assembly's version of the resolution was to have also requested authority for the Philippine Government to negotiate "in its discretion commercial treaties with other countries. " This was Assemblyman Carlos Lerma's contribution. Diario de sesiones, I, 160.

26. For these bills and the hearings conducted as a consequence of their introduction, see Reyes, op. cit. , pp. 101-10, and Abelarde, op. cit. , pp. 77-92.

27. See supra p. 140, and n. 77. The truth is, up to 1905 and well into 1908, the Spanish Chamber of Commerce in Manila appeared to have been the only open advocate of complete free trade relations between the Philippines and the United States. Such an advocacy was probably prompted by the Chamber's desire to have Spanish products also admitted duty free, at least until April 11, 1909. See "Petition to Secretary of War Taft and Congressional Party, " Manila, September 20, 1905, NA, 1239-60. English translation.

28. Edwards, Chief of the Bureau of Insular Affairs, to Smith, October 17, 1908, NA, C-1089-94.

29. Smith to SecWar, March 25, 1909, loc. cit. , C-1250-74. Smith had earlier estimated that free trade would mean a loss of almost ₱5,000,000 in customs receipts. Idem, January 8, 1909, loc. cit. , C-1089-96. Both of the above communications were cablegrams.

30. La Democracia, August 26, 1908, English translation of clipping in NA, C-1246-77.

31. Daniel O'Connell to Smith, November 17, 1908, loc. cit. , C-1246-78, transmitting petition of the Association. The petition, O'Connell wrote, "has in the neighborhood of 200,000 signatures. "

32. Resolution adopted February 1, 1909, quoted in Forbes, op. cit. , II, 158.

33. U.S., Statutes, XXXVI, Pt. 1, 11-118, Section V.

34. See supra, p. 122.

35. The Payne-Aldrich Tariff Act was superseded by
the Underwood-Simmons Act of October 3, 1913, which
removed the quota limitations on sugar and tobacco, thereby establishing complete free trade between the Philippines
and the United States. For the Underwood-Simmons Act,
see U.S., Statutes, XXXVIII, Pt. 1, 113.

36. The significant exceptions among the elite were
the three Progresista members of the Philippine Commission in 1909. They voted with their American colleagues
in favor of a proposed resolution which would have placed
the Legislature behind the Payne Bill. The lone Nacionalista member of the Commission voted against the resolution. See Commission Journal, III, 275-79.

37. These were Concurrent Resolution No. 36, March
27, 1909 (ibid., pp. 264-66), and the Assembly's negative
report on Commission Joint Resolution No. 8, which was
offered as a substitute to its own resolution (ibid., pp.
365-69). Quezon was behind both Assembly actions.

38. See the statements of Resident Commissioners
Legarda and Ocampo, respectively, in U.S., Congressional
Record, 61st Cong., 1st Sess., 1909, Pt. 1, pp. 930-31,
and in NA, 17086-3 (reprint). They are dated, respectively,
April 3, 1909, and April 2, 1909.

For Quezon's views as Resident Commissioner, see
the unpublished memorandum of the Bureau of Insular Affairs entitled, "Mr. Quezon's Stand on Free Trade Relations between the United States and the Philippine Islands,"
dated November 12, 1931, and a supplementary memorandum, dated November 7, 1932. Both are in NA, C-1250-
211.

39. The attitudes of the Filipino elite toward the future
political status of the Philippines are discussed in the next
chapter.

40. Concurrent Resolution No. 36, loc. cit.

41. Legarda's statement, loc. cit. Legarda's argument did not make sense at the time, since one of the
reasons why preferential treatment for Philippine sugar
and tobacco in the United States was being sought was the
need for favored markets! Of course, Legarda was right

in the long run, although it is arguable whether he was
really against free trade. See supra, pp. 131-33.

42. Quezon, op. cit. , p. 108. Quezon further recalled in his autobiography that his official opposition to
the Payne Bill was "my first clash with the American
Government while serving in the National [Philippine]
Assembly. " Ibid. , p. 107.

43. Minutes of the Meeting of the Committee of the
Assembly and of the Commission on the Payne Bill, March
29, 1909, in the Smith Papers. Prepared by Wm. H.
Donovan, Secretary of the Philippine Commission, and
cited hereafter as Donovan, "Minutes. "

When the Assembly passed Concurrent Resolution No.
36 on March 27, 1909, it appointed a Select Committee to
discuss the resolution with the Philippine Commission.
The members of the Committee were Quezon, Alberto
Barretto, Vicente Singson Encarnacion, Filemon Sotto,
Matias Gonzales, Salvador Laguda, and Juan Villamor.
The Committee had two sessions with the Commission in
Baguio on March 29, 1909.

The minutes of the sessions or discussions are among
the Smith Papers in the Washington State Historical Society
at Tacoma, Washington. Thanks to a grant from the Yale
Southeast Asia Studies Program, I was able to consult
these minutes last July, 1964. They consist of 46 double-
spaced typewritten pages of legal size paper, and were
transmitted by Donovan on August 9, 1909 to Governor
Smith, then spending his terminal leave in the United
States. In his letter of transmittal, Donovan wrote: "This
discussion was had without an interpreter and I utilized
the services of a Spanish stenographer, but... he was undoubtedly confused and failed to do as well as he might
have done otherwise. I translated and took notes at the
same time as a check on him, but you will realize that to
make a running translation and write as fast as a man
talks at the same time is at best not an easy matter. I
send it to you. ... This record will not be printed in the
journal, but will be filed with other similar records in my
office. " The Commission Journal (III, 264 and 266) mentions the Commission's meeting with the Select Committee
on March 29, 1909, but that is all, and Forbes (op. cit.)

is conspicuously silent on this meeting.

44. Donovan, "Minutes. " See also Resident Commissioner Pablo Ocampo's interview with the Washington Post, May 17, 1909, as quoted in Abelarde, op. cit. , pp. 99-100.

45. Concurrent Resolution No. 36, loc. cit. See also, for Quezon's re-statement of the argument, Donovan, "Minutes. " Legarda (loc. cit.) and Ocampo (loc. cit.) also cited the loss of revenues as part of their opposition to the Payne Bill.

46. Supra, n. 43 of this chapter.

47. Forbes merely states (op. cit. , II, 157-58) that the Assembly's action was a mistake and "not representative of all the intelligent opinion in the Islands.... " Cf. Kirk, op. cit. , p. 59.

48. Forbes to Edwards, April 7, 1909, Personal, NA, 13931-A-79.

49. Forbes to Wright, April 3, 1909, Confidential, Forbes Papers.   Former Governor-General Luke E. Wright was then the Secretary of War.

50. Smith to SecWar, April 3, 1909, NA, C-1250-78. Laguda represented the third district of Iloilo and was a member of the Assembly's Select Committee.

51. Forbes believes (Forbes to Wright, loc. cit.) that this was part of the Progresista strategy to embarrass the Nacionalistas, who had up to that time been working harmoniously with the administration on legislative matters, and whom the Progresistas charged with having "sold out" to the Americans. It was probably also part of the Progresista effort to appear before the electorate as pro-independencia as the Nacionalista majority of the Assembly, and therefore prove they were entitled to a larger share of the Assembly seats in the 1909 elections. See Chapter VIII.

52. See Donovan, "Minutes, " loc. cit.

53. Taft, then President of the United States, was in favor of free trade. See Stanley D. Solvick, "William Howard Taft and the Payne-Aldrich Tariff, " The Mississipi Valley Historical Review, L (December, 1963), 442.

While Taft could afford to smile at the Assembly's stand on free trade, he could not have tolerated any further vacillation on the part of Governor Smith or, for that matter, on the part of the Commission as whole.

54. See his letters to General Edwards and General Wright, loc. cit.

55. I have discussed the Public Lands Act more fully in a later section of this chapter.

56. Donovan, ''Minutes.'' The succeeding presentation is based on Donovan's ''Minutes.''

57. I must emphasize here that this conclusion is only a tentative one. For the details, see Chapter VIII. One wonders whether Speaker Osmena was really sick at the time the Assembly passed the crucial resolution against free trade. It certainly was a bad time to be absent.

58. Text in Commission Journal, III, 275-78. See also supra, n. 36 of this chapter, for the stand of the Filipino members of the Commission on the resolution.

59. Forbes to Edwards, April 7, 1909, loc. cit. See also Smith to Wright, April 5, 1909, Confidential, loc. cit., C-1250-79. ''Main difficulty,'' Smith cabled, ''seems to be the making of an honorable retreat.''

60. Edwards to Smith, April 9, 1909, NA, C-1250-83. Cablegram. The draft of the cable shows that it was prepared by John S. Hord.

61. Forbes says that General Manuel Tinio, a ranking revolutionary leader and the cacique par excellence of Nueva Ecija province during the American regime, ''had opposed free trade because he could not see how a better market for sugar and tobacco was going to help his province, which was principally devoted to rice culture. He was frank enough later to admit he saw his mistake when he found that the rice crop brought a higher price and that his people were also engaging in the production of sugar and tobacco.'' Op. cit., II, 251. See also Hayden, op. cit., pp. 278 and 285, for a characterization of Tinio.

62. See supra, n. 38 of this chapter.

63. Edwards to Fred W. Carpenter, Secretary to President Taft, March 24, 1909, Personal and Confidential, Edwards Papers. Taft read this letter.

64. See supra, p. 125.

65. John S. Hord to Edwards, April 3, 1909, NA, C-1250-80.

66. Abelarde, op. cit., p. 111. Forbes (op. cit., I,

245) characteristically attributes the slump to what he
calls a "serious disturbance in Philippine trade by reason
of the radical political platform inaugurated at the beginning
of the Democratic regime. " Forbes' argument, however,
is negated by an increase in the total value of Philippine
trade with the United States (including Hawaii and Porto
Rico) of 3,206,389 dollars in 1913 over 1912. See P.I.,
Bureau of Customs, Annual Report of the Insular Collector
of Customs...June 30, 1913 (Manila: Bureau of Printing,
1913), p. 20. Cited hereafter as Collector of Customs,
Annual Report.

    67. Collector of Customs, Annual Report, 1907, pp.
21 and 25.

    68. Unfortunately, I could not locate specific data on
American investments in agriculture. Those given in the
statistical bulletins of the P.I. Bureau of Commerce and
Industry are for both agriculture and the extractive industries. My source for the above statement is Abelarde
op. cit., p. 112 (who cites no figures), and is corroborated
by deductions made by A. V. H. Hartendorp, History of
Industry and Trade of the Philippines (rev. ed.; Manila:
American Chamber of Commerce of the Philippines, Inc.,
1958), p. 22, n. 3, who says that as late as 1930, more
than 75 percent of American capital invested (160,000,000
dollars) "was in government securities and public utilities."

    69. Forbes, op. cit., I, 323. Forbes wanted very
much to have the limitations on the amount of public lands
that corporations and individuals might acquire modified
to enable them to acquire substantially larger areas. See
his personal letter to Henry L. Stimson, then Secretary
of War, October 16, 1911, in Henry L. Stimson Papers
(Yale Sterling Library, New Haven, Connecticut).

    70. Cf. Forbes, op. cit., II, 89-90.

    71. Act No. 1189 of the Philippine Commission. For
an excellent summary of its provisions as well as a brief
background and results of application after two years, see
Hord, Internal Taxation in the Philippines, pp. 11-43.
Hord assisted Commissioner Henry C. Ide in drafting the
law and became the first internal revenue collector, a
position created by the new internal revenue act.

    72. As a matter of fact, some scheduled increases in

taxes, such as the tax on cigarettes, did not go into effect
much later. Cf. Tavera to Taft, March 25, 1905, Taft
Papers. I have used the English translation.

73. P.I. Finance and Justice, Report, 1902, p. 40.
A more or less complete draft, however, was not prepared until June-August, 1903. See Hord, op. cit., p. 19.

74. For a brief discussion of the system of taxation
under Spain, see supra, pp. 13-14. The details are in
Plehn, "Taxation in the Philippines," loc. cit., and Hord,
op. cit., pp. 7-11. Hord's is a summary of the more complete work by Plehn.

75. I have discussed this subject more fully elsewhere.
See supra, pp. 45-51. The disposition of the friar lands is
discussed in the next section of this chapter, supra, pp.
151-152.

76. See, for the reduction in the proposed taxes, P I
Finance and Justice, Report, 1904, pp. 53-55; Wright,
then Governor-General, to Taft, July 23, 1904, NA, 9639-
21; Smith to Wright, March 25, 1909, loc. cit., C-1250-74;
and Ide's Memorandum to the Chief of the Bureau of Insular
Affairs, March 30, 1909, in loc. cit., C-1250-with 74. The
latter is a copy of the original. For the suspension of the
land tax, see supra, 145-146.

77. The Internal Revenue Law, wrote Ide in 1903, "is
considered to be a very important one, in view of the fact
that ultimately it is most probable that the tariff barriers
between the United States and the Philippines will be more
largely broken down,... The new system ought to furnish
other sources of revenues so as to make the abolition of
duties in whole or in part more feasible." P.I., Finance
and Justice, Report, 1903, p. 70.

78. A brief summary of the protests against the Internal Revenue Law is in ibid., 1905, pp. 52 et. seq. See
also Hord, op. cit., pp. 20-24. Those received directly
by the Bureau of Insular Affairs, addressed to the Secretary of War, are in FILE 1228 of the records of the former Bureau of Insular Affairs in the National Archives.
They include the following: Herrera's cables to Taft,
April 14 and 22, 1904, Incls. 15 and 20; Chambers of
Commerce, Cagayan and Isabela and Governor, Cagayan,
to SecWar, April 18, 1904, Incl. 16 (cable); Philippine

Chamber of Commerce to the Secretary of War, June 22, 1904 Incl. 19 (cable).

79. Legarda to Taft, September 2, 1905, Personal, Taft Papers (English translation); Wright to Taft, August 21, 1904, NA, 1228-28 (cable

80. See Wright to Taft, August 21, 1904, loc. cit. , wherein he states that Tavera "never suggested an objection to the bill" before the Commission and that Legarda submitted his objections in writing, since he had been hesitant to do so openly because of his interests. For a corroboration of the latter, see Legarda to Taft, August 11, 1904, loc. cit. , 6830-33 (English translation).

81. Taft informed Governor Wright that he would not take action on the law as passed by the Commission until Wright had discussed its contents further with the Honorary Commission (which included Legarda and Tavera) then in the United States. See Taft to Wright, August 24, 1904, loc. cit. , 1280-30 (Confidential cable). For the amendments incorporating some of the Filipinos' proposals, see Philippine Commission Report, 1905, Pt. 4, pp. 28-29; 159-60.

82. Honorary Commission to Taft, August 10, 1904, NA, 1228-20. English translation.

83. They were in the United States at the time as Members of the Honorary Commission to the St. Louis Exposition. See supra, n. 17 of this chapter.

84. Williams to Taft, August 31, 1905, Personal, Taft Papers. For information about Williams, see supra, n. 33 of Chapter IV.

85. Legarda to Taft, October 17, 1904, Personal, Edwards Papers. My translation.

86. Tavera to Taft, January 13, 1905, Edwards Papers. English translation.

87. Tavera to Roosevelt, March 10, 1905, and same to Taft, May 19, 1905, Taft Papers. English translations. The disenchantment of the Federalistas with the government under Wright must have deeply worried Taft. This is seen from his personal letter to Tavera, in which he wrote: "I note with the greatest sorrow that the present government in the Philippine Islands seems to have lost the affectionate support of yourself, Benito Legarda and

Luzuriaga, on whom I counted as the pillars of my government in the Islands. This has given me the greatest concern,...I shall be with you, I hope, early in August, and shall be glad to talk over with you all the affairs in which we both have such a profound interest. " Taft to Tavera, June 19, 1905, Taft Papers.

88. So claims Mrs. Wm. H. Taft in her Recollections of Full Years (New York: Dodd, Mead and Company, 1914), p. 277.

89. No less than Mayor Herrera of Manila, who was also president of the Federal Party, openly criticized Governor and Mrs. Wright, mentioning the latter by name, at a breakfast with some members of the Taft Party, ranking insular officials and at least two American provincial governors. Herrera's action, if ungentlemanly, probably reflected the depth of dissatisfaction with the administration's policies, not the least of which was the internal revenue law. An eyewitness account of the "Herrera Affair" is Morgan W. Shuster, Collector of Customs, to Ide, August 30, 1905, Confidential, Taft Papers. Mayor Herrera was dismissed from office for making this criticism. Wright to Taft, September 17, 1905, Confidential, NA, 1239-53.

90. Taft to Mrs. Wm. H. Taft, September 24, 1905, Taft Papers.

91. This is not surprising since Ide drafted the Internal Revenue Law. But see Tavera to Congressman Henry A. Cooper, September 8, 1905, and Legarda to Taft, December 22, 1905. The English translations of both these confidential letters are in the Taft Papers.

92. Ide to Taft, December 14, 1905, and February 4, 1906, loc. cit. Cf. Forbes to Taft, September 21, 1906, Forbes Papers. This confidential letter was never sent.

93. From Vichy, France, Legarda felicitated Smith upon his appointment, saying: "Even the most uncompromising have affection for you. " Legarda to Smith, September 17, 1906, Smith Papers. My translation.

94. Wright was also unpopular with the Filipino elite because he adopted as his slogan "An Equal Chance for All, " instead of Taft's "The Philippines for the Filipinos." Wright further infuriated the Federalistas by not confining political appointments to their recommendations. Further-

more, his administration was marked by economic hardships and the breakdown of peace and order, especially in
Cavite and Batangas. In an attempt to deal with the situation effectively, the Constabulary, which was officered
almost entirely by Americans, committed excesses, con-
doned somewhat by the suspension of the writ of habeas
corpus. See James H. Blount, The American Occupation
of the Philippines, 1898-1912 (New York: G. P. Putnam's
Sons, 1912), chaps. XVIII-XIX; Pier, op. cit. , pp. 37-49;
Williams to Taft, August 31, 1905, Taft Papers; and
Tavera to Cooper, loc. cit.

As regards Ide, the elite simply believed that he was
as nonchalant as Wright and perhaps even more tactless.
Tavera and Legarda naturally viewed Ide's gestures as
insincere, if not wholly artificial. Tavera to Taft, December 7, 1905, Confidential, Taft Papers (translation) and
Legarda to Taft, April 13, 1906, Personal and Confidential,
loc. cit. (translation).

95. Hord, op. cit. , p. 40.

96. Cf. Taft to Ide, January 22, 1906, Personal and
Confidential, Taft Papers.

97. P. I. Finance and Justice, Report, 1904, pp. 50-
53; Hord, op. cit. , p. 23.

98. Philippine Commission Report, 1901, Pt. 1, p.
26. The taxes thus collected supported the public schools
and municipal and provincial improvements.

99. See supra, p. 13. The tax nearest to a real estate
tax under Spain was the urbana tax, which was collected on
rentals of urban property.

100. See Agoncillo, Malolos, pp. 258-61.

101. Philippine Commission Report, 1901, Pt. 1,
p. 26.

102. Ibid. , 1902, Pt. 1, p. 26, and Ibid. , 1907, Pt.
1, p. 86.

103. Wright to Taft, September 14, 1904, Edwards
Papers. Wright was evidently referring to overassessments of the properties of those who had no connections or
influence with the local authorities. In all likelihood,
many of these appeals came from small landowners who
were probably unaware of the machinery for appeals from
overassessments by local boards.

104. Ibid.
105. Legarda to Taft, December 22, 1905, Personal, Taft Papers. English translation.
106. Ibid.
107. Ibid. See also Tavera to Taft, December 7, 1905, Confidential, Taft Papers. English translation.
108. Forbes, op. cit., I, 255-56.
109. Philippine Commission Report, 1906, Pt. 1, pp. 49-50.
110. Ibid., 1907, Pt. 1, p. 84.
111. Ide to Taft, March 4, 1906, Confidential, Taft Papers. Italics mine.
112. Taft to Ide, April 18, 1906, Personal and Confidential, loc. cit.
113. Philippine Commission Report, 1907, Pt. 1, p. 85. Beginning in 1908, the suspension or re-institution of the land tax was left entirely to the provincial boards.
114. The Spaniards introduced the concept of land ownership as distinct from land use. For a fuller discussion, see Phelan, op. cit., pp. 116-18.
115. Forbes, op. cit., I, 315.
116. Act No. 496.
117. For the composition of this Court during the Taft Regime, see supra, p. 73, Table 3.
118. Quoted in P. I. Finance and Justice, Report, 1903, p. 15.
119. Philippine Commission Report, 1910, p. 10.
120. Forbes, op. cit., I, 316.
121. Philippine Commission Report, 1910, pp. 10-11. See also Forbes, op. cit., I, 317-18.
122. Ibid., I, 319. See also Worcester-Hayden, op. cit., pp. 547-48. Worcester claims that the Assembly insisted on the appointment of "incompetent" Filipino surveyors.
123. See supra, p. 73, Table 3.
124. Taft Commission Report, p. 33. One hectare equals 2.471 acres.
125. Public No. 235, July 1, 1902, loc. cit., Secs. 13-15 and 75.
126. Census of 1918, III, 873. The official who prepared the section on the public lands referred to the

estimate of 6,642,571 hectares as having been made "some few years ago."

127. Forbes (op. cit., I, 323-24) believes that this limitation was due to the machinations of the American beet sugar interests. See also Reyes, op. cit., pp. 144-47.

128. Act No. 926.

129. For the proclamation declaring that the act was in force, see Philippine Commission Report, 1907, [Pt. 2], Appendix, p. 474.

130. Ibid., p. 448. It is stated that 49.8 per cent of the lands used for agriculture by the Christian Filipinos were less than one hectare in size.

131. Cf. Census of 1918, Vol. III, pp. 880-81.

132. Cablenews-American (Manila), May 9, 1912, as quoted in Forbes, op. cit., I, 325, n. 1. To a certain extent, the above observation still applies to the Philippine farmer today, except that the overcrowding on the farm has been more acute than in the past and has compelled him to settle in virgin areas under the resettlement programs sponsored by the government.

133. Census of 1918, III, 882 and 884.

134. Ibid., p. 883.

135. For an idea of the distribution of the friar lands, see supra, p. 10.

136. For the evolution of United States friar policy, see supra, pp. 45-49.

137. See supra, p. 50.

138. For the Aglipayan Schism or Movement, see supra, pp. 97-107.

139. The agreements conveying the estates of the Dominicans, Augustinians, and Recollects to the government were signed on December 22, 1903. See Philippine Commission Report, 1903, Pt. 1, pp. 204-12, "Exhibit H." The purchase price of 6,930,462.70 dollars is given in Bureau of Insular Affairs, The Philippine Islands, 1913. It is lower than the original purchase figure of 7,239,784.16, but since it is the latest official figure, I am accepting it as more accurate.

It should be mentioned here that according to Professor Pelzer (op. cit., p. 91) the estates sold in 1903 were not the only friar lands. There were also "diocesan" lands, to

distinguish them from the "friar" lands, which were not
sold to the government.

140. Act No. 1120, passed by the Philippine Commission on April 26, 1904. The text may be found in Philippine Commission Report, 1907, [Pt. 2], Appendix, pp.
485-90.

141. Taft, Special Report, p. 20.

142. P. I. , Commission, The Friar Land Inquiry-
Philippine Government (Manila: Bureau of Printing, 1910),
p. 71.

143. Ibid.

144. Act No. 1847, June 3, 1908. The original Friar
Lands Act (loc. cit.) had made the area requirements of the
public land act applicable to the disposition of the friar
estates.

The sale of the huge San Jose Estate in Mindoro
(55, 000 acres) to a single individual in 1909 was made
possible by Act No. 1847. Although the action of the
Philippine government was upheld by the Committee on
Insular Affairs of the U. S. House of Representatives
after a thorough investigation, the Secretary of War found
it prudent to advise the Philippine government that subsequent transactions should conform to the area requirements of the public land act. As late as 1912, the Director
of Lands was asking for the revocation of this order, since
sales of the uncultivated friar lands "which could have
been made have been declined. " P. I. , Bureau of Lands,
Annual Report of the Director of Lands For the Fiscal
Year Ended June 30, 1912 (Manila: Bureau of Printing,
1912), p. 22.

Chapter VIII

1. There are a number of published works on Ameri-
can policy toward Philippine independence during the Taft
Era as well as on the Filipino reaction to such a policy.
Among these works may be mentioned the following:
Elliott, Commission Government; Forbes, op. cit. ;
Grunder and Livezey, op. cit. ; Maximo Kalaw, op. cit. ;
Kirk, op. cit. ; Rafael Palma, Our Campaign for Independ-
ence From Taft to Harrison (1901-1921), with annotations

by Teodoro M. Kalaw (Manila: Bureau of Printing, 1923);
and Willis, op. cit.

Our main effort in this chapter is to examine the
Filipino response to American policy as revealed primarily
in unpublished data which were either inaccessible to
earlier writers, or which some, like Forbes and Maximo
Kalaw, probably did not find it appropriate to include in
their works. It should not be surprising, therefore, if
some of my findings turn out to be different from those
found in earlier studies on the subject of Philippine
independence.

2. For a background of American policy as embodied
in the Philippine Bill of 1902, see supra, pp. 34-43.

3. Taft, Special Report, p. 74.

4. Morgan, op. cit., p. 421, citing the Literary
Digest, XVIII (January 28, 1899), 93-94.

5. See, for instance, his personal letters to H. K.
Love, November 24, 1900; to Charles W. Eliot, Novem-
ber 14, 1900 and June 20, 1904; and to Senator George F.
Hoar, June 16, 1902, which are found, respectively, in
Roosevelt Letters, II, 1442; II, 1415 and IV, 839; and
III, 276.

6. See his message to Congress, December 8, 1908,
quoted in Forbes, op. cit., II, 343.

7. Roosevelt to Taft, August 21, 1907, Roosevelt
Letters, V, 762. This letter was not made public until
1914.

8. Cf. Taft, Special Report, p. 74.

9. Cf. McKinley's story to the Methodist ministers,
supra, p. 108.

10. Taft to John N. Blair, March 16, 1905, NA,
364-73. Cf. Taft, Special Report, pp. 74-75.

11. Forbes (op. cit., II. 348-350) prints excerpts of
Taft's later statements on Philippine independence.

12. Roosevelt to Hoar, June 16, 1902, loc. cit.;
Roosevelt, An Autobiography (New York: The Macmillan
Company, 1913), pp. 543-44; and Taft to the Rev. Lawrence, February 16, 1904, Taft Papers. Taft's was in
answer to the latter's inquiry as to whether he should join
forty-nine other prominent Americans in urging Republi-
cans and Democrats to include in their 1904 platforms a

a promise to grant ultimate independence to the Filipinos.
Cf. supra, n. 6 to Chapter IV.

13. "The Philippine Government [i.e., the Americans]," General James F. Smith told President Roosevelt in 1903, "has been charged with having fostered and encouraged the Federal Party. This is true. ... " Smith to Roosevelt, October 24, 1903, Smith Papers. Italics mine. For Smith's career, see supra, n. 79 to Chapter III. Cf. Forbes, op. cit., I, 143, and II, 101.

14. The best single monograph on the history of Philippine political parties during the American regime, based on published sources, is Dapen Liang, The Development of Philippine Political Parties (Hongkong: South China Morning Post, 1939). See also Maximo Kalaw, op. cit. For an unpublished contemporary account on the formation of the Partido Federal, see Taft to Root, December 27, 1900, Taft Papers.

15. Taft to Root, January 9, 1901, Confidential Cable, NA, 141-40.

16. For the Hay Plan, see supra, p. 28.

17. For the platform of the Federal Party, adopted on December 23, 1900, see Florentino Torres, "Origin and Formation of the Federal Party," in General Arthur MacArthur's Report, 1901, Exhibit C, pp. 122-23.

18. T.H. Pardo de Tavera, Benito Legard[a], and Jose R. de Luzuriaga, "A History of the Federal Party," in Philippine Commission Report, Pt. 1, p. 164.

It is doubtful whether the Federalistas really subscribed to the goals set forth above. As a matter of fact, in light of their subsequent attitudes (about which more presently), the above statement appears to be completely devoid of sincerity. Perhaps the Federalistas advanced the above aims in an effort to dramatize their advocacy of statehood within the United States and to ingratiate themselves quickly and completely with Taft. In fairness to the Federalistas, however, it should be borne in mind that their goals were formulated during an abnormal period in Philippine history. As Dr. Tavera later said: "In proclaiming that our aspiration was some day to form a part of the American Union we rejected every form of colonial submission, and declared that if we could not

obtain national independence it was our desire to adopt
such independence as that had by the States of the Union. . . .

"A more mature consideration of the conditions affecting the American and the Filipino people led, as you know,
to the substitution of the idea of an impossible federation by
that of a complete independence, and the Federal Party became the present Partido Progresista. " "Address of Dr.
T. H. Pardo de Tavera at the Farewell Banquet. . . 17 of
April, 1909, " p. 4.

19. Taft to Root, January 13, 1901, Taft Papers.

20. Philippine Commission Report, 1901, Pt. 1, p.
165. The figures were supplied by the Secretary of the
Federal Party. Liang says that as of April, 1901, "there
were actually more than 200,000 persons affiliated with
this [i. e. , Federal] party. " Op. cit. , pp. 62, 63.

21. With very few exceptions, the Federal Party won
all contested posts before 1907. Cf. Liang, op. cit. , p. 66.

22. Quoted in Senate Doc. 331, Pt. 1, p. 67.

23. Section 10 of the Sedition Law (Act No. 292,
Philippine Commission, November 4, 1901) provided:

"Until it has been officially proclaimed that all war
or insurrection against the authority of the sovereignty of
the United States no longer exists in the Philippine Islands,
it shall be unlawful for any person to advocate orally or by
writing or printing, or like methods, the independence of
the Philippine Islands or their separation from the United
States, whether by peaceable or forcible means, or to
print, publish, or circulate any handbill, newspaper, or
other publication advocating such independence or
separation. "

24. Fro the text of this proclamation, see Forbes,
op. cit. , II, Appendix X.

25. Cf. supra, pp. 140-143.

26. Taft's policy of appointing only Federal Party
men to important posts was abandoned by Wright (supra,
Chapter VII, n. 94), and never revived by his successors.
In Smith's time, in fact, membership in one of the national-
ist groups was just as important as being a Federalista for
purposes of appointment (cf. supra, Chapter IV, n. 53);
Rafael Palma, a Nacionalista, was appointed to the
Philippine commission during his administration.

27. Liang, op. cit. , p. 75.

28. Quoted in Manifesto of the Federal Party: Recommendations to the Congress and Insular Governor...
(Manila: Establecimiento Tipografico "La Democracia,"
1905), p. 5. A copy is available at the NA, 2833-6.

29. Smith to Taft, September 24, 1906, Taft Papers.

30. Sumulong, loc. cit. , p. 867.

31. P. I. , Commission, Minutes of the Executive
Session of the Philippine Commission and the Secretary
of War and... the Congressional Party... Held at Manila,
August 11, 1905 (Manila: Bureau of Printing, 1905),
p. 57.

32. Maximo Kalaw, op. cit. , pp. 292 and 306; Liang,
op. cit. , pp. 77-79.

33. Tavera to Taft, January 9, 1907, NA, 2833-8.
My translation.

34. Legarda to Taft, January 17, 1909. Taft Papers.
I have used the English translation.

35. Tavera wrote Taft (loc. cit.) that Commissioner
Morgan W. Shuster "lends me his valuable assistance
[and] Governor Smith has given his entire approval" in
his (Tavera's) efforts to popularize the Progresista Party.
Such an attitude on the part of at least some of the American authorities was probably due to their personal knowledge that the Federalistas had changed their platform and
later party label not because they had become more
nationalistic or radical than before (more about this later).
Consequently, Dapen Liang's statement or conclusion
(op. cit. , p. 79) that the change "was highly significant in
itself" because "it marked an actual triumph of Filipino
nationalism,..." is open to question.

36. Taft to Root, November 11, 1902, Taft Papers;
idem. November 22, 1902, loc. cit. See also Maximo
Kalaw, op. cit. , pp. 287-89. Hereafter, all references
to Kalaw will be to Maximo (not Teodoro) Kalaw.

37. Ibid.

38. Ibid. , p. 289. Cf. Liang, op. cit. , pp. 66-68 for
the abortive nationalist parties before 1906.

39. Kalaw, op. cit. , pp. 300-301, and Liang, op. cit. ,
p. 72.

40. Smith to Taft, September 24, 1906, Taft Papers.

Cf. Dr. David J. Doherty to Taft, August 17, 1906, loc. cit. Both accounts are contemporary primary sources on the pre-Assembly Philippine political parties.

41. Kalaw, op. cit., pp. 302-303, and Liang, op. cit., p. 72.

42. Kalaw, op. cit., p. 302.

43. The full text of the Nacionalista Party platform is in ibid., pp. 304-6. See also the Manila Times, July 30, 1907. Liang (op. cit., p. 74) gives a short summary of the platform.

44. Philippine Commission Report, 1908, Pt. 1, p. 87. Previously, the provincial governor had been elected by the votes of the municipal vice-presidents and councilors of the province. Filipino "third" members of the provincial boards were also elected for the first time in 1907; heretofore, the governor had been the only elected member of the provincial board. Cf. supra, p. 56.

45. Philippine Commission Report, 1908, Pt. 1, p. 87.

46. Executive Secretary Frank W. Carpenter hastened to assure the Taft Party, then on its way to the islands for the opening session of the Assembly, that all statements and apprehensions on the upsurge of radicalism in the Philippines were "premised upon either honest ignorance or malicious misinformation." Carpenter to General Edwards, September 6, 1907, Confidential, Taft Papers. For Carpenter's Philippine career, see supra, Chapter VI, n. 107. He had excellent command of Spanish and Tagalog, and his position enabled him to enjoy a fairly representative circle of friends and acquaintances. According to him, he got his information "first hand" — "not via 'secret' service, or my muchacho, nor by observations through the bleary lens of 'Scotch and soda'." As we shall see later, Carpenter was right.

47. Cf. Carpenter, loc. cit. Many Nacionalistas, he wrote, were "men relatively of real worth and conservative to quite as a great a degree as any of our Progresista friends...." He also said of Osmena: "Although a Nationalist he is ultra-conservative and anxious to... [cooperate] with the Government."

Col. H. H. Bandholtz, then Acting Director of the
Philippine Constabulary, gave a pre-election assessment
in his letters to Taft, December 5, 1906, Taft Papers,
and to General Allen, May 16, 1907, Confidential, loc. cit.
Bandholtz told Taft before the merger of the nationalists
and the change in the name of the Federal Party that the
political groups were distinguishable from each other only
by their names, and that some Federalistas were as radical as the Urgentistas, and many of the Urgentistas "are
as conservative as any Federal." Bandholtz informed
Allen that Osmena and Quezon had assured him "that no
radical propositions will emanate from them."

48. For Filipino participation in the higher levels of
the government, see supra, p. 69.

49. Kalaw, op. cit., p. 317.

50. Forbes to SecWar, November 29, 1910, Cablegram, NA, 17073-71. Italics mine. In the 1909 elections,
the Nacionalistas had obtained four more Assembly seats
and about three times more popular votes than in the
elections held in 1907.

51. Cf. supra, n. 23 of this chapter, for the Sedition
Act. The Flag Law (Act No. 1696, Philippine Commission,
August 23, 1907) prohibited the display of the Philippine
flag, and was the direct result of the prominence given to
it, compared with the inconspicuous display of the American flag, by jubilant followers of the young Fernando Ma.
Guerrero while celebrating his election as Assembly delegate for the 2d district of Manila. This harsh action by
the Commission was received by cries that the administration was reverting to the "days of empire." Cf. Carpenter, loc. cit. The existence of the Sedition Law and later
the Flag Law has led Professor Kalaw to describe most of
the Taft Regime as "the period of suppressed nationalism."
Op. cit.

52. Cf. Kalaw, or. cit., pp. 317-22; Forbes to Sec-
War, loc. cit.; same to Jacob McG. Dickinson, Secretary
of War, February 12, 1911, Confidential, Forbes Papers;
same to Wright, March 15, 1911, Confidential, loc. cit.;
and same to T. N. Perkins, July 5, 1911, loc. cit.

The "chronic discord" between the Assembly and the
Commission was not terminated until 1914, when the

Democratic administration was already in power. This situation led President Wilson's special investigator in 1913 to observe that the relations between the Assembly and the Commission as separate chambers of the Legislature "are diplomatic rather than legislative. " Ford, "Main Report, 1913, " loc. cit. , p. 57. It will be recalled that Professor Henry Jones Ford spent sixty-six days investigating conditions in the Philippines in the spring of 1913. Cf. supra, p. 85.

53. Tavera to Smith, February 16, 1910, Smith Papers. My translation.

54. Ibid.

55. In December, 1906, as part of a contemplated merger with the Union Nacionalistas, the Federalistas almost joined the latter in urging Congress to declare its ultimate policy toward the Philippines. Secretary of War Taft, however, frowned upon both the merger and petition, when consulted by the Federalistas. See cablegrams, Smith to SecWar, December 24, 1906, and Taft to Smith, December 27, 1906, in Kalaw, op. cit. , pp. 306-7, n. 2; Smith to Sumulong, January 8, 1907, Smith Papers.

56. Quezon and Legarda to Dickinson, April 25, 1910, NA, 364-118. I have used the English translation.

57. Tavera to Quezon, February 10, 1910, NA, 18073-19. I have used the English translation. Tavera was no longer connected with the government at the time.

58. Ibid.

59. Forbes to Edwards, June 28, 1910, NA, 364-121. See also, for Forbes' later relationship with the nationalists, Forbes to Taft, April 8, 1911, Personal and Confidential, Forbes Papers.

60. Dickinson to Taft, August 7, 1910, copy in Dickinson, "Diary: 1910 — The Philippines, " Vol. I, in Jacob McGavock Dickinson Papers (Tennessee State Library and Archives, Nashville, Tennessee). I have a microfilmed copy of Secretary Dickinson's three-volume diary or journal of his Philippine tour (July 24 to September 3, 1910). See also his Special Report, p. 33.

61. Ford, "Main Report, 1913, " p. 95. Forbes (op. cit., II, 206) all but ignored this comment by Ford in his refutations of some of the latter's findings.

62. Ford, "Main Report, 1913," p. 96.

63. El Ideal, September 22, 1910, English translation of clipping in the Forbes Papers. For more information about El Ideal, see Valenzuela, op. cit., pp. 153-55.

El Ideal's editorial was inspired by Secretary Dickinson's statements during his Philippine trip (n. 60, supra),
in which he had reaffirmed Taft's earlier declarations on
American policy. Dickinson also said that the assumptions
upon which such a policy had originally been based were as
valid as ever, conditions having changed but little. There
was still a prevalence of caciquism, mass illiteracy and
the lack of an intelligent public opinion. Cf. Dickinson's
"Diary," passim. (Dickinson's views were later summarized in his Special Report, pp. 6-9.)

While Dickinson was still in the Philippines, El Ideal
refuted his remarks, branding as absurd the hypothesis
that if independence were to be granted to the Filipinos,
the ignorant masses would be exploited by a handful of
"intriguers and caciques." "Will the Filipinos not be
more interested in the education of these ignorant masses
than anybody else?" it asked. "Would they be so supinely
stupid as not to understand that the strength of the nation
lies in the education of the entire people? The defects
now observed in the Filipino race will be corrected as
soon as they are independent,..." El Ideal, August 30,
1910, translation of clipping in NA, 364-133.

64. La Vanguardia was "the reincarnation of El
Renacimiento," which had folded as a result of Worcester's libel suit against it in 1908. Cf. supra, Chapter III,
n. 81, and Valenzuela, op. cit., pp. 129-31 and 155.

65. La Vanguardia, May 10, 1911, English translation of clipping in the Forbes Papers.

66. Same, November 7, 1912 (translation), loc. cit.

67. Cf. Kalaw, op. cit., p. 334.

68. La Vanguardia, November 7, 1912, loc. cit.

69. Elliott, Commission Government, p. 417;
Forbes, op. cit., II, 203.

70. Bell to Forbes, November 20, 1912, Forbes
Papers.

71. Quoted in Forbes, op. cit., II, 358. The
Assembly's petitions generally consisted of the speech of

the Speaker at each concluding session, expressing it as
the wish of the entire chamber that the Filipinos desired
"immediate" independence, and adopted as a resolution
of the Assembly to be forwarded to the American Congress,
or of instructions to the Resident Commissioners to speak
in behalf of "immediate" independence in Congress. Cf.
Liang, op. cit. , pp. 91-92.

72. Quoted in Forbes, op. cit. , II, 358, n. 1. Wilson
delivered his speech in December, 1912.

73. In this respect, the position of some of the Filipino elite was similar to their stand on free trade relations
with the United States. See supra, pp. 125-133.

74. Quezon saw service in the Philippine-American
War. He was elected governor of Tayabas (now Quezon)
province in 1906 and to the Assembly in 1907 where he became the majority floor leader. In 1909, he was chosen
as one of the resident commissioners in the United States
and openly campaigned there for Philippine independence.
He served in that capacity until 1916, when he was elected
to the Senate of the Jones Law legislature and became its
president. In 1933, having maneuvered the rejection of
the Hare-Hawes-Cutting Act by the Philippine Legislature, he went to the United States and returned with the
Tydings-McDuffie Act of 1934, which was essentially the
Hare-Hawes-Cutting Act under a different name, and
which provided for the establishment of the Philippine
Commonwealth, under which a ten-year transitional government would be set up prior to independence. He became the first President of the Commonwealth, as expected, and had he not died in 1944, he would certainly
have also become the first President of the Philippine
Republic.

Osmena, who was less flamboyant than Quezon, was
a former editor of the nationalistic paper El Nuevo Dia
(Cebu). He was elected Governor of Cebu in 1906, and
later became the Speaker of the lower house of the
Philippine Legislature until 1922, when he was elected
to the Senate. He obtained, with Manuel A. Roxas, the
Hare-Hawes-Cutting Act in 1933, was elected first Vice
President of the Common wealth, and finally became its
President in 1944 upon Quezon's death.

75. To dispose of the books immediately, mention might be made of the works by Elliott, Commission Government (pp. 445-48), and Forbes (op. cit., II, 372, 385-87). Both Elliott and Forbes were ranking officials of the Taft Regime. They describe the wealthy landowners and businessmen as constituting the class which was generally opposed to independence, and Forbes referred to, and even quoted some, specific statements of attitudes expressed by individuals, but withheld the identity of his sources. See also Mrs. William H. Taft, op. cit., p. 112.

76. Op. cit., p. 9. Cf. Taft, Special Report (1908), pp. 74-75.

77. Cf. supra, Chapter VI, n. 47.

78. Cf. supra, Chapter VIII, n. 46, and Chapter VI, n. 47.

79. Forbes to R. E. Forbes, August 14, 1907, Forbes Papers. Italics mine.

80. Forbes to Taft, December 14, 1907, Confidential, Taft Papers. Bandholtz told Allen in May, 1907, that Forbes would be the "one Commissioner" who would have influence in the Assembly. Bandholtz to Allen, May 24, 1907, Confidential, loc. cit.

81. Forbes to Taft, July 14, 1910, Confidential, Forbes Papers.

82. H. B. 22143 (U. S. Congress, 62nd Cong., 2nd Sess., 1912). Cf. Kirk, op. cit., p. 44, and Elliott, Commission Government, p. 417.

83. Cf. Edward Bowditch, Jr., to Forbes (then in the United States), October 19, 1912, Forbes Papers. Bowditch, who was Forbes' Secretary, wrote that since Quezon's return from the United States he had been making a round of speeches almost every night, telling his listeners that Philippine independence was "in sight and that the Jones Bill will surely pass." Italics mine. Quezon was probably convinced that because of the Republican split, the Democrats would gain control of the White House and Congress in the November elections.

84. Bell to Forbes, November 20, 1912, loc. cit.

85. Forbes to Roosevelt, June 1, 1916, in Theodore Roosevelt Papers (The Houghton Library of Harvard University, Cambridge, Massachusetts).

86. On this point, see also NA, 364-178. This is an unsigned memorandum prepared by Forbes for Congressman William Redfield of Massachusetts for use in answering the first Jones. Bill. Cf. Forbes to Secretary of War Jenry L. Stimson, May 26, 1912, Personal and Confidential, loc. cit. , 364-177.

87. Forbes to Roosevelt, loc. cit. They do not appear in Forbes' two-volume work.

88. Professor Ford had two interviews with Speaker Osmena in 1913, during which Osmena said that the aim of the Nacionalista Party was "the organization of an independent government. . . . " The qualifier "immediately" does not appear. In his report to President Wilson, Ford said that while the United States should state positively that the Filipinos would not be held subjects against their will, "to fix a date at which complete independence should automatically take effect would be wanting in due regard for their situation. " It may be inferred from Ford's statement that from his conversations with Filipino leaders, including Osmena, he noticed that they were afraid that the Jones Bill might be passed. If so, he did not specify the probable bases for such fears, except to state that independence "is so involved in external considerations that it would be wise to postpone action" on it until later. Ford, "Main Report, 1913" pp. 73, 97.

89. Copies of these memoranda are in NA, 4325-158. These memoranda were prepared by McIntyre for Secretary of War Lindley M. Garrison, and will be cited hereafter as McIntyre, "Memorandum No. 1 — 1913" and "Memorandum No. 2 — 1914. " "Memorandum No. 1 — 1913, " dated December 29, 1913, covers the conversations of December 28-29. "Memorandum No. 2 — 1914" covers the points discussed on January 2, 5, 6, 12, 15, and 16, and is dated January 17. They were transmitted to President Wilson by Secretary Garrison on January 19, 1914, the President acknowledging their receipt in a letter to Secretary Garrison dated January 21, 1914. See, for the correspondence, NA, 4325-158.

90. Quezon had by this time acquired an excellent command of English. It might be pointed out at this point that although Quezon had an able secretary in Maximo

Kalaw, a scholar and former Dean of the University of the
Philippines College of Liberal Arts, it is not known
whether he was with Quezon during the nine times that
Quezon and McIntyre met. McIntyre does not mention
Kalaw, and Kalaw (op. cit.) does not even allude to such
conversations (neither does Quezon, op. cit.)! It is most
likely that the talks were held "behind closed doors."
    91. McIntyre, "Memorandum No. 1 — 1913."
Italics mine.
    92. McIntyre, "Memorandum No. 2 — 1914." All
subsequent citations are from this memorandum.
    93. Italics mine.
    94. Cf. supra, pp. 67-68, for the impact of Ameri-
can policy upon the party system in the Philippines.
    95. See, for Japanese plans, Willard H. Elsbree,
Japan's Role in Southeast Asian Nationalist Movements,
1940-1945 (New York: Institute of Pacific Relations,
1953.
    96. Forbes, op. cit. , II, 372, 385-88.
    97. Cf. Agoncillo, Malolos, pp. 429-32, citing and
quoting liberally from primary American sources.
    98. The Filipino elite, except for a few, did not join
the first phase of the Philippine Revolution (1896-1897)
not because of the fear of anarchy, but because they believed that the Filipinos were then ill-prepared to defeat
the Spanish forces and did not with to suffer the dire consequences of failure. Cf. supra, pp. 14-15, for this and
other reasons, none of which had any connection with the
fear of anarchy.
    99. Forbes himself (op. cit. , I, 224-35) discusses
the efforts of Government forces, at times assisted by
American regular troops, to put down fanatical outbreaks
and instill respect for law and order. I point out some of
these fanatical groups in the next section of this chapter,
but see, for the details, the annual reports of the Director of the Philippine Constabulary, 1902-1913, and
General Leonard Wood to President Roosevelt, November 18, 1906, Personal, in Leonard Wood Papers
(Library of Congress, Washington, D. C.)
    100. Elliott, Commission Government, p. 466.
    101. For the Philippine Government during the

revolutionary period, see supra, pp. 16-19.

102. Cf. Corpuz, "Western Colonisation and the Filipino Response," loc. cit., p. 18.

103. Cf. supra, pp. 14-16.

104 Cf. supra, p. 26; 45-46; 53-54; 92-93.

105. Cf. supra, pp. 135-139.

106. The Filipinos got independence and free trade in 1946, but it was not conceived that way during the Taft Regime, or even during the Commonwealth period.

107. See, for instance, Forbes, op. cit., I, 225.

108. Among these may be mentioned Felipe Salvador, really a marginal case, leader of the Santa Iglesia (Holy Church) movement in Central Luzon; the bandits Oruga and Otoy of Laguna and Samar, respectively; "Popes" Isio, Ablen, Faustino, Tiducduc, etc. Forbes, op. cit., I, 228-29. For the Santa Iglesia movement, see also P. I., Bureau of Constabulary, Annual Report of the Director of the Constabulary...July 1, 1905 — August 31, 1906 (Manila: Bureau of Printing, 1906), pp. 4-5, composed of excerpts from the report of the Senior Inspector of the First Constabulary District. Hereafter cited simply as Director of Constabulary, Annual Report.

109. Taft to Root, April 26, 1903, Root Papers.

110. Although "pulahan" (literally bandit or fanatic outbreaks in Samar and Leyte in 1904-1906 at one time involved the operations of several hundred Philippine Constabulary troops, Philippine Scouts (Filipino units of the regular army of the United States), and American troops, unlike the Sakay movement, the authorities did not regard such outbreaks as independence movements.

At the height of "pulahanism" in Samar and Leyte in 1906, Governor Smith, in company with Osmena, Sumulong and Barretto (representing the political parties), visited affected towns in those provinces. His cablegram, to Taft on November 27, 1906 (NA, 4865-40), reads in part: "Am convinced educated and civilized people have not been in sympathy with Pulahan fanatic movement.... Trouble in Leyte had no political significance.... Civilized instructed Filipinos of Samar have not been identified with and there is not the least evidence to show, as far as I could discover, that they have been involved in the Pulahan disturbances. '' For a similar view by another observer, see Doherty to Taft, August 17, 1906, Taft Papers. But Blount (op. cit., pp. 256ff.) says that as "pulahanism" remained unchecked in some parts, it began to develop as a political movement. Nevertheless, the outbreaks did not originate as political movements.

The "ladrone" outbreaks in Batangas-Cavite-Laguna, however, took on the semblance of an insurrection, although Tavera was quick to deny it, especially when the Constabulary suspected the prominent and wealthy Roxas family of complicity in the movement led by Sakay and his lieutenants. Cf. Tavera to Taft, March 3, 1905, Confidential, Taft Papers. English translation.

111. Cf. Armando J. Malay's "Introduction" in Memoirs of General Artemio Ricarte (Manila: National Heroes Commission, 1963), p. xx. Cited hereafter as Ricarte Memoirs. See also Philippine Commission Report, 1907, Pt. 1, pp. 37-38 for information about Sakay and his men.

112. Ibid., 1906, Pt. 1, pp. 29-30.

113. Ibid., 1907, Pt. 1, p. 40, gives specific date.

114. A surgeon, Dr. Dominador Gomez studied in Spain and was a member of the Madrid Junta opposing American annexation of the Philippines. He returned to the islands after the end of hostilities and soon took over the presidency of the Union Obrera Democratica from Isabelo de los Reyes, of Aglipayan fame. In 1906, he was the president of the Partido Urgentista. See ibid., 1903, Pt. 1, pp. 36-37; Smith to Taft, September 24, 1906, Taft Papers, and Doherty to Taft, August 17, 1906, loc. cit.

115. This view is insisted upon despite the official claim that Sakay and aides had "unconditionally surrendered." Director of Constabulary, Annual Report, 1907, p. 4. Cf. Governor Ide's cablegram to Taft, July 20, 1906, stating that "absolutely no promises [have been] made, except a fair trial, " in Forbes, op. cit., I, 229, and n. 2, and Philippine Commission Report, 1907, Pt. 1, pp. 39-40. The administration seemed to have really made promises of some sort, but it protested too much that it had not. See, however, footnote 116 below.

116. Governor Ide stated in his cable to Taft (loc.

cit.) that "no promises as to his litigation have been
authorized or made" to Dr. Gomez. This is not true, as
may be seen from Forbes' confidential letter to Taft regarding the matter:

'In the last two weeks things have become almost un-
bearable. Ide undertook to interpret a trade which Bandholtz had made in regard to reward made for the surrender
of certain bandits [sic] in a different sense from the way
Bandholtz and his agent [Gomez] understood it, thus practically repudiating an obligation which he and I previously
authorized Bandholtz to make. I have personally guaranteed
to Bandholtz that this difference be made good although it
comes to several thousand pesos,... " Forbes to Taft,
September 21, 1906, Forbes Papers. Italics mine. The
Philippine Constabulary was then under Forbes' department.
— Commerce and Police.

    117. Acting Constabulary Director at the time.

    118. It is evident that the "Bandolerismo Statute" of
November 12, 1902 had been passed just for the purpose
of "undignifying" even patently nationalist activities. The
law was even harsher than the Sedition Law, since no
prima facie evidence was necessary for conviction, which
carried the maximum penalty of death: all that was required was a mere reasonable inference that one had committed robbery through membership in an armed band.
Section 4 of the statute was a warning to nationalists suspected of conniving with or abetting "ladrones" in that it
imposed a punishment of imprisonment ranging from ten
to twenty years upon conviction. Philippine Commission
Report, 1903, Pt. I, pp. 34-35.

    119. Ibid., 1907, Pt. 1, p. 37. Some prominent
Filipinos of Manila prayed for pardon or clemency for
Sakay and Vega, but to no avail. Ibid., p. 39.

    120. The biographical data on Ricarte have been
taken from Malay's "Introduction" to the Ricarte Memoirs, pp. xv-xxv. The data on his movement have been
taken from the appendixes to the Ricarte Memoirs.

    The Memoirs proper go down only to December 1897.
Ricarte wrote them while in prison after 1903 at the request of William Brecknock Watson, an English journalist
in Manila at the time. The appendixes were themselves

part of the "Watson Collection." These will be identified
properly as citations are made to them in the succeeding
pages.

121. The text of Ricarte's proclamation is in the
Ricarte Memoirs, Appendix I. Italics mine. The proclamation, dated December 25, 1903, was published in English by the Cablenews (Manila) on January 3, 1904.

122. The "commissions" were sold at prices ranging
from ₱0.25 for Lieutenants to ₱1.25 for Colonels. Watson,
"The Christmas Eve Fiasco and A Brief Outline of the
Ricarte and Other Similar Movements from the Time of the
Breaking Up of the Insurrection of 1899-1901," in Ricarte
Memoirs, Appendix N, p. 179. Cited hereafter as Watson,
"Christmas Eve Fiasco."

123. I have based the narrative up to this point on the
stenographic report of Ricarte's interrogation by the Constabulary and the Manila Police in April, 1904, and on
Watson, "Christmas Eve Fiasco," loc. cit., pp. 122-30.
(Appendix K) and pp. 180-88, respectively.

124. Ibid., p. 188. General Ricarte stayed in Hongkong until 1915, when he moved to Japan, settling down in
Yokohama. He returned to the Philippines in December,
1941, with the Japanese invasion forces and died as a full-
fledged Japanese collaborator on July 31, 1945. Malay,
loc. cit.

125. Watson, "Christmas Eve Fiasco," loc. cit.,
pp. 207-8.

126. Ibid., pp. 208-9.

127. Ibid., p. 210.

128. Ibid., pp. 210-11.

129. August 26, 1896 is the traditional date of the so-
called "Cry of Balintawak," which marks the beginning of
the revolution against Spain. It was actually the "Cry of
Pugadlawin," and it took place not on August 26 but on
August 23, 1896. See Agoncillo, The Revolt of the
Masses, pp. 146-50.

130. Confidential Memorandum by Colonel J.G.
Harbord, Acting Director of the Philippine Constabulary,
August 27, 1912, in the Forbes Papers.

131. Ibid.

132. Cf. ibid., wherein it is mentioned that Joaquin

Luna and Lope K. Santos, members of the Assembly, were allegedly "in" on the August 26 plot, but got scared and called it off.

133. Kalaw, op. cit., p. 334.

134. Cf. La Democracia's editorial in its issue of September 11, 1912 (English translation of clipping in the Forbes Papers) on the August 26 plot.

Professor Ford made the following report to President Wilson:

"In all parts of the Philippines I found the belief was held by those most closely in touch with the situation that another insurrection is impending, and that it is stayed for the present only through hopes that the policy of the United States under the present administration will avert the necessity of conflict." Ford, "supplementary Report, 1913," p. 1.

This is a somewhat overdrawn observation, since the bulk of the elite were against any insurrection and did not even desire "immediate" independence.

Chapter IX

1. Cf. Corpuz, Bureaucracy in the Philippines, p. 165.

2. Forbes, op. cit., II, 158.

3. Theodore Friend, Between Two Empires: The Ordeal of the Philippines, 1929-1946 (New Haven, Connecticut: Yale University Press, 1965), p. 4 et passim. Unfortunately, I was not able to profit more from the insights of Professor Friend's monograph, since it was released only after I had completed the final draft of the main body of my thesis.

BIBLIOGRAPHY

BIBLIOGRAPHY

A. BIBLIOGRAPHICAL AIDS

ELSNER, Emma Osterman. Checklist of Publications of the Government of the Philippine Islands, September 1, 1900, to December 31, 1917. Manila: Bureau of Printing, 1918.

GRIFFIN, A. P. Bibliography of the Philippine Islands. Washington: U. S. Government Printing Office, 1903.

HAMER, Philip M. (ed.) A Guide to Archives and Manuscripts in the United States. New Haven, Connecticut: Yale University Press, 1961.

MUNDEN, Kenneth. (comp.) Records of the Bureau of Insular Affairs Relating to the Philippine Islands, 1898-1935: A List of Selected Files. (Special List No. 2.) Washington, D. C., The U. S. National Archives, 1942.

University of Chicago Philippine Studies Program. Selected Bibliography of the Philippines: Topically Arranged and Annotated. Preliminary edition. New Haven, Connecticut: Human Relations Area Files, 1956.

B. PUBLISHED DOCUMENTS

Manifesto of the Federal Party: Recommendations to the Congress and Insular Governor... Manila: Establecimiento Tipografico "La Democracia," 1905.

P. I. Board of Educational Survey. A Survey of the Educational System of the Philippine Islands. Manila: Bureau of Printing, 1925.

P. I. Bureau of Constabulary. Annual Reports of the
    Directors of the Constabulary (1902-1913).
    Manila: Bureau of Printing, 1902-1913.

P. I. Bureau of Customs. Annual Reports of the Insular
    Collector of Customs (1907, 1913, 1921, 1925).
    Manila: Bureau of Printing, 1907, 1913, 1921,
    1925.

P. I. Bureau of Lands. Annual Report of the Director
    of Lands... June 30, 1912. Manila: Bureau of
    Printing, 1912.

P. I. Census Office. Census of the Philippine Islands
    Taken... in the Year 1918. 4 vols. Manila:
    Bureau of Printing, 1921.

P. I. Commission. The Friar Land Inquiry — Philip-
    pine Government. Manila: Bureau of Printing,
    1910.

--- Hearings Before the Secretary of War and the
    Congressional Party Accompanying Him to the
    Philippine Islands, Manila, August 29-30, 1905.
    Manila: Bureau of Printing, 1905.

--- Minutes of the Executive Session of the Philippine
    Commission and the Secretary of War and... the
    Congressional Party... Held at Manila, August
    11, 1905. Manila: Bureau of Printing, 1905.

P. I. Department of Finance and Justice. Annual Re-
    ports of the Secretary of Finance and Justice
    (1902-1913). Manila: Bureau of Printing, 1902-
    1913.

P. I. Department of Public Instruction. Annual Re-
    ports of the Secretary of Public Instruction (1902-
    1913). Manila: Bureau of Printing, 1902-1913.

P. I. Legislature, Philippine Assembly. Diario de
    sesiones de la Asamblea Filipina, 1907 to 1916.
    11 vols.

--- Philippine Commission. Journal of the Philippine
    Commission, 1907 to 1916. 9 vols.

P. I. Public Laws Passed by the Philippine Commission
    [and Legislature]. (9 vols. covering the period of
    the Taft Regime.) Manila: Bureau of Printing,
    1903-1915.

RICHARDSON, James D. A Compilation of the Mes-
    sages and Papers of the Presidents. 20 vols.
    New York: Bureau of National Literature, Inc.
    [1917?]. Vol. XV.

U. S. Adjutant-General's Office. Correspondence Re-
    lating to the War with Spain. . . . from April 15,
    1898, to July 30, 1902. 2 vols. Washington,
    D. C. : U. S. Government Printing Office, 1902.
    Vol. II.

U. S. Bureau of Insular Affairs. The Philippine
    Islands. Washington, D. C. : U. S. Government
    Printing Office, 1913.

U. S. Congressional Record. Vol. XLIV.

U. S. Department of State. Foreign Relations of the
    United States: 1898. Washington, D. C. : Gov-
    ernment Printing Office, 1862-

U. S. Philippine Commission. Report of the [Schur-
    man] Philippine Commission to the President. 4
    vols. Washington, D. C. : U. S. Government
    Printing Office, 1900-1901.

U. S. Senate, Committee on the Philippines. Hearings,
    Affairs in the Philippine Islands. Document No.
    331, Part 1, 57th Cong. , 1st Sess. , 1902.

U.S. Senate. Lands Held for Ecclesiastical or Religious Uses in the Philippine Islands. Document No. 190. 56th Cong., 2d Sess., 1901.

--- Public Hearings on the Philippine Tariff...Held during the Month of August Before the Secretary of War and the Congressional Party [in]...the Philippine Islands. Document No. 227, Appendix, 59th Cong., 1st Sess., 1905.

--- Reports of the Taft Philippine Commission. Document No. 112. 56th Cong., 2d Sess., 1901.

U.S. Statutes at Large. Vols. XXX, XXXI, XXXV-XXXVI, XXXVIII-XXXIX.

U.S. War Department. Annual Reports for the Fiscal Year Ended June 30, 1900, Vol. I: Report of the Secretary of War. Washington, D.C.: U.S. Government Printing Office, 1900. Part 1.

--- Annual Reports for the Fiscal Year Ended June 30, 1901, Vol I, Part 4: Report of the Lieutenant-General Commanding the Army. Washington, D.C.: U.S. Government Printing Office, 1901.

--- Reports of the Philippine Commission (1901-1913). Washington, D.C.: U.S. Government Printing Office, 1901-1913.

--- Five Years of the War Department...1899-1903, As Shown in the Annual Reports of the Secretary of War. Washington, D.C.: U.S. Government Printing Office, [1904?].

--- Report of Major-General E.S. Otis, U.S. Volunteers, on Military Operations and Civil Affairs in the Philippine Islands, 1899. Washington, D.C.: U.S. Government Printing Office, 1899.

--- Special Report of J. M. Dickinson, Secretary of
War, to the President on the Philippines. Washington, D. C. : U. S. Government Printing Office,
1910.

--- Special Report of Wm. H. Taft to the President
on the Philippines. Washington, D. C. : U. S.
Government Printing Office, 1908.

C. PUBLISHED LETTERS, MEMOIRS,
AND AUTOBIOGRAPHIES

CALDERON, Felipe G. Mis memorias sobre la
revolucion Filipina. Segunda etapa. Manila:
Imp. de El Renacimiento, 1907.

CANNING, Eyot (ed.). The Story of the Lopez Family.
Boston: J. H. West Company, 1904.

DEWEY, George. Autobiography. New York: Charles
Scribner's Sons, 1913.

Memoirs of General Artemio Ricarte. Manila:
National Heroes Commission, 1963.

MORISON, Elting, et al. (ed.). The Letters of
Theodore Roosevelt. 8 vols. Cambridge, Mass:
Harvard University Press, 1951-1954.

QUEZON, Manuel Luis. The Good Fight. New York:
D. Appleton-Century Company, Inc., 1946.

ROOSEVELT, Theodore. An Autobiography. New
York: The Macmillan Company, 1913.

SARGENT, Nathan (comp.) Admiral Dewey and the
Manila Campaign. Washington: Naval Historical
Foundation, 1947.

TAFT, Mrs. William Howard. Recollections of Full
Years. New York: Dodd, Mead and Company, 1914.

WILLIAMS, D. R.   The Odyssey of the Philippine
Commission.   Chicago: A. C. McClurg and
Co., 1913.

D.   BOOKS

ABELARDE, Pedro E.   American Tariff Policy Toward
the Philippines, 1898-1946.   Morningside Heights,
N. Y.: King's Crown Press, 1947.

ACHUTEGUI, Pedro S. de, S. J., and Bernad, Miguel
A., S. J.   Religious Revolution in the Philippines:
The Life and Church of Gregorio Aglipay, 1860-
1960, Vol. I: From Aglipay's Birth to His Death,
1860-1940.   Manila: Ateneo de Manila, 1960.

AGONCILLO, Teodoro A.   Malolos: The Crisis of the
Republic.   ("The Philippine Social Sciences and
Humanities Review" [hereafter "PSSHR"], Vol.
XXV, Nos. 1-4.) Quezon City: University of the
Philippines, 1960.

--- The Revolt of the Masses: The Story of Bonifacio
and the Katipunan.   ("PSSHR," Vol. XXI, Nos.
1-4.) Quezon City: University of the Philippines,
1956.

ALZONA, Encarnacion.   A History of Education in the
Philippines, 1565-1930.   1st ed.   Manila: University of the Philippines Press, 1932.

BAZACO, Evergisto, O.P.   History of Education in the
Philippines.   Vol. I: Spanish Period — 1565-1898.
Manila: University of Santo Tomas Press, 1939.

BEMIS, Samuel Flagg.   A Diplomatic History of the
United States.   4th ed.   New York: Henry Holt
and Company, 1955.

BLOUNT, James H.   The American Occupation of the
Philippines, 1898-1912.   New York: G. P. Putnam's
Sons, 1912.

BRIGGS, Charles W. The Progressing Philippines. Philadelphia: The Griffith and Rowland Press, 1913.

COQUIA, Jorge R. The Legal Status of the Church in the Philippines. Washington: The Catholic University of America Press, 1950.

CORPUZ, Onofre D. The Bureaucracy in the Philippines. Manila: University of the Philippines, 1957.

DAUNCEY, Mrs. Campbell. An Englishwoman in the Philippines. New York: E. P. Dutton and Company, 1906.

del PILAR, Marcelo H. La frailocracia Filipina. Barcelona: Imp. de F. Fossas, 1888.

--- La soberania monacal en Filipinas. Barcelona: Imp. de F. Fossas, 1888.

DEUTSCH, Karl W. Nationalism and Social Communication: An Inquirty into the Foundations of Nationality. Cambridge, Mass.: Technology Press, and New York: John Wiley and Sons, 1953.

[DUNNE, Finley Peter], Observations by Mr. Dooley. New York: Harper and Brothers, 1906.

DUNNE, Philip (ed.) Mr. Dooley Remembers: The Informal Memoirs of Finley Peter Dunne. Boston: Little, Brown and Company, 1963.

ELLIOTT, Charles Burke. The Philippines: To the End of the Military Regime. Indianapolis: The Bobbs-Merrill Company, 1916.

--- The Philippines: To the End of the Commission Government — A Study in Tropical Democracy. Indianapolis: The Bobbs-Merrill Company, 1917.

ELLIS, Elmer. Mr. Dooley's America: A Life of Finley
    Peter Dunne. New York: Alfred A. Knopf, 1941.

ELSBREE, Willard H. Japan's Role in Southeast Asian
    Nationalist Movements, 1940-1945. New York:
    Institute of Pacific Relations, 1953.

FEE, Mary H. A Woman's Impressions of the Philippines.
    Chicago: A. C. McClurg and Co., 1910.

FERNANDEZ, Leandro H. The Philippine Republic.
    ("Columbia University: Studies in History, Economics
    and Public Law, " Vol. CXXII, No. 1.) New York:
    Columbia University Press, 1926.

FORBES, W. Cameron. The Philippine Islands. 2 vols.
    Boston: Houghton Mifflin Company, 1928.

FRIEND, Theodore. Between Two Empires: The Ordeal
    of the Philippines, 1929-1946. New Haven, Connecti-
    cut: Yale University Press, 1965.

GOWING, Peter G. Mosque and Moro: A Study of Muslims
    in the Philippines. Manila: Philippine Federation of
    Christian Churches, 1964.

GRISWOLD, A. Whitney. The Far Eastern Policy of the
    United States. New York: Harcourt, Brace and Co.,
    1938.

GRUNDER, Garel E., and Livezey, William E. The
    Philippines and the United States. Norman, Oklahoma:
    University of Oklahoma Press, 1951.

HAGEDORN, Hermann. Leonard Wood: A Biography. 2
    vols. New York: Harper and Brothers, 1931.

HALLE, Louis J. Dream and Reality: Aspects of Ameri-
    can Foreign Policy. New York: Harper and Brothers,
    1959.

HALSTEAD, Murat. The Story of the Philippines. Chicago: Our Possessions Publishing Co., 1898.

HART, Albert Bushnell. The Obvious Orient. New York: D. Appleton and Company, 1911.

HARTENDORP, A. V. H. History of Industry and Trade of the Philippines. Rev. ed. Manila: American Chamber of Commerce of the Philippines, 1958.

HAYDEN, Joseph Ralston. The Philippines: A Study in National Development. New York: The Macmillan Company, 1955. (First published in 1942.)

HERRERO, Fr. Casimiro. Resena que demuestra el fundamento y causas de la insurreccion del 20 de enero en Filipinas. Madrid: Imp. de Segundo Martinez, 1872.

HORD, John S. Internal Taxation in the Philippines. ("Johns Hopkins University: Studies in Historical and Political Science," Series XXV, No. 1.) Baltimore: The Johns Hopkins Press, 1907.

IRELAND, Alleyne. The Far Eastern Tropics: Studies in the Adminstration of Tropical Dependencies. Boston: Houghton Mifflin and Company, 1905.

JESSUP, Philip C. Elihu Root. 2 vols. New York: Dodd, Mead and Company, 1938.

KALAW, Maximo M. The Development of Philippine Politics, (1872-1920). Manila: Oriental Commercial Company, Inc., [1926].

KALAW, Teodoro M. The Philippine Revolution. Manila: Manila Book Company, 1925.

KENNAN, George F. American Diplomacy, 1900-1950. Chicago: The University of Chicago Press, 1951.

KIRK, Grayson L. Philippine Independence: Motives,
    Problems, and Prospects. New York: Farrar and
    Rinehart, Inc. , 1936.

LAUBACH, Frank Charles. The People of the Philippines:
    Their Religious Progress and Preparation for Spiritual
    Leadership in the Far East. New York: George H.
    Doran Company, 1925.

LEECH, Margaret. In the Days of McKinley. New York:
    Harper and Brothers, 1959.

LeROY, James A. The Americans in the Philippines. 2
    vols. Boston: Houghton Mifflin Company, 1914.

--- Philippine Life in Town and Country. New York:
    G. P. Putnam's Sons, 1905.

LIANG, Dapen. The Development of Philippine Political
    Parties. Hongkong: South China Morning Post, 1939.

LOPEZ-JAENA, Graciano. Discursos y articulos varios.
    Manila: Bureau of Printing, 1951.

McDEVITT, Brother V. Edmund, F. S. C. The First
    California's Chaplain. Fresno, Calif. : Academy
    Library Guild, 1956.

MAJUL, Cesar Adib. Mabini and the Philippine Revolution.
    Quezon City: University of the Philippines, 1960.

--- The Political and Constitutional Ideas of the Philippine
    Revolution. ("PSSHR, " Vol. XXII, Nos. 1-2.)
    Quezon City: University of the Philippines, 1957.

The Malolos Congress. Manila: Philippines Historical
    Committee, 1963.

MORGAN, H. Wayne. William McKinley and His America.
    Syracuse, N. Y. : Syracuse University Press, 1963.

MOYNIHAN, James H. The Life of Archbishop John Ireland. New York: Harper and Brothers, 1953.

O'CONNOR, Richard. Black Jack Pershing. Garden City, N. Y. : Doubleday and Company, Inc. , 1961.

OLCOTT, Charles A. The Life of William McKinley. 2 vols. Boston: Houghton Mifflin Company, 1916.

PALMA, Rafael. Our Campaign for Independence from Taft to Harrison, (1901-1921). With Annotations by Teodoro M. Kalaw. Manila: Bureau of Printing, 1923.

PELZER, Karl J. Pioneer Settlement in the Asiatic Tropics: Studies in Land Utilization and Agricultural Colonization in Southeastern Asia. New York: American Geographical Society, 1945.

PHELAN, John Leddy. The Hispanization of the Philippines: Spanish Aims and Filipino Responses, 1565-1700. Madison, Wis. : The University of Wisconsin Press, 1959.

PIER, Arthur S. American Apostles to the Philippines. Boston: The Beacon Press, 1950.

PONCE, Mariano. Cartas sobre la Revolucion: (1897-1900). Manila: Bureau of Printing, 1932.

PRATT, Julius W. America's Colonial Experiment: How the United States Gained, Governed, and in Part Gave Away a Colonial Empire. New York: Prentice-Hall, Inc. , 1950.

PRINGLE, Henry F. The Life and Times of William Howard Taft. 2 vols. New York: Farrar and Rinehart, Inc. , 1939.

REYES, Jose S. Legislative History of America's
    Economic Policy Toward the Philippines. ("Columbia
    University: Studies in History, Economics and Public
    Law, " Vol. CVI, No. 2.) New York: Columbia
    University Press, 1923.

RIZAL, Jose. The Reign of Greed. Translated by Charles
    E. Derbyshire. Manila: Philippine Education Com-
    pany, 1912.

--- The Social Cancer. Translated by Charles E. Derby-
    shire. Manila: Philippine Education Company, 1912.

RODRIGUEZ, P. Isacio R. , O.S.A. Gregorio Aglipay y
    los origenes de la Iglesia Filipina Independiente,
    (1898-1917). 2 vols. Madrid: Departamento de
    Misionologia Espanola, 1960.

SCHURMAN, Jacob Gould. Philippine Affairs: A Retro-
    spect and Outlook. New York: Charles Scribner's
    Sons, 1902.

STUNTZ, Homer C. The Philippines and the Far East.
    Cincinnati: Jennings and Pye, 1904.

TAYLOR, Carson. History of the Philippine Press.
    Manila: n. p. , 1927.

TAYLOR, George E. The Philippines and the United
    States: Problems of Partnership. New York: Council
    on Foreign Relations, 1964.

VALENZUELA, Jesus Z. History of Journalism in the
    Philippine Islands. Manila: Published by the author,
    1933.

WHITTEMORE, Lewis Bliss. Struggle for Freedom: His-
    tory of the Philippine Independent Church. Green-
    wich, Connecticut: The Seabury Press, Inc. , 1961.

WILLIAMS, D. R. The United States and the Philippines.
Garden City, N. Y.: Doubleday, Page and Company,
1924.

WILLIS, Henry Parker. Our Philippine Problem: A
Study of American Colonial Policy. New York:
Henry Holt and Company, 1905.

WOLFF, Leon. Little Brown Brother: How the United
States Purchased and Pacified the Philippine Islands
at the Century's Turn. Garden City, N. Y.: Doubleday and Company, Inc., 1961.

WORCESTER, Dean C. The Philippines: Past and Present. Edited by [Joseph] Ralston Hayden. 2 vols.
New ed. New York: The Macmillan Company, 1930.

ZABRISKIE, Alexander C. Bishop Brent: Crusader for
Christian Unity. Philadelphia: The Westminster
Press, 1948.

ZAIDE, Gregorio F. The Philippine Revolution. Manila:
Modern Book Company, 1954.

ZWIERLEIN, Frederick J. Theodore Roosevelt and
Catholics, 1882-1919. Rochester, N. Y.: Printed
for the Reverend Victor T. Suren by the Art Print
Shop, 1956.

E. ARTICLES, PERIODICALS AND PAMPHLETS

BOURNE, Edward Gaylord. "Historical Introduction,"
in The Philippine Islands, 1493-1898. Edited by
Emma Helen Blair and James Alexander Robertson.
55 vols. Cleveland, Ohio: The Arthur H. Clark
Company, 1903-1909, I, 19-87.

CORPUZ, Onofre D. "Western Colonisation and the
Filipino Response," Journal of Southeast Asian
History, III (March, 1962), 1-23.

CRAIG, Austin. "History of the University of the Philippines, " in Builders of a Nation. Edited by M.M.
Norton. Manila: n. p. , [1914], pp. 89-92.

La Democracia. 1900-1913.

FARRELL, John T. "Background of the 1902 Taft Mission
to Rome, " The Catholic Historical Review, XXXVI
(April, 1950), 1-32; XXXVII (April, 1951), 1-22.

FREI, Ernest J. "The Historical Development of the
Philippine National Language. " (Published serially in
PSSHR, XIV-XV [1949-1950]).

GILMORE, Eugene A. "The Development of Law in the
Philippines, " Iowa Law Review, XVI (June, 1931),
465-79.

HOFSTADTER, Richard. "Manifest Destiny and the Philippines, " in America in Crisis. Edited by Daniel Aaron.
New York: Alfred A. Knopf, 1952. Ch. VIII.

El Ideal. 1910-1913.

LARDIZABAL, Amparo Santamaria. "Pioneer American
Teachers and Philippine Education, " in Tales of the
American Teachers in the Philippines. Edited by
Geronima T. Pecson and Maria Racelis. Manila:
Carmelo and Bauermann, 1959.

LEOPOLD, Richard W. "The Foreign Relations Series:
A Centennial Estimate, " The Mississippi Valley
Historical Review, XLIX (March, 1963), 595-612.

LeROY, James A. "The Philippines, 1860-1898 — Some
Comment and Bibliographical Notes, " in The Philippine Islands, 1493-1898. Edited by Blair and Robertson. LII, 112-207.

McGAVRAN, Donald Anderson. "The Independent Church in the Philippines: The Story of a Spiritual Quest," Encounter (Indianapolis), XIX (Summer, 1958), 299-321.

Manila Times. 1901-1913.

MINGER, Ralph Eldin. "Taft, MacArthur, and the Establishment of Civil Government in the Philippines," The Ohio Historical Quarterly, LXX (October, 1961), 308-31.

NIEVA, Gregorio. "The Philippine Assembly," in Builders of a Nation: A Series of Biographical Sketches. Edited by M. M. Norton. Manila [1914], pp. 73-88.

PARKER, Donald D. "Church and State in the Philippines, 1896-1906," Philippine Social Science Review (hereafter PSSR), X (November, 1938), 354-371.

PLEHN, Carl C. "Taxation in the Philippines," PSSR, XIII (February, 1941), 79-117.

REGALA, Roberto A. "The Development of Representation in the Philippines," Philippine Law Journal, X (September, 1931), 63-88; (October, 1931), 111-139.

El Renacimiento. 1901-1908.

RIVERA, Juan A. "The Aglipayan Movement," PSSR, IX (December, 1937), 301-28; X (February, 1938), 9-30.

ROBERTSON, James Alexander. "The Evolution of Representation in the Philippine Islands," Journal of Race Development, VI (October, 1915), 155-66.

--- "The Extraordinary Session of the Philippine Legislature and the Work of the Philippine Assembly," American Political Science Review, IX (November, 1910), 516-36.

SALAMANCA, Bonifacio S. "Was the Philippine Encomienda a Land Grant?" Historical Bulletin, VII
(March, 1963), 34-51.

SOLVICK, Stanley D. "William Howard Taft and the
Payne-Aldrich Tariff, " The Mississippi Valley
Historical Review, L (December, 1963), 424-442.

SUMULONG, Juan. "The Philippine Problem from a
Filipino Standpoint, " North American Review,
CLXXIX (December, 1904), 860-867.

TAVERA, T. H. Pardo de. "Address...at the Farewell Banquet...of 17 April, 1909. " Manila.
(Pamphlet.)

La Vanguardia. 1910-1913.

VILLANUEVA, Honesto A. "A Chapter of Filipino
Diplomacy, " PSSHR, XVII (June, 1952), 103-178.

--- "The Diplomacy of the Spanish-American War. "
(Published serially in PSSHR, XIV-XVI [1949-1951]).

WICKBERG, E. "The Chinese Mestizo in Philippine
History, " Journal of Southeast Asian History, V
(March, 1964), 62-100.

YABES, Gregorio Y. "Philippine Representation in the
Spanish Cortes, " PSSR, VII (February, 1936), 36-
67; (June, 1936), 140-60.

ZAFRA, Nicolas, "The Northwest Territory and the
Ordinance of 1787. " PSSR, XIII (February, 1941),
1-29.

F.   UNPUBLISHED MATERIAL AND MANUSCRIPT
     COLLECTIONS

ALLEN, Henry T. Papers. Library of Congress,
Washington, D. C.

CLIFFORD, Sister Maria Dorita. "Aglipayanism as a
    Political Movement. " Unpublished Ph. D. dissertation
    Dept. of History, St. Louis University, 1960. (Micro-
    film.)

DICKINSON, Jacob McGavock. Papers. Tennessee State
    Library and Archives, Nashville, Tennessee. (Micro-
    film.)

EDWARDS, Clarence R. Papers. Massachusetts Historical
    Society, Boston, Massachusetts.

ELIOT, Charles W. Papers. The Houghton Library of
    Congress, Washington, D. C.

ELLIOTT, Charles Burke. Papers. Library of Congress,
    Washington, D. C.

FORBES, W. Cameron. Papers. The Houghton Library
    of Harvard University, Cambridge, Massachusetts.

McKINLEY, William. Papers. Library of Congress,
    Washington, D. C. (Microfilm.)

"The Muslim Minority in the Philippines. " Cebu City,
    Philippines, June, 1962. (Typewritten, Professor
    Harry J. Benda's Copy.)

ROOSEVELT, Theodore. Papers. The Houghton Library
    of Harvard University, Cambridge, Massachusetts.

ROOT, Elihu. Papers. Library of Congress, Washington,
    D. C.

SMITH, James F. Papers. Washington State Historical
    Society and Musuem, Tacoma, Washington.

STIMSON, Henry L. Papers. Yale Sterling Library, New
    Haven, Connecticut.

STOREY, Moorfield. Papers. Library of Congress,
Washington, D. C.

TAFT, William Howard. Papers. Library of Congress, Washington, D. C. (Part microfilm.)

U. S. Bureau of Insular Affairs. Records on the Philippine Islands, 1898-1946. Record Group 350. U. S.
National Archives, Washington, D. C.

WISE, Francis H. "The History of the Philippine
Independent Church. " Unpublished Master's
thesis, Department of History, University of
the Philippines, 1954.

WOOD, Leonard. Papers. Library of Congress,
Washington, D. C.

G. OTHER SOURCES

Personal Interview with Mrs. Lillian Smith Berg,
granddaughter of General James F. Smith
Tacoma, Washington, July 24, 1964.

DATE DUE

NOV 21 73			
NOV 21 73			
MAR 17 '88			
GAYLORD			PRINTED IN U.S.A.

DATE DUE

OCT 2 0 2006		
NOV 1 8 2006		
JAN 0 9 2007		
JAN 2 3 2007		
MAR 1 4 2007		
APR 0 2 2007		
SEP 1 7 2007		
OCT 0 8 2013		

Demco, Inc. 38-293

SEP 1 7 2107